YAHWEH AND THE GODS OF CANAAN

YAHWEH AND THE GODS OF CANAAN

A Historical Analysis of
Two Contrasting Faiths

by

WILLIAM FOXWELL ALBRIGHT

•

THE JORDAN LECTURES 1965
DELIVERED AT THE SCHOOL OF
ORIENTAL AND AFRICAN STUDIES
UNIVERSITY OF LONDON

•

GARDEN CITY, NEW YORK
DOUBLEDAY & COMPANY, INC.
1968

The Louis H. Jordan Bequest

The will of the Reverend Louis H. Jordan provided that the greater part of his estate should be paid over to the School of Oriental and African Studies to be employed for the furtherance of studies in comparative religion, to which his life had been devoted. Part of the funds which thus became available was to be used for the endowment of a Louis H. Jordan Lectureship in Comparative Religion. The lecturer is required to deliver a course of six or eight lectures for subsequent publication. The first series of lectures was delivered in 1951.

Library of Congress Catalog Card Number 68–22541

Printed in the United States of America

Preface

This volume contains the lectures under the Louis H. Jordan Bequest, delivered in May 1965, at the School of Oriental and African Studies in the University of London. The original series consisted of seven lectures, entitled 'Canaan, Phoenicia, and Israel: An Historical Analysis of Two Contrasting Faiths'. The first three lectures appear as Chapters I–III, with the same headings, but the four remaining lectures have been compressed into two chapters with new headings. The title of the published volume is taken from the heading of Chapter IV. The content of the volume reflects my own research during the past decade. In preparing it for publication, I have expanded my treatment of basic topics considerably, while I have deleted material which can readily be located, or which will be published elsewhere in the near future.

No attempt to be exhaustive is made in the footnotes. Fortunately for the reader who wishes to acquaint himself with both historical positions and current views in Old Testament scholarship, we now have an excellent guide in H. H. Rowley's *Worship in Ancient Israel* (London, 1967), which reached me just after I finished reading galley proofs of the present volume. My old friend's exact and comprehensive knowledge of pertinent bibliography is well known; readers who find my approach to Old Testament problems disconcerting, may see our problems in wider perspective after studying Professor Rowley's book.

Since the preparation of the final copy was extended over a year and a half (owing chiefly to a major operation in August 1965), it has proved necessary to include several pages of Addenda in order to bring the reader's information measurably up to date. But for the competent aid of Dr Leona G. Running, who was my research assistant in 1965–6, I might not have been able to complete the manuscript at all.

I wish to thank the Director and Academic Board of the School for the invitation to give these lectures. I also wish to express my hearty thanks to the Secretary of the School, Mr J. R. Bracken, and his staff for never-failing courtesy and competent assistance at all times. To the members of the faculty of the School I am indebted for friendship and hospitality.

I am greatly obligated to many scholars at home and abroad who have helped me with information and suggestions; I shall thank them in the notes.

I take exceptional pleasure in dedicating this volume to my old friend, Professor Otto Eissfeldt of Halle, whose indomitable spirit and acuteness in exploring *terra incognita* have so often opened new paths for me.

Lastly, I want to thank my wife once again for her patience with an odd specimen of an odd species, *Homo eruditus. Ad multos annos!*

W.F.A.

Baltimore, 1 July 1967

Contents

In Honour of the
Eightieth Birthday
1 September 1967
of Otto Eissfeldt
Whose Scholarly Exploration
Has Made This Volume Possible

Abbreviations

AAA	*Annals of Archaeology and Anthropology* (Liverpool)
AASOR	*Annual of the American Schools of Oriental Research*
ADS	*Le antiche divinità semitiche* (*Studi Semitici*, Rome, 1958), by M. J. Dahood, S.J.
AfO	*Archiv für Orientforschung*
AHAEBT	*Archaeology, Historical Analogy, and Early Biblical Tradition*, by W. F. Albright (Baton Rouge, La. [Louisiana State Univ. Press], 1966)
AHW	*Akkadisches Handwörterbuch*, by Wolfram von Soden (Wiesbaden, 1959)
AJA	*American Journal of Archaeology*
AJSL	*American Journal of Semitic Languages and Literatures*
ANEP	*The Ancient Near East in Pictures*, ed. James B. Pritchard (Princeton, 1954)
ANET	*Ancient Near Eastern Texts*, ed. James B. Pritchard (Princeton, 1955)
AOB	*Altorientalische Bibliothek*
APN	*Die ägyptischen Personennamen*, by H. Ranke (Glückstadt, 1935–)
APNMT	*Amorite Personal Names in the Mari Texts*, by H. B. Huffmon (Baltimore, 1965)
ARI	*Archaeology and the Religion of Israel*, by W. F. Albright (Baltimore, 1942, 4th edition, 1956)
ARM	*Archives Royales de Mari* (ed. A. Parrot and G. Dossin, Paris, 1940–)
ArOr	*Archiv Orientální*
BA	*Biblical Archaeologist* (American Schools of Oriental Research)
BAeV	*Die Beziehungen Aegyptens zu Vorderasien im 3. und 2. Jahrtausend v. Chr.*, by Wolfgang Helck (Wiesbaden, 1962)

BANE	*The Bible and the Ancient Near East,* ed. G. Ernest Wright (Essays in Honor of William Foxwell Albright, Garden City, N.Y., 1961)
BASOR	*Bulletin of the American Schools of Oriental Research*
BE	*Babylonian Expedition,* ed. Hilprecht (Philadelphia)
BiOr	*Bibliotheca Orientalis* (Leiden)
BJRL	*Bulletin of the John Rylands Library* (Manchester)
BMB	*Bulletin du Musée de Beyrouth*
BPAE	*The Biblical Period from Abraham to Ezra,* by W. F. Albright (Harper Torch Book, 1963)
BWANT	*Beiträge zur Wissenschaft vom Alten und Neuen Testament*
BZATW	*Beihefte zur Zeitschrift für die Alttestamentliche Wissenschaft*
CAD	*Chicago Assyrian Dictionary*
CAH^2	*Cambridge Ancient History,* rev. ed.
CBQ	*Catholic Biblical Quarterly*
CḪ	Code of Ḫammurapi
CML	*Canaanite Myths and Legends,* by G. R. Driver (Edinburgh, 1956)
COWA	*Chronologies in Old World Archaeology,* ed. Robert Ehrich (Chicago, 1965)
CRAI	*Comptes Rendus de l'Académie des Inscriptions et Belles-Lettres* (Paris)
CTBT	*Cuneiform Texts from Babylonian Tablets (in the British Museum)*
DMOA	*Documenta et Monumenta Orientis Antiqui* (Leiden)
DOTT	*Documents from Old Testament Times,* ed. Winton Thomas (London, 1958)
EA	*Die El-Amarna-Tafeln,* ed. J. A. Knudtzon (Leipzig, 1915). The following numbers apply to individual letters.
E.B.	Early Bronze Age
EM	*Entsiqlopediya Miqra'it* (Jerusalem, 1950–)
FCTBS	*The Four Canaanite Temples of Beth-shan,* by A. Rowe (Philadelphia, 1940)

FF	*Forschungen und Fortschritte* (East Berlin, DDR)
FSAC	*From the Stone Age to Christianity*, by W. F. Albright (1939)
Ḫab	*The Ḫab/piru*, by Moshe Greenberg (New Haven, Am. Or. Soc., 1955)
HACH	*History, Archaeology, and Christian Humanism*, by W. F. Albright (New York, 1964)
HSSt	*Hebrew and Semitic Studies* (G. R. Driver Festschrift, Oxford, 1963)
HTR	*Harvard Theological Review*
HUCA	*Hebrew Union College Annual*
ICC	*International Critical Commentary*
IEJ	*Israel Exploration Journal*
JA	*Journal Asiatique* (Paris)
JAOS	*Journal of the American Oriental Society*
JBL	*Journal of Biblical Literature*
JBR	*Journal of Bible and Religion*
JCS	*Journal of Cuneiform Studies*
JEA	*Journal of Egyptian Archaeology* (London)
JNES	*Journal of Near Eastern Studies*
JPOS	*Journal of the Palestine Oriental Society* (Jerusalem, before 1948)
JSS	*Journal of Semitic Studies* (Manchester)
JTS	*Journal of Theological Studies*
KBo	*Keilschrifttexte aus Boghazköi*
KSGVI	*Kleine Schriften zur Geschichte des Volkes Israel*, I–III, by A. Alt (Munich, 1953–1959)
L.B.	Late Bronze Age
LC^2	*The Legacy of Canaan*, by John Gray, 2nd ed. (Leiden, 1965)
LS	*Ha-Lashon ve-ha-Sefer* (Essays by Harry Torczyner, I–III, Jerusalem, 1948–1955)
M.B.	Middle Bronze Age
MDOG	*Mitteilungen der Deutschen Orient-Gesellschaft*
MIOF	*Mitteilungen des Instituts für Orientforschung* (Berlin, DDR)
MOPH	*Molk als Opferbegriff im Punischen und Hebräischen und das Ende des Gottes Moloch*, by Otto Eissfeldt (Halle, Saale, 1935)

MSD	*Mélanges syriens offerts à M. René Dussaud*, I–II (Paris, 1939–1940)
NMTRM	*Les nomades en Mésopotamie au temps des rois de Mari*, by Jean-Robert Kupper (Paris, 1957)
NPN	*Nuzi Personal Names*, by I. J. Gelb and others (Chicago, 1943)
OEKS	*Kleine Schriften*, I–III, by Otto Eissfeldt (Tübingen, 1962–1966)
OLZ	*Orientalistische Literaturzeitung* (Leipzig)
Or	*Orientalia*
OTMS	*The Old Testament and Modern Study*, ed. H. H. Rowley (Oxford, 1951)
PAPS	*Proceedings of the American Philosophical Society* (Philadelphia)
PEPI	*Patterns in the Early Poetry of Israel*, by Stanley Gevirtz (Chicago, 1963)
PḪ	*Le problème des Ḫabiru*, by Jean Bottéro (Paris, 1944)
PPG	*Phönizisch-Punische Grammatik*, by Johannes Friedrich (Rome, 1951)
PRU	*Palais Royal d'Ugarit* (Paris)
PSID	*The Proto-Sinaitic Inscriptions and Their Decipherment* (*Harvard Theological Studies* XXII [Cambridge, Mass., 1966])
RA	*Revue d'Assyriologie*
RB	*Revue Biblique*
RHR	*Revue de l'histoire des religions*
SBPM	*Samuel and the Beginnings of the Prophetic Movement*, by W. F. Albright (Cincinnati, Hebrew Union College Press, 1961)
SKL	*The Sumerian King List*, by Thorkild Jacobsen (Chicago, 1939)
SLTN	*Sumerische literarische Texte aus Nippur*, by S. N. Kramer and Inez Bernhardt (Berlin, 1961)
SOTP	*Studies in Old Testament Prophecy* (T. H. Robinson Festschrift), ed. H. H. Rowley (Edinburgh, 1950)
ThSt	*Theological Studies* (Woodstock, Maryland)
TN	*Die Inschriften Tukulti-Ninurtas I. und seiner*

	Nachfolger (*AfO*, *Beiheft* 12, 1959), by Ernst Weidner
UAR	*Urkunden des Alten Reiches*, by K. Sethe (Leipzig, 1903)
VESO	*Vocalization of the Egyptian Syllabic Orthography*, by W. F. Albright (New Haven, 1934)
VT	*Vetus Testamentum* (Leiden)
WBA	*Biblical Archaeology*, by G. E. Wright (Philadelphia, 1957)
WBäS	*Wörterbuch der ägyptischen Sprache*, by Erman-Grapow
WM	*Wörterbuch der Mythologie*, ed. H. W. Haussig (Stuttgart, 1965–)
WVDOG	*Wissenschaftliche Veröffentlichungen der Deutschen Orient-Gesellschaft*
ZA	*Zeitschrift für Assyriologie*
ZÄS	*Zeitschrift für Ägyptische Sprache*
ZAW	*Zeitschrift für die Alttestamentliche Wissenschaft*
ZDMG	*Zeitschrift der Deutschen Morgenländischen Gesellschaft*
ZDPV	*Zeitschrift des Deutschen Palästina-Vereins*
ZZB	*Die 'Zweite Zwischenzeit' Babyloniens*, by D. O. Edzard (Wiesbaden, 1957)

I

Verse and Prose in Early Israelite Tradition

A. POETRY VERSUS PROSE: THEIR RELATIVE DATE AND TRANSMISSION

In the early years of modern Biblical research, it seemed reasonable enough to men like J. G. Herder[1] and Heinrich Ewald[2] to suppose that early Hebrew poetry dated back in general to the beginnings of Hebrew literature and that prose followed early poetry just as was true of other Old World literatures. The romantic movement was then so strong that the relative priority of verse appeared to be self-evident. Then came a period dominated by Julius Wellhausen, in which the date of Hebrew poetry was lowered more and more as literary critics came to accept as normative for Israel Wellhausen's Hegelian[3] view of religious history as a development from 'fetishism', through henotheism, to monotheism. Under his influence, an increasingly large number of scholars in the first half of this century came to believe that virtually all

[1] Especially in *Vom Geiste der ebräischen Poesie* (1782–3).

[2] Especially in *Geschichte des Volkes Israel* (1843–59).

[3] The basic Hegelianism of Wellhausen has been strangely denied by some recent writers. His 'Hegelian' insistence that prophecy came before codified religious law led him to date most prophetic verse before *tôrah*. On the other hand, his unilinear system of religious evolution (which is partly Hegelian) resulted in his dating non-prophetic verse (Psalms, Wisdom literature) in the Persian and Greek periods. From the standpoint of consistency in dealing with literary forms, chaos resulted, as pointed out by H. Gunkel and his disciples and now demonstrated by comparative literary evidence.

extant Biblical Hebrew poetry is extremely late—in fact that much of it was composed in the Hellenistic age between the late fourth and the first century B.C., chiefly because of the 'advanced' concepts which were characteristic of it, generally presupposing monotheism.

The approach introduced by Wellhausen still holds sway today in many circles of Biblical scholarship, in spite of the swelling tide of archaeological finds which is making it an historical anachronism. It is surprising to see how many Old Testament scholars still deny that we have any appreciable amount of poetry antedating the monarchy—except for the Song of Deborah and a few fragments.

Yet, if the still current view is correct, the Hebrew Bible would probably be alone among Old World literatures in having the earliest poetry follow the oldest prose instead of precede it. The reason for the relative antiquity of verse is very simple: poetry was then regularly sung or chanted to the accompaniment of stringed instruments such as the harp and the lyre, especially various forms of the lyre, which were known in both Egypt and Babylonia before the middle of the third millennium. Since the lyre appears in rock carvings in central Arabia at an even earlier date, it must have been known in Mesopotamia from Chalcolithic, if not Neolithic, times.[4] Illustrations of the priority of verse are innumerable. Among historical civilizations (as opposed to the archaeologically-known cultures of the Old World and the little-known native cultures of the New), we need point only to Greek and Latin, Germanic and Romance, Slavic and Ugro-Finnic, Indic and Iranian, Chinese and other East-Asian literatures. In the ancient Near East we can point to Sumerian (we now have actual literary compositions from the Fara period before 2500 B.C.),[5] Accadian (hymnal-

[4] My information comes through Emmanuel Anati, the noted authority on rock carvings in southern Europe and the Near East.

[5] According to information received from Dr. Robert D. Biggs,

epic), Canaanite (Ugaritic), Hurrian and Hittite, and pre-Islamic Arab. Egyptian is not an exception, since the Pyramid Texts certainly go back in part to the First Dynasty or earlier—no later than about 2900 B.C.[6]

When clear analogies are so numerous, we are in a position to construct a loose model on which to pattern a viable theory of literary sequence-dating in Israel. Naturally, we cannot attain certainty unless we can confirm the applicability of the model in question to a given literature by checking it with all available empirical data. As we shall see, we can now parallel changing poetic style with historically meaningful content, a method which gives us approximate dates for stylistic modifications. After establishing phases of style, we can often employ stylistic methods to date archaic survivals from original poems embedded in prose narratives.[7] The value of this tool for determining the age of literary tradition should be obvious.

Poetic style does not change at a uniform rate. There are periods when it remains virtually unchanged for centuries; there are other times when it shifts so rapidly that

---

who is preparing the tablet material from Tell Ṣalābīkh for publication.

[6] Following the late Herman Junker, some Egyptologists insist that the Pyramid Texts are little, if any, older than the Pyramids in which they are found. Their definitive editor, Kurt Sethe, who was a far better linguist-philologian, insisted correctly on their relatively early date, in accord with what we know of similar religious poetry elsewhere. The archaism of language and especially the phonetic spelling used in these texts, are indications that they had been handed down from earlier times by scribes who knew that exact reproduction of their content was essential to their efficacy.

[7] Illustrations of this principle are common in the Bible; cf., for example, Jacob M. Myers, *The Linguistic and Literary Form of the Book of Ruth* (Leiden, 1955). Early and medieval Arabic literature abounds with poetry embedded in a prose matrix, either of descriptive or narrative character.

it is impossible to make a clear distinction between chronological stages. A good example of these two extremes is to be found in Greek poetry, where all known early verse appears in dactylic hexameters; then suddenly in the seventh century B.C. lyric verse emerges in the perfection of Archilocus, becoming stylistically complex as we approach fifth-century Pindar, in whose work many prosodic styles are combined. Particularly open to sequence-dating are early Roman and early Romance poetry, and—perhaps the best example—Old and Middle English verse to the fourteenth century A.D. Accadian poetry can be dated stylistically with increasing precision.[8]

B. CANAANITE REPETITIVE STYLE

In the second millennium B.C. Canaan underwent many cultural and ethno-political changes as it moved from Middle Bronze through Late Bronze into Early Iron. Thanks to the excavation of Ugarit by C. F. A. Schaeffer and the publication by Ch. Virolleaud, of poetic epics in the cuneiform alphabet, our knowledge of Canaanite higher culture has been increasing by leaps and bounds since 1932. Our knowledge of the period between c. 1500 and c. 1233 B.C. has been enlarged beyond our wildest dreams of 1929. It was a time peculiarly suited for rapid change in literary style, just as in England between the time of *Widsith* and *Beowulf* and that of Chaucer.

The three Canaanite (Ugaritic) epics which we possess in large part, Baal, Aqhat and Keret, were put into approximately their extant form between the seventeenth

[8] Cf. in particular the work of B. Landsberger and his pupils, especially W. von Soden. Important contributions were also made by A. Schott and recently by W. G. Lambert. The latter has been treating the material from the point of view of its historical and theological content, while the others have laid chief stress on philological and linguistic analysis.

and the fifteenth centuries in the order given,[9] and are in substantially the same poetic style. In particular, each has roughly the same proportion of repetitive parallelism.

It was H. L. Ginsberg who first defined repetitive parallelism in Canaanite poetry.[10] The fundamental significance of 'climactic parallelism' for the Song of Deborah had been recognized by C. F. Burney nearly half a century ago,[11] and in 1922 I had followed Burney, differing from him chiefly in my linguistic and metric reconstruction, and in recognizing that additional cases of repetition must have dropped out by haplography.[12] (Some scholars had previously tried to eliminate most—or even all—cases of repetition, which they treated as dittographies.)[13] At the same time I pointed out similarities

[9] The Baal Epic was composed during the transition from use of *ba'lu* as pure appellation ('lord') to its use as a proper name (Baal), that is, in the latter part of the Middle Bronze Age. Needless to say, the present form of the Baal Epic, in which the mimation has been dropped, has been influenced by oral transmission in the Late Bronze Age, after the mimation had been lost. Much of the poetic form of the Baal Epic may be still earlier, going back into the early Middle Bronze Age. The myths are naturally older. The Keret Epic could not have been composed until after the time of Kirta, putative founder of the Mitanni kingdom in the sixteenth century B.C. There is much Hurrian influence in this epic.

[10] *Orientalia* v (1936), 180. The Ginsberg-Gordon treatment of the poetic structure of Ugaritic in Cyrus H. Gordon, *Ugaritic Grammar* (Rome, 1940), pp. 78 ff., does not dwell on this matter. It seems that I was actually the first scholar to emphasize the importance of repetitive parallelism in Ugaritic, following C. F. Burney on the Song of Deborah (see n. 11).

[11] See C. F. Burney, *The Book of Judges*, pp. 169 ff., and my further application of his principles, with correction of his linguistic approach and comparison with Accadian hymnal-epic style in JPOS II (1922), 69 ff.

[12] This observation of mine has turned out to be quite correct in principle, though not every case may stand.

[13] Cf. especially Paul Haupt in the Wellhausen *Festschrift* (Giessen, 1914), pp. 191 ff., in which he condenses the entire poem by 30 per cent to seventy cola, omitting every trace of repetitive parallelism. Rudolf Kittel's animadversions in his *Geschichte des*

between Old-Babylonian verse structure and that of the Song of Deborah.[14] I naturally could have no idea that the discovery and decipherment of the Ugaritic epics would eventually confirm Burney's point of view in essentials. At the same time, some renderings and emendations have proved to be wrong in the light of our growing knowledge of the poetic language of Canaan.

The classic example of Canaanite repetitive style is a tricolon (3+3+3, with the word-pattern abc:abd: ad′b′),[15] which appears in nearly the same (theologically superior) form in Psalm 92:10:

> *Behold, thine enemies*, O Baal,
> *Behold, thine enemies* shalt thou crush,
> Behold, thou shalt crush thy foes!

Another specimen of a repetitive tricolon of the same type (here abc:abd:b′b′d′) appears in Aqhat II, vi:26 ff.:

> *Ask thou for life*, O lad Aqhat,
> *Ask thou for life*, and I'll give it to thee,
> Immortality, and I'll grant it to thee![16]

Still another example may be quoted from Keret II, vi:54 ff. (abc:abd:a′a′d′):

Volkes Israel, 5th ed. (1922), II, 28 f., n. 7, were unfortunately quite justified.

[14] JPOS II, 70–3.

[15] Some scholars object to our substitution of the term 'colon', 'bicolon', 'tricolon' for 'stich' (or 'stichos'). The reason is that the term 'stich' is often used for a single verse unit (colon), whereas others prefer to use the term 'hemistich' for the same unit. In their terminology a 'stich' is the same as 'distich' in the alternative terminology. Since such confusion is intolerable, it is much better to employ the unambiguous term 'colon', as now done by my former students.

[16] For the translation, see Ginsberg, BASOR 98 (1945), 19, and note that we have two successive pronominal suffixes in the dative case, just as in Old and Middle Babylonian as well as in stereotyped expressions in Hebrew. A striking example in Ugaritic prose is found in PRU v, 84, No. 60, line 31, where we have *'eb. 'ltn*, 'the enemy has come up against me'; see Ch. IV, n. 22.

May Horan break, O my son,
May Horan break thy head,
May Glory-of-the-Name-of-Baal,[17] thy skull!

Again in Aqhat II, i:3–14 there are four successive occurrences of a single tricolon of similar type (abc: abd:ad′b′):

With honour (shall) Dan'el the gods.
With honour the gods shall he feed,
With honour shall he give drink to the sons of Qudshu.[18]

(Note that the third line of this tricolon has only three beats in Ugaritic.) There are many more complete examples of the repetitive tricolon in Ugaritic texts, but the above may suffice. Repetitive patterns of various types also appear in bicola. In the poetic liturgy of Shahar and Shalim we read, for instance,

In his (Death's) *hand is the staff* of bereavement (of children)
In his hand is the staff of widowhood.

Aqhat I:148–150 offers (abc:bca′):

The wings of the eagle *shall Baal break*,
Baal shall break their pinions.

This pattern was to become relatively commoner in early Israelite verse.

There are cases where single words are repeated in adjacent cola, though they are relatively scarce. We also have series of cola which begin with the same word or the same two words, showing a stylistic phenomenon quite common in archaic Hebrew poetry.

When we compare Canaanite with Hebrew poetic

[17] This is my translation of *'Aštart-Šem-Ba'al*. For details, see Ch. III below.

[18] For the meaning of *'uzr* see JAOS LXXI (1951), 262 f., where I wrongly treated it as in apposition to *Dn'el*. Here it is an adverbial accusative, as shown clearly in the same column, lines 22 f., where it has the enclitic *m* attached. In Punic it refers to a particularly important sacrifice; see J. G. Février, JA CCXLVIII (1960), 170 ff.

style[19] we must never forget that the resemblances in structure and wording go far beyond the phenomena we have just described. For example, there are over seventy specific pairs of vocabulary units (one word, occasionally two in each unit) in parallelism which appear in both Hebrew and Ugaritic, as shown by U. Cassuto and Moshe Held.[20]

This is not the place to discuss the origin of these complex patterns of repetitive parallelism. They unquestionably go back to Old Accadian, which was the spoken language of northern Babylonia during the Dynasty of Accad (24th–22nd centuries B.C.) and the Third Dynasty of Ur (c. 2060–1955 B.C.). At that time there developed a special generalized dialect of poetry, like Homeric Greek and the Canaanite of the Ugaritic epics (which was not the same as the dialect of the prose letters from Ugarit).[21] Called the 'hymnal-epic dialect' by B. Landsberger and W. von Soden,[22] it remained in use until the end of the First Dynasty of Babylon and was occasionally imitated later (not very successfully, as in the Creation Epic of the twelfth-eleventh centuries B.C.).[23] The earlier

[19] See below and Ch. III for discussion of the character and language of the Ugaritic epics, which are in a generalized Canaanite poetic dialect closely related to the South Canaanite *koinē* which we find underlying the Amarna Tablets and the early Canaanite alphabetic inscriptions, and which was ancestral to the various Hebrew dialects of Israel as well as to the dialects of Phoenicia.

[20] See M. D. (Umberto) Cassuto, *Ha-elah 'Anat* (Jerusalem, 1951), pp. 19 f., as well as his more detailed article in *Tarbiz* XIII (1942), 197–212. For many additional cases see Moshe Held, *Tarbiz* XXV (1954), 144–60. See also the useful monograph of Stanley Gevirtz, *Patterns in the Early Poetry of Israel* (Chicago, 1963).

[21] See my study in BASOR 150 (1958), 36 ff. and especially Mario Liverani, 'Elementi innovativi nell'Ugaritico non letterario', in *Accademia dei Lincei*, S. 8, CCCLXI (1964), 1–19.

[22] See W. von Soden, ZA XL (1932), 163 ff.; XLI (1933), 90 ff.

[23] This date has been demonstrated by W. G. Lambert in the T. J. Meek anniversary volume.

poems often show a complex and sometimes rather irregular repetition, whereas the later poems have become standardized by repeating the first half of a four-line stanza in the second half, with only one or rarely two verbal changes; the structure of a stanza generally consists of eight cola, each with two beats.[24] There are enough specific parallels in diction between this poetry and that of Canaanite literature from Ugarit and the early parts of the Hebrew Bible to make ultimate dependence reasonably certain, but it is possible that both poetic complexes go back to a common source antedating the Dynasty of Accad (instead of following it, as I formerly thought).

There is, however, one important area in which Hebrew prosody is intermediate between Accadian and Canaanite. In the former, metre is regularly 2 + 2, forming an accentual tetrameter. This is particularly clear in the hymnal-epic dialect, in which metre was probably native Accadian instead of being obscured by the influence of translations from Sumerian, as in the case of most lyric poetry of later date. On the other hand, Canaanite poetry is almost entirely accentual hexameter (3 + 3). Tetrameter (2 + 2) probably existed but has not yet been defined, and the mixed metres of early Israel have not been recognized in Ugaritic literature. Canaanite therefore agrees with Hittite (accentual) and early Greek (quantitative) models. It may be that Hebrew 2 + 2 metre goes back in part to Mesopotamian influence (see below).

As a result of the revolutionary changes in culture and political organization after the Amarna age, we find a rapid shift in poetic style as we move down from the fourteenth to the eleventh century B.C. Almost the only

24 There is a pronounced shift in this respect between the early texts of this category (as in *Cuneiform Texts* XV) and such relatively late texts as the Ammiditana hymn; cf. my remarks in SOTP, 1950, p. 8.

materials we have from this time are Egyptian magical texts translated from older Canaanite spells[25] as well as some early Hebrew poems. It is the Hebrew group that enables us to trace these changes. The standard repetitive parallelism gradually yields to new types and is finally displaced by paronomasia. The latter seldom occurs in Ugaritic poetry (so far) and is at best very rare in Babylonian literature, but it is almost universal in all known periods of Egyptian literature, so on these grounds alone it is reasonable to assume that it came relatively late in Syria–Palestine, perhaps appearing first in twelfth-century Phoenicia.[26] We shall consider the poems in stylistic sequence, which in general corresponds to the historical order which one would infer from their content. Style does not naturally develop according to any unilinear scheme, so that one should not expect the two sequences to be consistently parallel.

C. EARLY ISRAELITE REPETITIVE STYLE

The thirteenth century was just as transitional in poetic style as in the linguistic history of Israel. At about that time, in the areas for which we have data, several consonants coalesced with other consonants and final short vowels were dropped;[27] the disappearance of morphemes

[25] See R. T. O'Callaghan, *Orientalia*, XXI (1952), pp. 37–46, and W. Helck, BAeV, pp. 580 f.

[26] There is evidence for a pronounced growth of Egyptian influence on Phoenicia about the end of the Empire, as illustrated by the Wen-Amun Report from c. 1060 B.C. Cf. my remarks in JAOS LXXI (1951), 100 f. We know that there was a great expansion of Egyptian influence in Phoenicia in the Amarna and Ramesside periods (see my discussion, JEA XXIII [1937], 190 ff., and now Helck, BAeV, *passim*). We shall also see below that it is hard to place the introduction of a number of Egyptian divine names into Phoenicia at any other period.

[27] Cf. my remarks on the interpretation of the alphabetic cuneiform incantation from Beth-shemesh in BASOR 173 (1964), 51 ff.

made it necessary to depend on fixed word order instead of on morphemic controls for intelligibility. At about that time the accent moved to the final syllable of most words and short accented vowels were lengthened.[28] Many other minor changes accompanied these major shifts, and verse structure was greatly affected, much as the change of Greek and Latin metre in the early Middle Ages from vowel length and syllabic quantity to stress accent brought with it major changes in prosody and poetic style generally.

At first Hebrew poetry preserved many of the old endings, in order not to change familiar word groups and phrases. For instance, the final short *i* of the gerundive *qatâli*, *qatôli* was lengthened and kept in such archaic passages as Gen. 49:11 and Ex. 15:6: in the Balaam Oracles the hero is called *bĕnō Bĕ'ôr*, 'son of Beor', where the first word stands for the older *bĭnŭ*, 'son of (nominative)', thus keeping the old metre which would otherwise have disappeared.[29] There can be no doubt that in many cola (verse-units) which are too short in their later Hebrew pronunciation, the same phenomenon was at work. Even in much later times, some of these archaic endings were used in accordance with old models. How the phonetic revolution worked in practice may be illustrated from the early thirteenth-century Song of Miriam (Ex. 15), where we have in verse 11a (3 + 3):

Who is like Thee among the gods, O Yahweh?
Who is like Thee, feared among the holy (ones)![30]

[28] For an account of the relation between these phenomena (though his dating is too low), see Zellig Harris, *The Development of the Canaanite Dialects* (1939), *passim* (see his Index under 'Stress').

[29] See JBL LXIII (1944), 216, n. 54.

[30] In Canaanite and Phoenician, *qdšm* has the same meaning as *'elm*, 'gods', and in later Hebrew it became 'angels' like *'ēlîm*. The LXX preserves the original plural. See F. M. Cross, Jr., and D. N. Freedman, JNES XIV (1955), 247, n. 35.

The first phrase appears as a single beat, *mî-kāmôkā*, in Classical Hebrew, but a little before the time of Moses it was still pronounced in two beats, *miya kamôka*.[31] The metric structure remained a bicolon with 3 + 3 beats, but the prototype was shorter; it may have run:

Who is like unto thee, O Baal?
Who is like unto thee among the gods?[32]

Here we have a typical Canaanite abc:abd sequence, such as we have seen so often elsewhere.

The oldest Israelite poetry of any length, judging from stylistic indications, confirmed by the content, is the Song of Miriam, which I should date in the thirteenth century B.C., preferably in the first quarter. It belongs to a wider category of triumphal songs (or hymns) which includes the long poems celebrating the 'victory' of Ramesses II at Kadesh, the triumph of Marniptah over the Libyans, and the victory of Tukulti-Ninurta I over the Cossaeans of Babylonia—all from the same century B.C. The general fidelity with which the Song of Miriam has been transmitted may be partly due to its popularity as a kind of Israelite national anthem. In the Song there are three instances of full repetitive parallelism (for traces of a fourth see below):

Thy right hand, O Yahweh, is fearsome in might,
Thy right hand, O Yahweh, has crushed the enemy. (verse 6)[33]

[31] In Amarna, *miya* or *miya-mi* and in Ugaritic, *my*, *my-m* (so!).

[32] In Stratum F of Ḥamā, dating from about the thirteenth–twelfth century B.C., Harald Ingholt discovered a cylinder seal of the Cossaean period containing an invocation to the goddess Ishtar which ends with the words '*mannu išan(n)anki* ^d^*Nin-Eanna*' (or *Bêlit-Ayakki*), 'who can rival thee, O Lady of Eanna?' (name of the temple of Ishtar at Erech).

[33] On the archaism *ne'dârî* see JNES XIV (1955), 245 f., which refers to previous work on the form. This is another example of an archaic North-west Semitic ending (see W. Moran, JCS IV, 169 ff.).

Who is like Thee, among the gods, O Yahweh?
Who is like Thee, feared among the holy (ones)?
(verse 11)

While Thy people cross, O Yahweh,
While the *people cross* whom Thou hast created.
(verse 16)

The first two represent the fully-developed 2 + 2:2 + 2 pattern ab:cd/ab:ef, while the third example follows a 3 + 3 abc:abd pattern. This is sufficient to indicate that full repetitive parallelism was still alive, though slightly modified in structure. Furthermore there is an instance of partial repetitive parallelism (ab:ac) in verse 3:

Yahweh is a warrior (?),[34]
Yahweh is His name.

The Song of Deborah may be dated about 1150, or a little later.[35] It shows marked deterioration in the form of repetitive parallelism since the Song of Miriam, though the somewhat fragmentary nature of the text-tradition may obscure an originally good example here and there. As it is, words are sometimes repeated in contexts where the poetic structure is not clear. Although there are some eighteen examples of repetitive parallelism in Judges 5, the resulting mosaic of patterns becomes very complex, consisting mostly of secondary imitations of the standard structures of the Bronze Age. In this respect the Song of Miriam is far more conservative in patterning. Both poems seem to have been composed in strophes, with alternating 3 + 3 bicola and several lines of 2 + 2 bicola,

[34] I have given the conventional translation of the Hebrew, but my long-standing opinion is that it meant originally 'He brings warriors (collective) into being ⟨through⟩ His name Yahweh'.

[35] All my dates have had to be raised by the recent demonstration (included in the revised edition of CAH) that Ramesses II became king in 1304 B.C., and that the date of Ramesses III's accession must thus be raised again to between c. 1200 and 1195 B.C. This means that my original arguments for a date c. 1150 stand and my subsequent dating about 1125 must be given up.

but it is not possible to reconstruct the inferred strophic structure with certainty.[36] The prevalence of the two-beat rhythm accounts in part, no doubt, for the decline of the older Canaanite tricolon pattern; the shift is perhaps due both to the development of lyric patterns in preference to epic and to the phonetic changes which we have described above. It should be added that the tricolon 3 + 3 + 3, with or without repetitive pattern, still dominates Canaanite magical spells from Egypt and Palestine in the fourteenth–thirteenth centuries B.C.[37]

The old normative abc:abd bicolon appears in Judges 5:30:

> *Spoil of dyed stuff* for Sisera,
> *Spoil of dyed stuff* embroidered.

The almost equally popular Canaanite pattern abc:bcd is found in 5:23:

> For they came not *to the help of Yahweh,*
> *To the help of Yahweh* sending their warriors.

Note also the very ancient pattern in 5:12, which continued in occasional use long after the repetitive style had otherwise vanished:

> *Awake, awake,* O Deborah,
> *Awake, awake,* chant a song!

Repetitive patterns in 2 + 2 beat are quite common, as in 5:3: '*Even I* to Yahweh *Even I* will sing!' Just as in the Oracles of Balaam and the Song of Moses, etc.,

[36] In my paper, JPOS II (1922), 69 ff., I reconstructed the Song of Deborah as 3 + 3 followed by 2 + 2:2 + 2, or 2 + 2:2 + 2:2 + 2, with the latter predominating. In my own unpublished reconstruction the Song of Miriam seems to follow a somewhat similar plan, but Cross and Freedman (*loc. cit.*) have proposed a much more irregular reconstruction in which most cola have only two beats. More work will be needed on the verse structure of the poem.

[37] See Helck, BAeV, pp. 580 f., and my article in BASOR 173, 51 ff.

such repetition of single words in different patterns becomes dominant; sometimes there is only one such repetition and sometimes the single word recurs in different positions through a series of cola. It is noteworthy that not one instance of repetitive parallelism occurs in the list of tribes in verses 14 to 18. This style was perhaps foreign to Israel when such descriptions were being composed. On the other hand we find assonance replacing strict repetitive parallelism in verses 2, 6, 19, and especially 30.

The Oracles of Balaam (c. 1200 B.C.)[38] contain one perfect example of a repetitive pattern familiar from Ugarit (abc:acb′):

And Edom *shall be dispossessed,*
And dispossessed shall be Seir. (Num. 24:18)

There are also five instances where one word (one accentual unit) is repeated in parallelism, e.g.:

Utterance of Balaam who is Beor's son,
Utterance of the man whose eye is true. (Num. 24:3, 15)[39]

[38] This date may have to be raised; it is based primarily on recognition of the fact that Num. 24:23 refers to events connected with the irruption of the Sea Peoples, presumably between the first great invasion of the south-eastern Mediterranean about 1234 B.C. (revised CAH chronology) and the date of the decisive occupation of the seacoast of Palestine by the Philistines and their allies. Since my article in JBL LXIII (1944), 207–33, important new material on Balaam has come in from the Idrimi stele. Here we have the first occurrence of the already known Egyptian name *'Amaw* as cuneiform *Amau* (genitive *Amae*); see BASOR 118 (1950), 15 f., n. 13. That the city of Emar on the Euphrates was in the land of 'Amau is not certain but probable. The first location of Emar by G. Dossin at Meskene on the basis of the Mari texts has been corrected by A. Goetze in BASOR 147 (1957), 22 ff., to a location half-way between Meskene and Carchemish (see also JCS XVIII [1964], 115 f.). This new location is close to the site of ancient Pitru = Pethor, home of Balaam in the land of 'Amau (according to the Hebrew consonantal text, confirmed by LXX).

[39] This slight modification of Wellhausen's 'whose eye is perfect' is confirmed by the first Arslan Tash incantation; see my remarks in

In four instances part of an accentual unit is repeated, especially an emphatic negative, e.g.:

For there is *no* omen against Jacob,
And *no* spell can work against Israel. (Num. 23:23)

Lastly we find a group of oracles where the repetitive style is entirely absent (Num. 24:20–24); the oracles may originally have been unconnected items reported from the Negeb, where the three peoples in question still existed in the Late Bronze Age. The third of these oracles, verses 22–3, may well go back to Balaam's time.[40] In 23:8, 10, 20, and 24:4, 7, 10, etymological assonance has clearly begun to displace the older repetitive type, which now seems to be limited to a few specific words. Examples of etymological assonance are:

How shall *I curse* whom El *hath* not *cursed*,
How *shall I doom* whom Yahweh *hath* not *doomed*? (23:8)

Blessed is he who doth bless thee
And cursed is he who doth curse thee! (24:10)

JBL LXIII (1944), 216, n. 56 (with references to my own previous study and that of T. H. Gaster).

[40] My present interpretation of this oracle of Balaam differs somewhat from my first translation, *ibid.*, pp. 222 and 226. We must replace the lost three words at the beginning of verse 23 from the Greek, taking the variant 'Gog' (Num. 24:7) as probably the best reading, and recognizing as I have for a number of years that *Aššûr* in this verse is not Assyria but is a synonym of *'Eber*. We may then follow my previous rendering of 23b and 24a but accept the Masoretic text of the rest of verse 24, with the following translation: 'And he saw Gog and delivered an oracle about him, saying,

The isles shall be gathered from the north
And ships from the farthest sea,
And they shall harass Aššûr and harass 'Eber,
But he (Gog) will perish forever.'

Gog refers, of course, to the northern barbarians, Amarna *Gagāya*. *'šr* is a synonym of *'Eber* and perhaps means 'caravaneers', lit. 'walkers' (collective); cf. my remarks in the Alt *Festschrift* (Tübingen, 1953), pp. 10 f., on the plural, *Aššûrîm,* which seems to have this meaning. For the date, see n. 38 above.

In the so-called Blessing of Moses (Deut. 33), Levi is very much in favour. Since the Levites were most popular before the Fall of Shiloh, we may infer that Deut. 33 must have been composed before the shrine fell. After the Fall, when the tabernacle lay in ruins and the priests had been slaughtered,[41] Samuel, as the new religious leader of the people, disregarded the Levites. Our inference is that Deut. 33 was composed about the middle of the eleventh century,[42] and its ascription to Moses presumably arose from the specific mention of him in verse 4.

There are three instances of one-word repetitive parallelism in the poem. The same word occurs at the beginning of several cola in verses 13–16: 'from the abundance of'. A single word is also repeated in verse 17b as well as in verse 26, where Cross and Freedman have restored a colon:

Who rides the heavens mightily,
Who rides gloriously the clouds.[43]

Paronomasia is found in verses 6 and 17, e.g.:

Let Reuben live, *let him* not *die*
Although *his men* be few.

In verse 8 there are two striking examples of the *figura etymologica*. We conclude that by this stage repetitive parallelism had become rare, and that paronomasia was being deliberately cultivated in different ways.

Deut. 32 probably dates from about 1025 B.C., well after the Fall of Shiloh.[44] It contains very few instances

[41] For this see Ps. 78:64 and Eissfeldt's convincing interpretation of the passage in *Das Lied Moses . . .* in *Verh. Sächs. Acad. Wiss. Leipzig, Phil.-hist. Kl.* 104, 5 (1958), 26–41.

[42] See Cross and Freedman, JBL LXVII (1948), 191 ff.

[43] See Cross and Freedman, BASOR 108 (1947), 6 f.

[44] See Eissfeldt, *op. cit.* (n. 41), and my discussion in VT IX (1959), 339–46.

of repetitive parallelism. In verse 2 both of two prepositions in the first colon are repeated in the second:

Like fine rain *on* the grass,
Like showers *on* the herbs.

Verse 6 repeats the pronoun

Is not *He* thy father who created thee?
He who made thee and formed thee?

The repetition in verse 14 is very likely a case of (vertical) dittography. However, in verse 17 the MT conceals a good example preserved by the Greek:

Gods whom they *know not*,
(And) whom their fathers *knew not*.[45]

Another parallel that I should restore from the Greek and a Qumran fragment[46] is at the beginning of verse 43:

Rejoice with Him, O heavens,
And bow before Him, O sons of God!
Rejoice with His people, O nations,
And honour Him,[46a] all sons of God!

In verse 39 the first personal pronoun is repeated four times:

Behold now, *I* am *I*,[47]
And there is no other God than *I*;
I kill and restore to life,

[45] See Albright, *ibid.*, p. 342, for the text.

[46] See *ibid.* for my latest treatment. The Qumran text was published by Patrick W. Skehan, BASOR 136 (1954), 12 ff.

[46a] This colon is preserved only in LXX, where the verb *enischusatōsan* has remained obscure. Delbert Hillers has cleared it up (private communication, Nov., 1964) by pointing out that *enischuō* is used to translate Hebrew *kabbēd* in four passages in Genesis. He has also pointed out that the original Hebrew probably read *wa-yĕkabbedûhu kol-bĕnê-'ēl.* With this he properly compares Ps. 22:24.

[47] For this translation, which is absolutely certain, see VT IX (1959), 342 f.

After I have smitten *I* heal,
And none can save from my hand!

There are nine indubitable cases of assonance. In one case phonetically similar words are set in parallelism (verse 22):

For a fire *is kindled* in my nostrils,
It *will burn* to lowermost Sheol.

In four verses a word appears in different forms, and in one verse (21) two words are so treated:

They set up a no-God *as My rival,*
They made Me angry by their follies;
So I *will set up* a no-people *as their rival,*
I will make them angry with a foolish nation.[48]

Assonance is also achieved by repetition of suffixes as in verse 6:

Is He not *thy* father who created *thee*,
He who made *thee* and formed *thee*?

We infer that Deut. 32 contains only echoes of true repetitive parallelism and that it dates from a time when assonance and paronomasia had become characteristic features of poetic style.

The Blessing of Jacob (Gen. 49) is favourable to Judah and Joseph, neutral towards Benjamin, and hostile to Levi; it should therefore date well after the Fall of Shiloh, but before the accession of Saul.[49] Its attribution to Jacob

[48] See *ibid.*, p. 344.

[49] Much confusion has been caused by mistranslation of Gen. 49:10, which must be rendered:

The (tribal) staff shall not depart from Judah
Nor the (tribal) chieftain from among his offspring.

In other words, this has nothing whatever to do (except according to later understanding) with the kingdom of David; it refers to the relative importance and stability of the tribe of Judah, protected on all sides by its mountainous terrain with steep ascents and deep gorges.

was presumably due to inference from verses 4 and 6 ff. Of five examples of repetitive parallelism, two are questionable (in verses 2 and 13), and one is still obscure (in verse 22). We shall limit ourselves to quoting two passages. Gen. 49:3:

Excelling in pride, and *excelling* in might.

In verses 25 f. we have virtually the same archaic oracle which we find in Deut. 33:13 ff.:

Blessings of the heavens above,
Blessings of the deep, which crouches beneath,
Blessings of breast and womb,
Blessings of thy father . . .[50]

Paronomasia abounds in the Blessing of Jacob, playing on the names of Judah (8), Dan (16), and Gad (19):

Judah, thy brothers *shall praise* thee,
  Thy hand shall be on the neck of thy foes.
Dan shall judge his people.
Gad will be raided by raiders,
But he *will raid* . . .

Verses 3–4 offer a case of *figura etymologica*:

Excelling in pride, and *excelling* in might,
  . . . those shall not *excel*.

In nearly every verse from v. 6 onwards, prepositions and suffixes are repeated, so that almost every bicolon has some element of assonance. Repetitive parallelism in the classic sense has, however, been virtually displaced by paronomasia throughout the Blessing of Jacob. And yet this Blessing contains some very archaic survivals from pre-Conquest days![51]

Some very archaic verse has been preserved as the

[50] The rest of the passage is defective, but 'blessings of' was repeated at least once more.

[51] Parade examples are Gen. 49:6 and 49:11. [See the Addenda.]

Song of Hannah (I Sam. 2:1–10). It is highly probable that it does go back to the time of Samuel, though rather to the end of his life than to its beginning. It is now possible to explain the final lines more appropriately:

It is Yahweh who crushes His opponents,
  It is the Exalted One who thunders in Heaven;
It is Yahweh who judges the ends of the earth,
  Giving power to His reign (!)
As He lifts the horns (!) of His anointed one.[52]

Note that in Psalm 72, which may be about a century later in date, it is not Yahweh, but the king, who is said to reign as far as the ends of the earth. In the Song of Hannah the kingship belongs to Yahweh, just as it does to Baal in the Ugaritic epics. The very archaic poem Psalm 29 begins by assigning 'power' (using the same word *'oz*) to Yahweh.

The early date of the poem is indicated by several archaic features. God is referred to as *Ṣûr* ('Mountain'), as well as by Canaanite *'Alî* or *'Elî*, 'The Exalted One'. Repetitive parallelism may be found in verse 1 (but the Greek and Old Latin read 'my God' the second time):

My heart rejoices *in Yahweh*,
  My horns (!) are exalted *in Yahweh*.

And once more there are a number of close parallels to

[52] The following changes are necessary in vocalization: Read an active for a passive form of the verb in the first colon. The first word in the second colon has been correctly explained by Nyberg as an appellation of Yahweh, 'the Exalted One', which also appears a number of times elsewhere in the Bible and is an appellation of Baal in the Ugaritic epics. The last word in the fourth colon must be vocalized *molkô*, 'his kingdom', as often elsewhere in the Bible as well as in Ugaritic and Phoenician. The second word of the fifth colon must be vocalized *qarnê*, i.e., dual instead of singular; it is an old metaphor representing the king as a wild bull. These are all archaic expressions whose meaning was often forgotten in later times.

the Song of Moses; Deut. 32:31, 37 are recalled by verse 2:

There is no Mountain like our God

and verses 6 ff:

Yahweh kills and revives,
  Sends down to Sheol and raises,
Yahweh dispossesses and enriches,
  Abases, yes, and exalts.

A few poetic fragments are extremely archaic in structure. Exodus 32:18 is a tricolon (3+3+3)—see below:

Not the musical tones of triumph,
  Nor the musical tones of defeat,
    But *the* (*musical*) *tones* ⟨of intoxication⟩ I hear![53]

Judges 15:16 (in the story of Samson) reads (two bicola, 2+2/2+2):

With the jawbone of a donkey
  Have I mightily raged,[54]
With the jawbone of a donkey
  Have I slain a thousand men!

Here are two perfect examples of repetitive parallelism, both similar in form to passages from Deut. 32. The second in particular has the same repetitive structure as

[53] I have restored this tricolon with the aid of the Greek and Syriac texts. The word *'annôt* should be so vocalized in all three occurrences of the consonantal frameword, not both *'anôt* and *'annôt*, as in Hebrew. This is in full agreement with the Greek and Syriac. In the third colon the Hebrew text omits the word after *'annôt*, but Greek and Syriac insert it as 'wine' and 'sin', respectively. In the context we have the word *br'* or *pr'*, with doubtful vocalization, in the meaning of 'intoxication' or 'disorderly conduct'. The Greek uses the former meaning ('wine') and the Syriac the latter (='sin').

[54] The Hebrew vocalization is corrupt; vocalize *ḥămôr ḥamartîm* but treat the final *m* as a normal enclitic and render 'mightily have I raged' instead of 'I have destroyed them'.

Deut. 32:43; it is characterized by assonance and word-play very similar to what we find in the Blessing of Moses (see below); the stem *ḤMR* appears four times in three different forms and meanings. Both these poetic quotations must date originally from between the thirteenth and the eleventh centuries.

A survival from more ancient times is to be found in II Kings 13:17:

A good omen of victory for Yahweh!
A good omen of victory over Aram!

This is a belomantic formula of obvious antiquity, as has been demonstrated by S. Iwry.[55]

Again, in Hosea 12:13–14 we read (3 + 3:3 + 3?):

For a woman did Israel serve,
And through a woman was he preserved ⟨from his foes (?)⟩;
Through a prophet was Israel brought up (from Egypt),
And through a prophet was he preserved ⟨from his enemies (?)⟩.[56]

The two women were, of course, Rachel and Deborah or Jael; the two 'prophets' were Moses and Samuel. This repetitive style, complex but regular in form, suggests the period of Samuel as a probable date of composition. More early material was quoted by the prophets than is commonly supposed.[57]

55 See JAOS LXXXI (1961), 27–34, especially p. 30.

56 On this passage cf. my *Samuel and the Beginnings of the Prophetic Movement* (Cincinnati, Hebrew Union College Press, 1961), p. 9. I have made some minor changes in the text in order to restore its approximate original form, which was certainly more poetic than it is in the extant text.

57 In the eighth- and seventh-century prophets we seem to have much less re-use of old material than we have in the latest pre-exilic and the exilic prophets, where quotations from much earlier texts, otherwise lost, are by no means uncommon—especially in Second Isaiah and Habakkuk. A clear case of prophetic re-use of older material is found in the oracles against Moab in Isaiah

Four poems attributed to David represent the next stage in the development of early Israelite verse. In David's lament over Saul and Jonathan (II Sam. 1:18–27) repetitive parallelism of single words still appears in three places (verses 20, 21, 26):

Lest the daughters of the Philistines rejoice,
   Lest the daughters of the uncircumcised exult.
For there was defiled *the shield of* the heroes,
The shield of Saul, not anointed with oil.
More wonderful was thy *love* for me
   Than the *love* of women.

Assonance appears in occasional repetition of unaccented negative particles, conjunctions and suffixes. There is a play on words at the beginning of verse 20: '*Tell it* not in *Gath.*' As might be expected in a lyric poem, we find a refrain: 'How have the mighty fallen!' and its archaic flavour is illustrated by the fact that it appears as the first element of more than one bicolon, in this respect like some of the earlier passages quoted above.

The last words of David in II Samuel 23:1–7 open with the Balaam formula, 'The oracle of . . .', in similar parallelism: 'The oracle of Balaam/David, son of Beor/Jesse// The oracle of the man . . .' One word is also repeated in parallelism in verses 3b, 4a, 5b, 5b–6. A single example of *figura etymologica* seems to occur in the last line. Confirming the antiquity of the poem, which the high ratio of repetitive parallelism would lead us to assume, is the use of the word *Ṣûr*, 'Mountain', for God (verse 3), which appears some eight times in Deut. 32.

Ṣûr is also used four times in our next poem (II Sam. 22 = Psalm 18); we must naturally include *Ṣûrî*, 'my God',

15–16 and Jeremiah 48, which are both probably adapted from a single ninth-century prototype. An earlier prototype has been suggested, but stylistic criteria are strongly opposed to an earlier date. In JBL LXI (1942), 119, I suggested that the original poem dated about 650 B.C., when Moab was inundated by nomad hordes. But this has become less and less probable.

among occurrences. In verse 47 its repetition in the Massoretic text is probably not original, since its second occurrence is *extra metrum*, and in fact does not appear in Psalm 18 (=II Sam. 22). The latter, together with the Greek and Syriac, also testifies against the repetition of 'I called' in verse 7. This leaves only one good case of repetitive parallelism, found in verse 32:

For *who* is a god, *except* Yahweh?
And *who* is a Mountain, *except* our God?

Assonance appears in several places, notably in verses 8, 11, and especially verses 26–27, where we can quote three good cases of *figura etymologica*:

With *the faithful He deals faithfully,*
With *the man of integrity He deals with integrity,*
With *the pure He deals purely.*

I date the composition of II Sam. 22 in the tenth century B.C., in agreement with the tradition; Cross and Freedman have shown that it is no later than the eighth century.[57a]

Psalm 78 is another archaic poem, as shown by Otto Eissfeldt.[58] The historical review in verses 9 ff., 56, comes down only to the Philistine destruction of Shiloh, ending with the rejection of Joseph–Ephraim and the establishment of David's kingship in Jerusalem. There is only one clear case of repetitive parallelism (verse 8):

A *generation* obstinate and rebellious,
A *generation* which did not make its heart true.

Occasionally we are strongly reminded of still earlier poems; for example, Deut. 32:16, 21 are recalled by verse 58:

They made Him angry with their high places,
And with their idols they made Him jealous.

57a F. M. Cross, Jr., and D. N. Freedman, 'A Royal Song of Thanksgiving: II Samuel 22 = Psalm 18', JBL LXXII (1953), 15–21.
58 See Eissfeldt (n. 41), pp. 26 ff.

There are several reminiscences of Ex. 15, e.g., in verse 54:

And He brought them to His holy mountain (!),[59]
The mountain which His right hand had created.

Psalm 68 offers a valuable supplement to the data which we have sketched, since it contains material going back into pre-thirteenth-century North-west Semitic tradition, as well as matter which can be dated in the thirteenth–twelfth and eleventh–tenth centuries B.C. Until 1951, when I published my detailed study of this chapter based on the analogy of the ancient Oriental catalogues of incipits, it had proved quite impossible to treat the 'Psalm' as a unified composition.[60] My approach was widely rejected because of its novelty, but during the past fifteen years we have learned a great deal more about such catalogues, which include a Yale tablet copied as early as about 2000 B.C. We also possess new Ugaritic texts of liturgical character,[61] with similar incipits, and it has become possible to make some improvements over my then-suggested renderings. It is now certain that a number of incipits are taken without significant modification from 'Canaanite' sources already available to us in Ugaritic: e.g., verses 5, 6, 14b, 23, 34. There are a number of passages in which Canaanite divinities are explicitly or implicitly mentioned, or where a similar source is highly probable. There are also verses referring explicitly to the background of Sinai and Transjordan, as well as to

[59] This is a clear reminiscence of Ex. 15:17, which is itself an equally clear reflection of passages in the Baal Epic. On the passage in Ex. 15 see Cross and Freedman, JNES XIV (1955), 249 f. For Ugaritic *gbl* 'mountain' see G. R. Driver, CML 146, n. 28 and M. Dahood, *Mél. Eugène Tisserant* I (Rome, 1964), 86.

[60] See my studies, HUCA XXIII (1950–1), 1–39 and the Mowinckel *Festschrift* (Oslo, 1956), pp. 1 ff. Since these treatments appeared there have been a number of corrections and confirmations of individual proposals of mine; cf. n. 62.

[61] E.g. PRU II, Nos. 1 and 2, pp. 3 ff.

the days of the Conquest of Canaan and the period of the Judges (e.g., verses 2–3, 13–14, 15, 28); other passages belong to the time of the United Monarchy (e.g., 19, 30, 32, and perhaps others). While early poems need not have repetitive parallelism, it is always gratifying to find archaism in content combined with archaism in form. Three incipits in particular stand out; two of them require new translations in the light of advancing knowledge: Psalm 68:23:

> The (primordial?) Serpent *I have muzzled,*
> *I have muzzled* the abyss of Sea![62]

Psalm 68:13:

> (When) kings (and) armies *fled in disorder,*
> (When) *fled in disorder* (. . .),
> In the tent camps the spoil was divided.[63]

Psalm 68:17:

'*O mountains* of God,	*Mountains of Bashan,*
O domed (?) *mountains,*	*Mountains of Bashan,*
Why do ye . . . (?)	*O domed* (?) *mountains,*
Mountains which *God* wanted	For His habitation!'

From Psalms 22 (II Sam. 18), 78 and 72 on through the pre-exilic period most Psalms, like most prophetic verse, eschew repetition and endeavour to vary the wording as much as possible. There are, of course, exceptions in such clearly archaic verse as Psalm 29 as well as in older material in Habakkuk and the other prophets, but in general it is not until exilic times that we have a renaissance of archaism in poetic style. The composers of the *Šîrê ham-Ma'alot* (Psalms 120–134) felt the effect of the ancient repetitive style, but obviously had no clear idea how to imitate it. Naturally, the results, though often impressive, had little or nothing in common with the ancient formulas

[62] See M. Dahood, JBL LXXX (1961), 270 f.

[63] The discovery that in the Mari texts the North-west Semitic word *nawûm/nawêm* meant 'camp' requires a change from 'meadows' to 'tent camps'.

except word repetition. Similarly, the scribes of Shamash-shum-ukin wrote incredibly bad Sumerian in the seventh century B.C., and in the sixth century the scribes of Nebuchadnezzar had no idea how to use the old Babylonian case-endings which they tried to imitate. During the Early Iron Age, then, we can trace the gradual abandonment of repetitive parallelism, and a tendency to substitute various forms of assonance and paronomasia. Used in conjunction with other lines of evidence, these two factors serve as valid criteria for dating verse reputed to have been composed, or suspected of being composed, in the eleventh century or earlier.[64]

D. THE JE COMPLEX

The state of documentary analysis in the field of Old Testament studies has been changing rapidly during the past decade, though many specialists fail to recognize the fact. Until the discovery of Cave IV at Qumran, in September 1952, there was no evidence except the Nash Papyrus for a really divergent Hebrew text of the Bible; this fragment was thought by some to be a kind of amulet with conflate text, which did not reflect a uniform older recension.[65] Since the serious study of the innumerable fragments from Cave IV at Qumran began in 1953, the existence of widely divergent recensions of the Hebrew text of the Old Testament has become certain. I discussed the evidence available to me in 1955,[66] and Frank M. Cross, Jr., presented it on the basis of much more extensive material in 1958.[67] It is now demonstrated that the

[64] See my remarks in the Mowinckel *Festschrift* (1956), pp. 6 ff.

[65] JBL LVI (1937), 145–76.

[66] BASOR 140, pp. 27 ff.

[67] Frank M. Cross, Jr., *The Ancient Library of Qumran* (New York, 1958), pp. 124 ff., 140 ff. The most important subsequent development has been the increasing recognition by Cross of the importance of the Lucianic recension, which goes back to an Old Palestinian prototype.

recensional differences between the Hebrew and the Greek texts go back in principle to different Hebrew recensions antedating the Hellenistic period. Nearly all of the more striking differences between Hebrew and Greek may now be explained by recensional divergences between the Hebrew prototypes, and only rarely by inner Greek corruptions arising between the third–second centuries B.C. and the fourth–fifth centuries A.D.

The discovery of relatively wide limits of textual variation antedating the third century B.C. makes the minute analysis of the Pentateuch which became fashionable after Wellhausen completely absurd. While it is quite true that there is less evidence for recensional differences in the Pentateuch than there is, for example, in Samuel–Kings, there is already more than enough to warn against elaborate hypothetical analyses and against finding different 'sources' and 'documents' wherever there appears to be any flaw or inconsistency in the received text. Such a subjective approach to literary-historical problems was always suspect and has now become irrational. The distribution of short passages and often of single verses among various independent strands of tradition has generally been gratuitous. We shall illustrate below, with two detailed examples, how exaggerated recent analysis has been. Both these examples contain matter hitherto distributed between J, E, and P, or other sources related to them. As a matter of fact, the material is so homogeneous and yet so archaic that we can safely refer it to the J complex put together from verse and prose tradition in the tenth century B.C.[68] E is merely a northern

[68] It is scarcely possible that the date for the composition of the original J history is later than the tenth century, because the secondary E tradition shows strong indications of being an official recension of it intended for the Northern Kingdom and therefore hard to date much later than the disruption of the Monarchy. Besides, wherever we have J material which can be used for dating purposes, a date under the United Monarchy becomes highly prob-

recension of J (or of part of it) dating from the century following the Division of the Kingdom (c. 922 B.C.).[69] We shall return to this point below.

There can be no doubt that nineteenth-century scholarship was correct in recognizing different blocks of material in the Pentateuch. D must stand as the 'Second Law' regardless of hypotheses about its origin and date. P remains a repertory of cultic tradition whatever its date and origin, and remains more closely related to E than to J. And the narrative sources J and E clearly reflect two different, though closely related, bodies of material. The great importance of the two chief divine names in distinguishing them has not been diminished by the finds at Qumran. J. Skinner's demonstration that MT and Samaritan agree in the use of the names *Yahweh* and *Elohim* over 97 per cent of the time, remains a convincing answer to those scholars who reject the Documentary Hypothesis *in toto*.[70]

---

able. An argument which I have often advanced in the past is that such J material as the Oracles of Balaam was transmitted in the defective orthography of the tenth century before *waw* and *yod* began to be used as vowel letters in final position. That this was the case at that time we know from the early Phoenician inscriptions as well as from such Israelite texts as the Gezer Calendar.

[69] We owe recognition of this fact to the combined work of P. Volz, W. Rudolph, M. Noth, and S. Mowinckel. I came to adopt this point of view only about a decade ago (after following R. Kittel for decades), but did not publish anything on the subject until 1963 (CBQ xxv, 9 ff.). See especially Rudolph, *Der 'Elohist' von Exodus bis Josua* (BZATW, No. 63, 1938); Noth, *Ueberlieferungsgeschichte des Pentateuchs* (Stuttgart, 1948), pp. 40 ff. and *passim*; Mowinckel, *Erwägungen zur Pentateuch-Quellenfrage* (Oslo, 1964), pp. 59–118; *Tetrateuch-Pentateuch-Hexateuch* (BZATW, No. 90, 1964), *passim*. In my opinion, Mowinckel is correct in emphasizing the continuity of oral tradition after the appearance of J, but wrong in supposing that all the historically significant E matter came from J. My position is, therefore, closer to that of Noth than to that of Mowinckel.

[70] Since 1937 I have pointed out that the script in which the Samaritan Pentateuch and other documents were written was not a

The first real break in the deadlock which has stopped debate on the origins of J and E came with the publication of Robert G. Boling's paper, '"Synonymous" Parallelism in the Psalms', in 1960.[71] In this study he investigated the structure of poetic parallelism in the Psalter, basing his approach on a still unpublished thesis of Moshe Held, *Studies in Ugaritic Lexicography and Poetic Style*.[72] Ugaritic poetry is characterized, as we have seen, by fixed pairs of synonyms or related words appearing in parallelism. The first, Held and Boling call 'A-words'; they were common in prose and enjoyed a preferred sequence over 'B-words', which usually only appear in verse. In early Hebrew verse the rules of parallelism were originally nearly the same, and such differences from Canaanite as occur in the earliest Biblical poems are clearly due to the fact that Ugaritic poetry was considerably older, as a rule. In most of our extant Psalter we have much variation from the original norms, because of the considerably later date of most Psalms. Where standard metrical schemes were followed, a more or less fixed pattern of word order prevailed, words in A position enjoying a privileged status relative to words in B position.[73]

Boling has carefully compared the occurrences of *Yah-*

---

continuation of the pre-exilic cursive, but was an archaistic revival in Hasmonaean times, presumably during the subjugation of Samaria to the Jews in the late second and early first centuries B.C. See FSAC (1940 ed.), pp. 266 and 336. This late date has been confirmed by the analysis of palaeo-Hebrew scripts in the Hasmonaean age by Frank M. Cross, Jr., and Richard S. Hanson; see the latter's paper in BASOR 175 (1964), 26–42 especially p. 42. Once the two recensions had separated, they did not influence one another again.

[71] JSS v (1960), 221–55. This is a condensation of his unpublished Johns Hopkins dissertation (1959).

[72] Unpublished Johns Hopkins dissertation (1957).

[73] There is a remarkably regular shift in A and B words between Bronze-Age Canaanite and Iron-Age Hebrew.

weh and *Elôhîm* in the Psalter. In the so-called Elohistic Psalms (42–83) we have the following relation:[74]

	A	B
Eloh(im)	30	3
Yahweh	5	11

In all the remaining Psalms (1–41, 84–150) we have the following relation:

	A	B
Yahweh	77	7
Eloh(im)	6	27

Where divine names occur in texts transmitted independently in different contexts (e.g., Psalm 40:17=70:5), each following a different stylistic preference, the order is reversed. Finally, a comparison of counts of all occurrences of the divine names in question in the Psalter yields the following table:

	J Psalms	E Psalms
Yahweh	584 (86·1%)	45 (17·6%)
Eloh(im)	94 (13·9%)	210 (82·4%)

In other words, we have not only a stylistic preference for a fixed order in both groups, but we have also five or six times as large a number of occurrences of the preferred divine name in each group, the ratio being about the same (inverted) in each. This leaves little room for doubt that the source of preference for one divine name over the other is the same in JE as in the Psalter. The time has passed when most of the Psalter was unceremoniously relegated to post-exilic and Hellenistic times; there is no good reason to date any of the Psalms after the fifth–fourth centuries B.C. and most of them are probably pre-exilic.

Reconsideration of the origin of the J and E narratives

[74] See Boling's analysis, JSS v (1960), 248–55, which I have reproduced in CBQ xxv (1963), 3.

in the light of the foregoing material indicates that a new approach is necessary. In the light of Boling's material, interpreted according to the evidence now available for much higher dating of archaic Israelite verse, we are forced to look for an earlier origin of the alternation between J and E. Re-study of the Pentateuchal poems composed between the Exodus and the establishment of the Monarchy makes it clear that Ex. 15 is essentially 'J', while the Oracles of Balaam in Num. 23–24 are essentially 'E'; Deut. 32 and 33 (Song of Moses and Blessing of Moses, both from about the middle of the eleventh century) are rather 'J' than 'E'; Gen. 49 (Blessing of Jacob, late eleventh century in its present form, but with much earlier material) is uncertain. The Song of Deborah (Judg. 5) is definitely 'J'.

Starting probably as a liturgical formula among the Hebrews (or possibly the Midianites),[75] *Yahweh* was adopted by Moses as the official name of the God of Israel and gained ground rapidly, being employed by Joshua in forming his Yahwist name, and appearing twice among the names of the family of Gideon (twelfth century). It may, accordingly, be supposed that the Song of Miriam and the Oracles of Balaam (probably from the early and late thirteenth century, respectively) also reflect rapid adaptation of the new monotheistic terminology to traditional poetic usage. In Ugaritic poetry we find constantly recurring parallelism between different names or appellations of the same divinity (e.g., *Athirat* and *Qudšu*, *Al'iyan Ba'lu* and *Zubulu ba'lu 'arṣi*) or of different deities. In Mosaic Israel only a single God could appear: thus, in the Balaam Oracles, we have *El* and *Šaddai* in parallelism. Similarly, *Yahweh* replaced *Ba'al* (or a synonymous appellation) in Yahwistic poems, while El names (*El-šaddai*, etc.) were replaced by *Elôhîm*. It is

[75] See my discussion in JBL LXVII (1948), 377–81 and D. N. Freedman, 'The Name of the God of Moses', JBL LXXIX (1960), 151–6, as well as Frank M. Cross, Jr., in HTR LV (1962), 250 ff.

not surprising that *El* and *Elôhîm* tended to be more popular on the edge of the desert, where El names long remained dominant as a heritage from early times.

The following synopsis reflects my present views: When the ancient traditions in verse and prose were collected in the tenth century B.C., a paraphrase was made in prose, with *Yahweh* dominant throughout, but after the Division of the Monarchy this was replaced in the North by an E redaction, as normal alternative (in keeping with the Northern tendency to archaize). About the early seventh century B.C. a new edition of the early narrative tradition was prepared, which took J as its basis, supplementing its narrative by divergent material from the E recension.[76] From the tenth century onwards there were, accordingly, definite 'scribal' schools which preferred one or the other of the divine names in position A. In composing religious poetry, we find similar priorities, which are illustrated by the J and E Psalters; the latter must have been re-edited as late as the seventh century B.C., when 'Elohim' replaced Yahweh in hymns referring specifically to Jerusalem as the Holy City.

There are several bodies of material in the Pentateuch which are clearly homogeneous, though usually considered as highly composite. Among them are particularly the account of the march from Rameses across the 'sea' into the desert (Ex. 12–14, Num. 33—where a common original text can be easily reconstructed with the aid of the LXX),[77] and a group of narratives referring to the Kenites. Systematic comparison of MT, LXX (particularly in Judges), and new Qumran material in such books as Exodus, Deuteronomy and Samuel, show that there has been much shortening of originally longer text by haplographies of all kinds, including especially *homoio-*

[76] See notes 68 and 69 above.

[77] The method employed here is closely parallel to that used in my study of the two recensions of the list of Levitic cities; see below, n. 78.

teleuton and *homoioarkton.* There is less evidence than might have been expected for conflate readings and virtually none for late glosses. Scribes and reciters from memory were clearly conscientious in not adding to the text, though humanly fallible in dropping words, letters, phrases and even whole passages. In Judges we have such striking recensional differences between the A and B recensions of LXX that we must recognize the existence of lost Hebrew prototypes for most of the differences. In their way these LXX recensions are as valuable for reconstructing the Hebrew original as the different Qumran recensions of I Samuel, in which the combined evidence of Qumran, LXX and MT makes it possible to restore, with a high degree of probability, a substantially longer original.

After presenting these two examples of a common prose source, with poetic quotations, which have hitherto been attributed to several different documentary sources, I shall illustrate the heavy indebtedness of historical tradition to orally transmitted poetic saga. The supposed independent confirmation from different sources (J, E, P), which we seem to have lost, we regain with compound interest when we recognize the basic historical significance of archaic verse tradition.

The first of the two examples of a common source comes from the list of stations along the Exodus route in Egypt and immediately after crossing into the desert; it is preserved in Ex. 12–15 and Num. 33. The passages listing the stations in question have been distributed by leading critical authorities from Baentsch to Noth and from Carpenter to Cuthbert Simpson among at least three sources—and individual attributions vary enormously. Among the most recent, Cuthbert Simpson employs J_2, J_3, E_2, and P, besides various additional *sigla.* And yet the Hebrew lists differ among themselves little more than the Hebrew does from the Greek, or even than the A and B recensions of the LXX differ among themselves. Under such conditions, one should look normally for recensional, not documentary, explanations of the divergences, especially when one observes that most variants can be easily explained as due to various simple types of scribal error. Here I recall my proof (1945) that the lists of the Levitic cities in Josh. 21 = I Chron. 6:54 ff. were two scribal recensions of the same written list and not distinct orally transmitted traditions, as thought by S. Klein.[78] My success was due to systematic application of the methods of Max Margolis to the Greek MS material, complemented by use of all then available data bearing on the history of occupation. Another important cause of scribal error in transmitting our lists of stations is the fact that they exhibit two types of epic material: prospective, or that in which a speaker tells what is to happen, or gives advance orders in detail; narrative, in which a speaker tells what happened or what was done. In the Ugaritic epics, especially in Keret, there are long doublets of this kind, and numerous obscurities have been cleared up and gaps filled by comparing prospective with narrative, and *vice versa.*

At the same time, the material from Cave IV at Qumran has proved that most of the Qumran Hebrew and LXX text of Samuel not found in Massoretic Hebrew is certainly or probably original; there has been a steady erosion of the text as passages with similar word-content have been dropped by copyists. In other words, we have few scribal glosses—the sacred text was exempt from such deliberate additions—but many inadvertent losses.

If we bear these principles in mind, and convert prospective passages into narrative, the basic text of the list of stations may be rendered *approximately* as follows:

And the children of Israel departed from Rameses to Suc-

[78] See 'The List of Levitic Cities' in the Louis Ginzberg Jubilee volume (New York, 1945), pp. 49–73, which was very well received by the late Peter Walters (Katz) and H. M. Orlinsky.

coth, and they encamped at Succoth (Ex. 12:37 combined with Num. 33:5);

And they departed from Succoth (to Othom), and they encamped at Othom on the edge of the desert (Ex. 13:20 = Num. 33:6);

And they departed from Othom . . . (Num. 33:7);

And they turned back towards (!) Pi-hahiroth, between Migdol and the sea, over against Baal-zephon (Ex. 14:2; Num. 33:7);

And opposite it they encamped by the sea (Ex. 14:2, 9);

And they departed from before Pi-hahiroth, and they passed through the midst of the sea into the desert (Num. 33:8);

And Moses caused them (!) to depart from the Sea of Reeds, and they went out into the desert of the Wall (Shur) . . . , and they came to Marah (Num. 33:8; Ex. 15:22).

In the midst of the condensed account in Exodus, we find the good poetic bicolon (3:3):

> Trapped are they in the land (Egypt),
> The desert has barred them in. (Ex. 14:3)

This quotation is so extraordinarily apt that one can scarcely doubt its antiquity. Our knowledge of the topography of north-eastern Egypt is now so precise that this reconstruction, based as it is on textual evidence throughout, is not likely to be appreciably wrong.[79] Of course, it lays no claim to be anything but an approximate condensation of a longer original, most of which has been irretrievably lost by the vicissitudes of oral and written transmission. That the original J text has come down to our Hebrew Bible through JE and P, I do not deny, but these are not in any sense independent sources, but

[79] My detailed analysis of the topographic material not yet published, is based on the Egyptian sources and on study of the terrain as it is today, as well as on a more precise linguistic approach to toponymy; for some preliminary observations see BASOR 109 (1948), 15 f. and the *Festschrift* Alfred Bertholet (Tübingen, 1950), pp. 1–14, especially pp. 12 ff.

rather very ancient recensions, all of which provide valuable clues in our efforts to reconstruct Biblical history.

Our second example of the homogeneity of material attributed by critical scholars since Wellhausen to different independent sources is the Kenite material in Exodus, Numbers and Judges.[80] As a result of the general misunderstanding of the nature of early Israelite historical tradition, a state of chaos continues to prevail among Biblical scholars with respect to the relation between Israel and the Kenites. The literary reflections of early Israelite oral tradition are confusing, since they appear to give three different names to the patron and father-in-law of Moses, who seems to be called Reuel, Jethro, or Hobab. The latter's affiliations are described as 'Midianite' and 'Kenite', a fact which seems to compound the difficulty.

The dilemma has been attacked with the aid of several techniques: (1) the texts can be harmonized, especially by giving *ḥôtén* a special sense, 'brother-in-law', when used of Hobab; (2) the different names can be assigned to different Pentateuchal documents: e.g., Hobab to J, Jethro to E; (3) Reuel (Ex. 2:18) can be considered secondary. Since Hobab (also Jethro, LXX B) is called a Kenite as well as a Midianite, it is often argued that the Kenites were a branch of the Midianites. But the problem is not solved by such superficial attempts to harmonize the text or by assigning variants to different sources. We must determine, if possible, the origin of the variations. While it is possible that there were different traditions about the name of the 'priest of Midian', it is wholly unnecessary to make this assumption. We need only analyse the texts and names in the light of modern knowledge in order to reach a reasonable solution of the present apparent dilemma.

As priest of Midian, Reuel is mentioned in MT only in

[80] See my discussion in CBQ xxv (1963), 3–9, which underlies the present treatment. For details consult the extensive material included there in footnotes.

Ex. 2:18, although this name has been introduced elsewhere in the recensions and is found almost exclusively in Josephus. In Num. 10:29 Reuel is stated explicitly to be the 'father' of Hobab. The name Reuel is clearly the clan name of Hobab, since in such early references to nomads the patronymic was usually a clan name. This name is actually preserved as that of a clan affiliated with Midian in the LXX of Gen. 25:3. Moreover, like many of these early tribal and clan names, Reuel also appears as a clan of the neighbouring people of Edom (Gen. 36, *passim*; I Chron. 1:35, 37). The situation here is similar to that of Kenaz and other groups, where a clan either shifts its tribal allegiance or is split into different parts, each of which becomes attached to a different group. Parallels in the tribal history of the Arabs are very numerous.

Accordingly, it is rather obvious that in Ex. 2:18, which mentions Reuel as the father of the daughters of Jethro (Ex. 3:1), we should read: 'And they (the daughters of the "priest of Midian" [v. 16]) came to ⟨Jethro⟩, son of Reuel, their father.' While this is not attested in any of the versions, it is most improbable that the original editors of the Pentateuch can have left such an obvious discrepancy standing. We may, therefore, eliminate the clan of Reuel as a competitor for the distinction of being the person intended to play the rôle of the priest of Midian, leaving only Jethro and Hobab to be considered.

Quite aside from the two distinct names, the rôles of Jethro and Hobab are entirely different. Jethro appears as an old man with seven daughters (Ex. 2:16), who advises his son-in-law from the wealth of his own experience (Ex. 18). Hobab, on the other hand, appears as a vigorous younger man whom Moses wants as a guide in the wilderness (Num. 10:29–32); the extant text assumes that Hobab did yield to pressure and act in this capacity. The antiquity of the passage—which is accepted by most critics—becomes even clearer when we note that a perfectly good poetic bicolon (3+3) is embedded in the words of Moses to Hobab:

Thou dost know how we camp in the desert
And thou shalt become our eyes.

We have only to change the vocalization from *ḥôtén* to *ḥătán* where Hobab is mentioned, and our difficulties vanish: render Num. 10:29, 'Hobab, the son of Reuel, the Midianite, son-in-law (!) of Moses.'[81] The fact that both Hobab and Jethro belonged to the clan of Reuel should cause no difficulty whatever, since the West Semitic nomads were as a rule endogamous; therefore one would expect Moses' son-in-law and father-in-law both to come from the same clan.

Although in Num. 10:29 Hobab is plainly identified as a Midianite, one may observe that elsewhere, in Judg. 1:16 and 4:11, Hobab is called a Kenite (*Qênî*): 'And the children of Hobab the Kenite, son-in-law (!) of Moses, went up from the Town of Date Palms (to dwell) with the children of Judah in the desert which is in the south of ⟨Judah, going down from⟩ Arad,[82] ⟨. . .⟩ and

[81] See *ibid.*, p. 7, n. 22, for the evidence.

[82] LXX B inserts in Judg. 1:16 . . . *Iouda hē estin epi katabaseōs Arad.* LXX A leaves out the first three words above but also inserts *epi katabaseōs Arad.* Since the word *katabasis* elsewhere translates Hebrew *môrād*, it follows that the Hebrew text read originally *be-môrad 'Arad*, just as we have *be-môrad Bêt-Hôrôn* (Josh. 10:11) and *be-môrad Ḥôrônaim* (Jer. 48:5). The haplography is so obvious that it is scarcely necessary to mention it. This reading disposes of the supposed conflict between the Hebrew text of the passage and the results of the excavation of the site by Yohanan Aharoni and Ruth Amiran, who have shown that Arad was not occupied between the early third millennium and the tenth century B.C. The Deuteronomic editor in the seventh century B.C. has been responsible for recent confusion. Either he or a precursor drew the natural inference that Arad was one of the Canaanite royal cities captured by Joshua (Josh. 12:14). This is on a par with several other reasonable inferences of his which happen to be wrong. On the other hand, this same editor has preserved several names of

they (!) went and dwelt with the Ama[lekites]. And Judah went with Simeon his brother and they defeated the Canaanite who resided in Zephath and devoted it to destruction, and they (!) called the name of the city Hormah' (Judg. 1:16f.). 'And Heber the Kenite left the Kenites who belonged to the children of Hobab, the son-in-law (!) of Moses' (Judg. 4:11). (Note that the changes of MT in angular brackets are from LXX A or B; the changes in square brackets are required by the context.)

It has long been recognized that *Qênî*, 'Kenite', is an occupational name derived from *qayn*, which meant originally 'metal-worker, smith', as in Aramaic and Arabic; the meaning is clearly preserved in the appellation of the third son of Lamech in Gen. 4:22, 'Tubal (the) smith, craftsman . . . worker in copper and iron.' Copper was extensively worked in Sinai from the third millennium on, and since there was more copper in Midian proper, the region east and south of the Gulf of 'Aqaba,[83] than there was in Sinai, we may safely suppose that copper working was just as ancient there. A passage in the 'Oracles of Balaam', which can scarcely be later than c. 1200 B.C., makes it clear that there was a metal-working tribe installed in the mountainous regions of Sinai or Midian at that time. From the two passages just cited, it is clear that metal-working was a speciality of the Midianite group among whom Moses settled. But it not necessary to connect the metal-working family of Hobab di-

towns captured by Israelites which are not preserved by any other source, so we owe a debt of gratitude to him for his effort not to miss anything. In my opinion, Zephath (later Hormah) was destroyed by the Israelites about that time; it is almost certainly modern Tell el-Milḥ south-east of Beersheba, where soundings have yielded remains of Middle and Late Bronze. For a different opinion, see B. Mazar in JNES XXIV (1965), 297–303, completed before my paper in CBQ appeared. Mazar's article contains important observations which would have been strengthened by use of the consistent LXX reading.

[83] On Midian see most recently my discussion, *ibid.*, pp. 7 ff.

rectly to the reference in the 'Oracles of Balaam'. To summarize: Hobab, son-in-law of Moses, was a Midianite belonging to the clan of Reuel and a smith by profession. The apparent contradictions are the result of scribal errors and misunderstandings, and have been further exaggerated by the unnecessary conjectures of modern literary analysts.

E. THE HISTORICAL SIGNIFICANCE OF ARCHAIC HEBREW VERSE

In the following pages, I shall give some illustrations of the special historical significance of archaic verse in Exodus–Numbers. These will be followed by a few examples drawn from the Patriarchal narratives. The best cases come, however, from the Mosaic and early post-Mosaic tradition.

First let us consider Num. 12:6–8, which has been attributed by leading Pentateuchal scholars to J_1 (L), the oldest commonly recognized source:

> Hear now the words of ⟨Yahweh⟩!
>
> If there be a prophet among you,[84]
> In a vision I will make myself known to him,
> In a dream I will speak with him.
> Not so is My servant Moses;
> Of all My household he is most faithful.
> Mouth to mouth will I speak to him;
> ⟨Not⟩ in a vision and not in riddles,[85]
> But the image of Yahweh shall he see.[86]

[84] We must read, with Old Latin and Vulgate, *nābî' bākem* instead of *něbîăkem.*

[85] We must prefix *lô'* ('not') to the colon; its loss is due to the fact that there are two other occurrences of *lô'* preceding and following in two successive lines. Incidentally, we should read *mar'eh* and not *mar'ah* in both cases.

[86] It is more than doubtful that the pointing *těmûnat* is correct. A more probable vocalization is simply *tamnît* (= *tabnît*), 'structure,

The archaism is clear from the stylistic resemblances (including some repetition) to passages in the Ugaritic Baal Epic. For instance, in both we find successive three-beat cola beginning with "In a dream . . . In a vision . . ." The important point is that here we can draw on an archaic verse account for a view of the relation of God to the prophets and Moses which antedates our extant prose tradition. A plausible conjectural date for the poem might be in the period of acute friction between priests and prophets in the time of Samuel (see Chapter IV).

The account of the Golden Calf episode of Ex. 32 is attributed by most critics to JE, with some earlier and later material distinguished. Actually it is very archaic and even totally unintelligible in places; it may not have been edited in approximately its present form until after the meaning of the text was no longer fully understood. Particularly archaic is the description (Ex. 32:20) of how the image of the young bull was destroyed, which shares three steps in progressive annihilation with the destruction of Death by the goddess Anath in the Baal Epic of Ugarit—each account using the same verbs, though in different order. The passages (verses 17, 22, 25) in which derivatives of a stem *BR'/PR'* seem to occur are almost wholly obscure. The tricolon (3 + 3 + 3) in 32:18 is especially significant—the repetitive part of it has been correctly preserved by LXX and Syriac, though with only imperfect comprehension (see above). In this fragment, just as in Ex. 15:11, two original beats had already been

form, image', especially since the same word may appear in Phoenician names as *Tbnt,* which is transcribed into Greek as *Tennēs* (probably from *Tennît*; see Ch. III on *Tnt.*). This word does not mean 'idol', nor 'similitude' or 'form', but rather an enveloping brilliance like Assyrian *melammû,* which made the presence of God known without permitting Him to be seen by mortal eye. LXX correctly renders the word *tmnt* as *doxa* and Syriac as *šubḥâ.* Note especially that *pānêkā* is in parallelism with *tĕmûnātkā* in Psalm 17:15. [See Addenda and Ch. III, n. 62.]

reduced to one by the loss of vocalic endings: *qôlu ghannôti* has become *qôl 'annôt*, literally 'the sound of music'. This suits a thirteenth-century date for the fragment very well; it may be contemporary with Ex. 15.

The Song of the Well (Num. 21:17–18) is another fragment going back to about the time of Moses. In it we seem to have a bicolon (2+2) followed by two bicola (3+3/3+3); the first line has been spoiled by the omission of a word and part of another word, both beginning with *'ayin*. The text is a play on the original meanings of the two place-names Beer and Mattanah, included in an early list of desert stations which are omitted from the P list in Num. 33:

⟨Sing⟩ about a well (Beer), Sing about it . . .
 Well which the notables dug,
  Which the leaders of the people sank;
From digging rock comes sustenance,
 And from the desert (comes) a gift (Mattanah)![87]

This fragment goes back to the Mosaic period or very soon afterwards. Immediately before it comes another fragment (Num. 21:14–15), which cannot be reconstructed, though it is explicitly quoted from 'The Book of the Wars of Yahweh'. One sign of its antiquity is the insertion of the enclitic *mem* in the middle of a construct chain: *naḥalê-m Arnôn*, 'branch-wadis of the Arnon', like *hararê-m Śē 'îr*, 'mountains of Seir', in Gen. 14:6.[88]

[87] This archaic fragment has suffered at the hands of later oral and written transmission. The first colon should probably be read ⟨*'annu*⟩ *'alê be'er*. In cola 4 and 5 there has been some wrong division of words, and there has also been confusion between the two initial consonants of the first three words. In other words, restore the Hebrew as *bĕmō ḥqq miš'enet* (cf. Is. 3:1, 'all *miš'an* of bread and all *miš'an* of water); the sixth colon then begins with *ū-bĕmō midbar mattānah*. Here is naturally a play on the meaning of the place-name *Mattānah*.

[88] This syntactic construction appears not infrequently in Ugarit and Amarna; more examples are being found all the time in biblical poetry or prose derived from poetry; see provisionally Albright,

Turning back to the Song of Miriam, with which we dealt above solely from the standpoint of its exceedingly archaic style, it must be emphasized that we not only have indications of great age in the prosodic structure, but we also have numerous survivals of Bronze Age grammatical phenomena, as well as allusions to ancient Canaanite poetry. For instance, in Ex. 15:17–18 we have a series of direct quotations from Canaanite sources, including especially the reference to 'the mountain of Thine inheritance, O Yahweh'—where 'Yahweh' replaces 'Baal'. In the light of this relationship, the often defended post-exilic date sounds absurd, to say the least.[89]

We can dispose of two alleged anachronisms without too much difficulty. In verse 8 we read (2 + 2/3 + 3):

By the breath of Thy nostrils The waters were heaped up,
They were raised like the dykes of the irrigators,
The deeps were curdled[90] in the midst of the sea.

The word *nēd*, for *nidd*, Arabic *nadd*, 'piled-up earth or sand' (also in Psalm 78:13),[91] refers to the raised banks of earth or sand (levees) which were thrown up along irrigation canals and ditches in order to prevent their water from escaping. In Egypt it was perfectly natural to employ such an allusion, and there is not the slightest reason to consider its use in the Song of Miriam as secondary to its use in the account of the damming up of the Jordan above the place where the Israelites crossed (Josh. 3:16). Exactly the reverse is true; the passage through the Sea of Reeds was so much more important than the crossing of the Jordan that borrowing must have

---

JBL LXIII (1944), 219, n. 83, and Horace D. Hummel, JBL LXXVI (1957), 99 ff. New examples are turning up constantly in Ugaritic.

[89] See the fuller treatment of the Song of Miriam above.

[90] In this connexion the translation 'congealed' is wrong, since *qp'* refers to churning of butter or curdling of milk and not to freezing, as there are no icy sheets of water in or around Egypt.

[91] Whether *nôzĕlîm* is correctly vocalized or not we cannot say; *nzlm* might mean either 'irrigators' or 'irrigation ditches'.

taken place along the normal stream of literary activity. Incidentally, the mixed metaphors in verse 8 are characteristic of North-west Semitic verse; cf. my comments elsewhere on the stylistically normal but illogical expressions used in Joshua's famous injunction to the sun and moon (Josh. 10:12), and in the Song of Deborah (Judg. 5:26), with Ugaritic parallels.[92] It was, accordingly, natural that the prose editor of Ex. 14:22 should understand the poetic tradition in the sense of walls of water standing on either side of the fleeing Israelites, whereas in Ex. 14:21, following independent tradition, he correctly explained the retreat of the water as caused by a strong east wind blowing all night before the Israelites crossed. In other words, all three descriptions are correct in essential respects: Ex. 15:8 in giving a vivid poetic description, entirely correct according to then prevailing stylistic norms; Ex. 14:21 in giving a factual account of what happened; Ex. 14:22 in translating vague poetic metaphors into literal prose at a time when the intentional vagueness of early verse was no longer understood.

One apparent anachronism in the Song of Miriam (verse 14) remains to be considered: the reference to the 'dwellers of Philistia', which employs the rare singular of the exceedingly common name 'Philistines', otherwise found only in a few late passages. Its location in the text immediately before the 'clans of Edom' and the '*êlê* Moab' is very strange.[93] Again the Oracles of Balaam

[92] On the proto-logical background of these devices, now so familiar from Ugarit, and their survival in the very oldest Israelite poetry, see HACH 95 f. It is interesting to note that all three passages were completely misunderstood by the empirically-minded Israelites of later times—in fact, in two cases (Ex. 14 and Judg. 4) an early poetic device has been misunderstood as a special cosmic miracle. A miracle was certainly involved, but it was historical rather than cosmic.

[93] Note that the translation of *êlê Mo'ab* is still very obscure. The rendering 'chieftains' is still the most likely, but it may refer to special social groups.

and the discoveries of Qumran come to our assistance. In
the former we have a reference to 'all the *Bĕnê Št*' in
parallelism with a reference to Moab (Num. 24:17). An
identification of *Bĕnê Št* with the nomadic or semi-
nomadic Shutu of the nineteenth century B.C., as well as
with other groups of the same or a similar name, provides
us with a clue.[94] If the original text in Ex. 15:14 read 'all
the children of Shut' and *KL*, 'all', was accidentally omitted, it would be very easy to insert the letters *KL* (which
in the cursive script of the seventh–sixth centuries
B.C. looked almost exactly like *PL*) after 'dwellers', thus
giving us the phrase 'the dwellers in Philistia', which MT
actually has.[95] I have therefore no hesitation in proposing
this emendation, though for the moment it must obviously
remain hypothetical. At all events, it is no longer necessary to insist on an anachronism in this passage, which
suits a thirteenth-century background so well.

For lack of space we shall not dwell at length on the
period of the Conquest and the Judges, though there are
a great many illustrations of the historical importance of
archaic verse embedded in narrative prose. We have already discussed one of the best examples of true, though
late, repetitive poetry quoted in prose context in the
Story of Samson (Judg. 15:16).

The most archaic anecdote preserved in connexion
with the capture by the Israelites of a Canaanite town is

[94] See my discussion in JBL LXIII (1944), 220, n. 89. Some new
material has come in since, and the identification becomes more
probable all the time. There is no evidence that the name of Seth
son of Adam was in any way connected with this nomadic group,
which may well have migrated into Transjordan from north-eastern
Arabia. There is no difficulty in the equivalence of sibilants, since
South-Canaanite *šin* (= Arabic *s*) was etymologically equivalent to
Amorite *s*.

[95] Note that the last colon of v. 15 has *kol yôšĕbê Kĕnaʿan*,
'all the dwellers of Canaan', so *kol* might be expected in a similar
position in v. 14.

found in Joshua 15:18–19 and Judges 1:14–15.[96] It does not seem to have been recognized in the past that this little story of Caleb's daughter Achsah's visit to her father on behalf of her husband, Othniel, is actually composed in scarcely disguised metrical form. While our extant fragment probably exhibits internal lacunae as it stands, it may be reconstructed roughly as follows:

And when she came, she urged him,
  To ask tilled land from her father.

And she alighted from the donkey,
  And Caleb said to her, "What's wrong?"
And she said to him, "Give me a blessing!
  Truly thou hast given me Southland;
    And now give me basins of water!"
So Caleb gave her
  The upper basins
    And the lower basins.

The alternation of a 3 + 3 tricolon with a 2 + 2 tricolon and the archaic forms *'illîyôt* (a *hapax*) and *taḥtîyôt* as well as the late repetitive style strongly suggest an early date, probably in the twelfth or eleventh century B.C.

How was this early verse transmitted? Undoubtedly in many different ways, but one kind of diffusion has been sadly neglected. As we shall see in Chapter II, the Hebrews first came to Palestine as donkey caravaneers, and we can trace this phase of their activity in Egypt down to the time of the Song of Deborah itself. In Palestine donkey caravaneering was still common at the time of the Amarna Tablets (fourteenth century B.C.),[97] and the

[96] For the identification of Debir (Kirjath-sepher) with Tell Beit Mirsim, see my essay in the forthcoming jubilee volume of the Society for Old Testament Study, *Archaeology and Old Testament Study* (ed. D. Winton Thomas). A much longer treatment of the topographical arguments will be found in the *Archaeological Encyclopedia* being prepared by the Israel Exploration Society.

[97] See the revised edition of CAH (II, ch. 20, published as a fascicle in 1966, p. 18) with the references cited there.

Hebrews probably took an active part in it until it was largely superseded by camel caravans about the eleventh century. The reference in the Song to the interruption of caravan trade at the time of Shamgar of Beth-anath almost certainly refers to the raids of the Sea Peoples, headed by the Philistines.[98] Verses 6–11 read as follows:

In the days of Shamgar ben Anath,
  . . . the caravans ceased,[99]
And the caravaneers
  Followed winding paths.[100]
Warriors[101] ceased,
  In Israel they ceased.

O riders on tawny she-asses,
  Ye who sit on caparisoned ⟨male donkeys⟩ (?)[102]

[98] See JPOS 1 (1921), 55–62, where I pointed out the historical position of Shamgar and his connexion with Beth-anath in Galilee. That his name is Hurrian was seen by M. Noth, who identified it with *Šimikari*. Suggestions frequently made that the name *Ben-'Anat* was a personal name are possible but improbable.

[99] The first word of this colon, 'in his days', is possible, but the reference to Shamgar in Judg. 3:31, followed immediately by a reference to Jabin, king of Canaan, suggests that we should insert 'Jabin' instead of the impossible 'Jael'. Incidentally, this name is an abbreviation of the longer *Yabni-Hadad* (name of a king of Hazor in the seventeenth century; cf. *Yabni-el*, name of a prince of Lachish in the fourteenth century). The final long vowel reflects a secondary North-Israelite stress lengthening of a short (anaptyctic) vowel in the jussive of several classes of weak verbs. This phenomenon is common in hypocoristica.

[100] As frequently in Hebrew poetic texts, there has been a secondary transposition of two words in parallelism; *hōlĕkê 'ŏrāḥôt* means 'those who walk in the caravans', see our discussion immediately following.

[101] The word *pĕrāzôn* does not mean 'villagers', as formerly thought, but is a collective from a Canaanite word for 'warrior', which appears in Pap. Anastasi 1, 23, line 4, in the correct consonantal transcription.

[102] *Yôšĕbê 'al mdn* is probably incomplete, since we should expect a 3 + 3 + 3 unit. It has been suggested to me orally by Delbert Hillers that *mdn* may be derived from a dissimilated by-form of the word which appears in Ugaritic as *mdl* (see Jonas Greenfield,

O ye who walk on the road, attend!
At the sound of the cymbals,
Between the watering places,[103]
There they will recite the triumphs of Yahweh,
The triumphs of his warriors in Israel!

In order to understand the terminology it must be remembered that in the Amarna Tablets and other cuneiform texts of the age, as well as in Hebrew, the word meaning 'to walk' (*alāku*, *hālák*) was often used specifically in the sense 'to be a member of a donkey caravan', and one of the commonest terms for a caravan was the derived *aliktu*, *alaktu*, Hebrew *hălîkāh*.[104] There is ample evidence that caravan leaders rode on donkeys while ordinary caravaneers walked behind the donkeys, each caravaneer taking charge of a number of donkeys. In the late nineteenth century B.C., representations at Serābîṭ el-Khâdem show the caravan leader (who may or may not have been an 'Apiru) riding a donkey while his immediate followers walk; incidentally, he bore the name *Khabadadum* and is called 'brother of the chief of Retjenu'.

Unfortunately, we have no way of knowing whether the stories of the Patriarchs were transmitted through caravaneers and similar non-religious groups or whether they came down through religious channels; presumably both modes of oral transmission co-existed. Both professional and amateur rhapsodists undoubtedly existed in early Israel. However this may be, most of the poetry embedded in the stories of Abraham and Isaac in Gen.

Biblica XLV [1964], 527 ff.). In Ugaritic we have *mdl ʿr*, 'caparison a young donkey!' parallel to *ṣmd pḥl*, 'harness a male donkey!' We must remember that donkeys were never saddled in our sense, but that heavy cloths were laid over them and fastened in place by straps. I suggest that we read *yōšĕbê ʿal mdn⟨ʿair⟩*, in which case the loss of *ʿair* after *ʿal* is simple haplography.

[103] *Mašʾăbîm* must be derived from *šʾb*, 'to draw water', which is common in Ugaritic as well as in Hebrew.

[104] On these words see especially CAD, s. vv. and R. Youngblood, BASOR 168 (1962), 24 ff.

12–27 cannot yet be dated stylistically. That the style is often archaic is clear, and I suspect that the original poetic form was Patriarchal Hebrew antedating the period of strong Canaanite influence. But I cannot find satisfactory parallels. Only in the case of Gen. 14, where much of the text can be put into rough metrical form by elimination of prose features and explanations, and where the presence of extremely archaic features cannot be denied, is an early date certain, in my opinion. In this chapter, which all serious critics recognize as an independent source, we find the caravaneering activities of Abraham brought so clearly to the surface that no other explanation of them is reasonable. Only a wealthy caravan leader would be likely to have 318 armed retainers (Gen. 14:14) and to be involved in covenant relationship with so many native chieftains, while he and his nephew remained foreign residents in towns ruled by others. Such a stirring saga may well have been transmitted by caravaneers, just as we have inferred from the Song of Deborah. As a fitting climax I quote the fragment put into the mouth of Abram's friend and ally Melchizedek[105] (Gen. 14:19f.); the metre seems to be $2 + 2 + 3/2 + 2 + 3$, which was still common among the archaic incipits listed in Psalm 68:

Blessed art thou (O Abram) Unto the Highest God,
Creator of Heaven and Earth;
Blessed ⟨art thou⟩ Unto the Highest God,
Who hath given thy foes into thy hands!

[105] See my discussion in BASOR 163 (1961), 52. My observations have been misunderstood by R. H. Smith in ZAW LXXVII (1965), 141 f. My proposal is to read *ū-Malkî-ṣédeq mélek šĕlôm⟨ōh⟩ hôṣî' léḥem wa-yáyin*, 'And Melchizedek, his allied king, brought out bread and wine'. The only 'emendation' required is insertion of *h* lost by haplography between ŠLM and HWṢY'. *Melek šĕlômoh*, 'the king allied to him', has exceedingly good Hebrew parallels (see *ad loc.*, n. 75), and the spelling is normal pre-exilic. On Melchizedek and the tradition, see further the important discussion by J. A. Fitzmyer in CBQ XXV (1963), 305–21, especially pp. 313 ff. [See also Addenda.]

The repetitive style is here definitely liturgical in character, and proves nothing about the original date of the quotation. The latter contains, however, some archaisms from an early source: the preposition *lĕ* may have the archaic sense 'from' instead of the usual Classical Hebrew 'to' in similar context. The divinity is now well known as Canaanite *El* (*'Elyôn*) *qônê 'ĕrĕṣ*, '(The Highest) God, Creator of Earth', who can be traced back through a Hittite adaptation of a lost Hurrian text in pre-Mosaic times.[106] *Miggēn*, 'he gave', appears in Ugaritic but is extremely rare in Hebrew. Even the strong monotheistic colouring is perhaps pre-Mosaic.

In this introductory chapter we have marshalled some of the evidence for early oral transmission of historical information through archaic verse. We have also presented evidence for the poetic background of early Hebrew prose. The examples of stylistic evolution which we have presented in chronological order (according to internal evidence) establish the soundness of our model, itself based on a very large number of analogies from all parts of the Old World, with no known exceptions. Two such consistent sets of evidence, each entirely independent of the other, force us to recognize that archaic Hebrew poetry furnishes invaluable confirmation—as well as correction—of the historical data in our early narrative sources.

[106] See the Mowinckel *Festschrift* (1956), pp. 7f.

II

The Patriarchal Background of Israel's Faith

A. RECENT ARCHAEOLOGICAL FINDS BEARING ON THE PATRIARCHAL AGE

During the forty years from 1925 to 1965 there has been extraordinary progress in our understanding of the Patriarchal background of Israel. First came thirty years of revolutionary advances, followed by steady consolidation of our gains during the past decade.[1]

In 1925 came the initial discovery of tablet archives at Nuzi in north-eastern Iraq, containing family records and legal documents belonging to a Hurrian (Biblical Horite) population in the fifteenth and early fourteenth centuries B.C. The Nuzi finds have proved that many curious details of customary law in the Patriarchal narratives are very ancient, and were no longer understood in tenth-century Israel and later times.[2]

The Nuzi discoveries were followed by the publication in 1926 and 1940 of the Egyptian 'Execration Texts'.[3]

[1] For successive surveys of our gains, see FSAC (1957 ed.), 25 ff.; OTMS 1–47; HACH 103 ff., 130 ff.

[2] See especially E. A. Speiser, *Genesis* (Anchor Bible, 1964), *passim*, and R. de Vaux's review in JBL LXXXV (1965), 74 ff. Speiser offers about twenty parallels between Patriarchal customary law and Nuzi. De Vaux's caveat about exaggerating the importance of Hurrian influence on the early Hebrews is not really necessary in view of the fact that the city of Nahor (Gen. 24:10) was actually ruled by Hurrian princes in the Mari period and that Harran itself was in an area inhabited by a mixed population of Hurrians and Semites. Cf. n. 31 below, as well as § F.

[3] On the initial publications by K. Sethe and G. Posener, cf. the

These texts are extremely significant because they contain long lists of place and tribal names together with the names of the chieftains who ruled these towns or tribes, dating from the late twentieth and nineteenth centuries B.C. In some respects, thanks to the light shed on the vocalization of these names by cuneiform transcriptions of West Semitic names, the Execration Texts are exceptionally important for our purpose, since all Asiatic names come from Palestine, Phoenicia and southern Syria.

The same year as the first publication of Execration Texts from Egypt, there appeared Theo Bauer's collection and analysis of North-west Semitic personal names from Babylonian tablets of the nineteenth to sixteenth centuries B.C.[4] Together with subsequent finds in Mesopotamia this has made it possible to place early Hebrew names in their correct setting and to use them as a key to Patriarchal chronology.

Since 1929 the epoch-making discoveries of tablets at Ugarit on the coast of northern Syria have greatly deepened our knowledge of native North-west Semitic language, religion and culture in the period between 1500 and 1200 B.C.[5] The Canaanite culture of the Late Bronze

references in OTMS, 43 f., n. 5. My own principal papers on the subject were published in JPOS VIII (1928), 223–56 and BASOR 83 (1941), 30 ff. Very important new material, confirming incidentally my chronology of these texts since 1940 (BASOR 83, 32 f.), has been discovered at Mirgissa, south of Wadi Halfa in Nubia. These new Execration Texts date between the Berlin vases and the statuettes of Saqqara, but are nearer the former than the latter in time. They may, therefore, be tentatively dated in the early nineteenth century B.C. On this discovery, which has not yet been formally published, see CRAI, 1963, 97–102, by J. Vercoutter and G. Posener. See also André Vila, *Journal des Savants*, 1963, 135–60.

[4] See his monograph *Die Ostkanaanäer*. The material has now been brought up to date by inclusion of all the Mari evidence as well as pertinent new material from Babylonian tablets in Herbert B. Huffmon, *Amorite Personal Names in the Mari Texts* (Baltimore, 1965).

[5] The literature on Ugarit is now so extensive that it is scarcely

Age was essentially a continuation of Middle Bronze civilization, so this material is vital for proper analysis of the differences between Canaanite and Sumero-Accadian elements in early Hebrew background. We need not dwell further on Ugaritic material here, since it has already been utilized so extensively in Chapter I and will be again in Chapter III.

Since 1933 A. Parrot's work at Mari in the Middle Euphrates Valley has yielded a mass of written material from the late eighteenth century B.C., some three centuries before the date of the Nuzi tablets. Publication is far from being completed, but we already know incomparably more than we previously did about the history, language and life of this key period of Patriarchal history. Inevitably, parallels of all kinds have been found between the contents of the Mari documents and early biblical traditions.[6]

Archaeological research during the past forty years has also been brilliantly successful in clearing up difficulties and filling in gaps in our previous knowledge of the general age in question, which extends from the late third millennium B.C. through the early centuries of the second. I must limit myself to a few hints of what has happened during the past few years. We can now date non-epigraphic finds belonging to the period between c. 2500 and 1500 B.C. with surprising precision, thanks especially

necessary to mention more than the two basic series, C. F. A. Schaeffer's *Ugaritica* (now in its 5th vol.) and *Le Palais Royal d'Ugarit* (consisting of texts mainly published by Ch. Virolleaud and J. Nougayrol). A good survey of the material has been published by John Gray, *The Legacy of Canaan* (2nd rev. ed., Leiden, 1965).

[6] The Mari material is being published in three series: (1) *Mission archéologique de Mari*, which deals with the non-epigraphic material; (2) *Archives royales de Mari*, nine volumes of which have appeared (cuneiform texts); (3) a series of *Archives royales de Mari* containing transcriptions and translations of the tablets, thirteen volumes of which have appeared so far.

to excavations in such sites as Byblos[7] and to the able work of Ruth Amiran and Olga Tufnell in analysing the material in question.[8] We now know that after a period of relative depopulation between c. 2200 and 2000 B.C., the causes of which we do not yet know, the population began to increase again in the nineteenth century B.C. During the period between c. 2200 and 1800 B.C. came a phase of material culture which Dr. Kenyon has recently named 'Early Bronze–Middle Bronze'. Her designation covers, however, both Early Bronze IV (or III B) and the following period of debased caliciform pottery which I have been calling Middle Bronze I since 1932. At first I dated the latter between c. 2050 and 1850; I now date it between the early twentieth and the end of the nineteenth century B.C.

This lowering of M.B. I dates has become possible largely because of recent work on the chronology of the tombs of early princes of Byblos found by P. Montet over forty years ago, but whose chronology had not been adequately clarified.[9] Since the pottery found in these so-called 'Royal Tombs of Byblos' is characteristic M.B. IIA, though much richer than corresponding finds in Palestine, we can date similar Palestinian ware at the same time or a little later, between the late nineteenth century and the end of the eighteenth century B.C. This represents a reduction of over half a century in dating, and there can be no doubt about the general accuracy of the results, which are established by numerous synchronisms with Egyptian reigns fixed within a few years by a combina-

[7] Of the publications by P. Montet and M. Dunand half a dozen separately bound parts of three volumes have so far appeared, and a great deal more remains to be published.

[8] See R. Amiran, IEJ x (1960), 204–25, and Tufnell, *Bulletin of the University of London Institute of Archaeology*, III (1962). See also my discussion of their results in BASOR 168 (1962), 36 ff.

[9] On this clarification, see my papers in BASOR 176 (1964), 38–46, and 179 (1965), 38–43. [See also the fuller treatment in BASOR 184 (1966), 26–35.]

tion of astronomical data with dead reckoning by regnal years.

I shall avoid details about the new light shed on the Hyksos period; we now know that from the end of the eighteenth century B.C. to about the middle of the seventeenth Egypt was ruled by princes with West Semitic names. Some of these princes bear names already known from the Bible, such as *Ya'qub-'al* (Jacob)[10] and Shesha (Sheshai). The bearers of these names belonged to the general class of semi-nomadic folk described in Genesis, and there may well have been an even closer connexion, but evidence is still insufficient.

This phase was followed, about the middle of the seventeenth century B.C., by an irruption of chariot warriors from the north-east. Some of their leaders bore Indo-Aryan names but most had names which have not yet been identified linguistically.[11] They established an empire of considerable magnitude and held sway over all or most of Egypt for more than a century, until they were driven out about 1540–1530 B.C.[12]

[10] Past readings such as 'Jacob-El' and my own *Ya'qub-Har* are both wrong. We have two clear writings, neither of which is a mistake for the other, on our scarabs of this reign: *Y'qbhr* and *Y'qb'r*. The second element is naturally the divine name *'Ali*, *'Eli* or *'Al*, on which see Ch. I, n. 52; it was first located in the Hebrew Bible by H. S. Nyberg, and has since been found elsewhere in the Bible. In Ugaritic texts it appears in the sense 'the Exalted One', an appellation of Baal. The alternative Egyptian writing with *h* is a simple dissimilation, in order to avert the repetition of a harsh Semitic *'ayin* in the same name. The Egyptian *'ayin* was much softer —just as today.

[11] I suggested many years ago in an unpublished paper that some of these names might be Luvian. Luvian names are quite common at Ugarit.

[12] Since the chronological evidence is more and more favourable, I adhere to my earlier suggestion that the Indo-Iranian name of the Manda chieftain *Zayaluti* or *Za'aluti* is identical with that of the first king of the Fifteenth Dynasty, Salitis; see BASOR 146 (1957), 31 f. It must be pointed out that among known Hyksos names there are also Egyptian, Semitic and Hurrian names. By the

B. TRADE AND COMMERCE IN THE ANCIENT EAST

One of the most important results of archaeological discovery during the past few years has been an enormous advance in understanding the trade relations of the ancient Near and Middle East. We now know that organized commerce was far earlier than we had imagined. The importance of trade in the development of civilization can scarcely be exaggerated. Without intensive trade, no great expansion of material civilization, or probably of higher culture, is possible. We can now trace commerce back to the pre-Pottery Neolithic of the seventh millennium B.C. at such sites as Jericho in Palestine and Çatal Hüyük in south-central Anatolia.[13] It was shown by Emmanuel Anati in 1962 that it is impossible to explain the massive fortification of Jericho nearly nine thousand years ago, or the high level of building art there at such an early time, without recognizing that the wealth of Jericho depended only in small part on its oasis, which covers a mere few hundred acres. While extremely useful as a source of food, it could not possibly be the source of the capital required by these indications of wealth. Jericho was, in fact, an important trade centre to which the mineral riches of the Dead Sea Valley, particularly salt, sulphur and asphalt, were brought in order to export them to surrounding regions. This implies some form of caravaneering, though we have no direct evidence for it.

---

time of the Fifteenth Dynasty, the ethnic composition of the foreign invaders must have been very mixed. The date of the final reconquest of Egypt by Amosis is now approximately fixed; the *terminus post quem* is his eleventh year (C. F. Nims, *Egypt of the Pharaohs*, 1965, 199, n. 2). Amosis became king after c. 1540 (Helck, 1962), after c. 1545 (Parker, 1964), after c. 1550 (Hornung, 1964).

[13] On Jericho see E. Anati, BASOR 167 (1962), 25 ff. On Çatal Hüyük see J. Mellaart, *Anatolian Studies* XIII (1963), 102 f. See also M. E. L. Mallowan, *Iran* III (1965), 1–8.

South-western Asia and Egypt, between 3200 and 2800 B.C., were closely linked together by trade. Somewhere about the thirty-first century B.C., during the 'Warka' period in Babylonia, whose influence already extended over most of south-western Asia, there was active trade between Mesopotamia and Egypt, reaching its climax in the so-called Djemdet Naṣr period about the beginning of the First Egyptian Dynasty. At that time many innovations were brought into Egypt from Babylonia, and it is probable that other novelties were exported from Egypt to Mesopotamia (though our evidence for the latter inference is still defective).[14] A little later, about the beginning of the First Egyptian Dynasty under Narmer, there was active commerce between Egypt and Palestine, as we know from the finds made at Gath in recent years by Samuel Yeivin,[15] confirmed by Ruth Amiran's work in Stratum 4 of Arad, in the extreme south of the hill-country of Judah. Her work in Stratum 3–1 at Arad has proved that there was equally active trade between Egypt in the middle and late First Dynasty and contemporary E.B. II Palestine.[16] It is most surprising to find such evidence of commerce across the central desert of Sinai at the very commencement of Egyptian Dynastic history, just as there was, though on a greatly expanded scale, in the days of the Patriarchs.

Under the Empire of Accad, which reached its acme in the twenty-third century B.C., we have a glorification of commerce which has seldom been surpassed in history. The most important, in fact almost the only, known epic from the time of this dynasty is 'The King of Battle' (*šar tamḫari*). The best known tablet deals at length with the activities of the merchants who were trading between

[14] On this general subject see W. Helck, BAeV, *passim*, and Helene J. Kantor, COWA, 1–46.

[15] See S. Yeivin, IEJ x (1960), 193 ff. and *Oriens Antiquus* II (1963), 205 ff., together with my brief discussion, COWA, 49 f.

[16] See Amiran, BASOR 179 (1965), 30 ff.

Babylonia and central Asia Minor, thanks to whose efforts the king of Accad, then in control of all Mesopotamia, was persuaded to extend Babylonian arms as far as Cappadocia, said to have been at a distance of 420 double-hours from Accad.[17] All through the Dynasty of Accad we have evidence from excavations in various parts of Mesopotamia that trade was highly regarded and was, in fact, the chief economic basis of the marvellous explosion of higher culture under these Semitic rulers of Babylonia.

The Third Dynasty of Ur, which flourished from the middle of the twenty-first century to the middle of the twentieth (about 2060–1955 B.C.)[18] was even more developed commercially than the Dynasty of Accad. It is true that trade may have become less glamorous, but it had also become better organized and was largely in the hands of the court, as we know from scores of thousands of accounting tablets, some of which show that double-entry book-keeping was already employed in Babylonia four thousand years ago.[19] From the economic texts of Ur III as well as from the tablets dated in the eighteenth century (long after Ur had been sacked by the Elamites), we know that it was still one of the greatest centres of commerce by sea and by land that the world had ever known.[20] Whether Ur was greater than the city of Accad

[17] See BASOR 163 (1961), 53, n. 76.

[18] In spite of the fact that the low chronology which I have defended for many years has been rejected by the editors of CAH[2] in favour of my middle chronology, which was shortly afterwards independently proposed by Sidney Smith, the evidence for the low dates has been steadily accumulating; see Helck, BAeV, 64 ff., and my remarks, BASOR 179 (1965), 42 f.

[19] This we know from the independent work of Tom B. Jones and W. W. Hallo, announced and discussed in various places but not yet fully published. On the economic life of the Third Dynasty in general, see C. J. Gadd, CAH[2] I, XXII, 28 ff., with the references.

[20] See especially A. L. Oppenheim, 'The Seafaring Merchants of Ur', JAOS 74 (1954), 6–17.

had been before its destruction by the Guti, we cannot say; the sea and land trade of the latter were both famous, as we know from contemporary inscriptions as well as from the Sumerian epic studied by S. N. Kramer, called 'The Curse of Accad'.[21]

At this time we find intensive trade between Assyria and Asia Minor, over a distance of nearly a thousand miles by road from Assyria proper, on the middle Tigris River, to Cappadocia, on the plateau of east-central Asia Minor. The so-called Cappadocian tablets are written in Old Assyrian and contain a vast amount of important information bearing on the history and economic life of the Assyrians and Anatolians (through the nineteenth century and for a short period in the third quarter of the eighteenth century B.C.).[22]

In the Egyptian Twelfth Dynasty, which lasted from 1991 to early in the eighteenth century B.C., Egypt turned towards Asia and extended its rule over Palestine, southern Syria and Phoenicia for the greater part of two centuries.[23] Egyptian finds from this dynasty have yielded

[21] See Kramer, *The Sumerians* (Chicago, 1963), 62 f.

[22] See most recently Hildegard Lewy in CAH[2] (1965) I, ch. xxiv. §§ vii–x; and for general orientation and chronology see BASOR 163 (1961), 40 f.

[23] Assertions to the contrary, insisting that Egypt did not control Palestine and adjacent parts of Syria during the Middle Kingdom, are frequently made by Egyptologists who should know better. For a good *mise-au-point* see G. Posener in CAH[2] (1965) I, ch. xxi, §§ i–iii. With the accumulation of data from the new Execration Texts (above, n. 3) it becomes completely absurd to suggest that all of these chieftains of Palestine, Phoenicia and southern Syria were only potential foes instead of being, like the Egyptians listed in the same documents, actual subjects and potential if not actual rebels. It must again be stressed that if our knowledge of Egyptian conquests in Nubia were limited to inscriptions found in Egypt itself (not including the Execration Texts), we should know next to nothing about them. No important public buildings from the Twelfth Dynasty have yet been excavated in either Palestine or Syria.

many objects imported from south-western Asia, including articles of Mesopotamian provenience. Objects sent out from Egypt are found in many excavated sites of this period in Syria and Asia Minor.[24] Byblos, the most important seaport of Phoenicia, had become an Egyptian harbour and was a focus of Egyptian influence throughout the eastern Mediterranean. For nearly two centuries there were no native Byblian princes as far as we know, but only Egyptian governors who ruled directly over the so-called 'tribes' of Byblos, as recorded in the Execration Texts. At the beginning of this period Byblos was still a vassal of Ur, but it was probably occupied by the Egyptians well before the death of Amenemmes I (1962 B.C.).[25]

One of the most important results of Nelson Glueck's explorations in the Negeb since 1952 (supplemented by those of Yohanan Aharoni and Beno Rothenberg in 1956–57) has been the tracing of caravan routes from the twentieth and nineteenth centuries B.C. (marked by settlements yielding M.B. I pottery) through the desert of north-central Sinai as far as just this side of Suez on the way into Egypt. Nelson Glueck had previously discovered scores of sites from this period distributed along the old north–south route through Transjordan.[26]

In the Negeb of Western Palestine Glueck has discovered hundreds more of these sites, and the Aharoni-Rothenberg expedition added scores more in the Kadesh

[24] See BAeV, 43 ff., and G. Posener, CAH[2] I, ch. XXI, § ii.

[25] See E. Sollberger, AfO XIX (1960), 120 ff.; and on the names, see BASOR 163 (1961), 45, nn. 44 and 45, as well as BASOR 179 (1965), 42 f.

[26] For a survey of the material found by Glueck and Rothenberg, see BASOR 163 (1961), 36 ff., to which must now be added the hitherto unpublished material discovered by Glueck and described in BASOR 179 (1965), 6–29, *passim*. On the chronology of the material, see BASOR 168 (1962), 36 ff.; 176 (1964), 38 ff.; and my remarks on COWA, especially pp. 52–7. [Also BASOR 184, 26–35.]

area and in Sinai proper. On the western side of Jordan we find, running down through the hill-country and spreading out in the Negeb, a whole series of sites with remains of occupation from this period. It is no accident that they are mostly located on the watershed-ridge road, since the trade routes in question started in Mesopotamia and Asia Minor, moving down from Aleppo and other Syrian cities to Damascus and then southward by way of Shechem, Bethel, and Jerusalem to Hebron and Gerar. From there easy routes led to Kadesh-barnea, where magnificent springs made it possible to establish a whole network of stations and posts. More sites are then found along the old caravan route through the desolate wilderness of north-central Sinai to just above Suez, as stated above. There are also many sites along the edge of the desert in Transjordan, as well as in the Jordan Valley as far south as Jericho and Bâb edh-Dhrâʻ.[27]

[27] The importance of nineteenth-century occupation at Jericho has been accentuated by Kathleen Kenyon's discovery of many tombs from the period in the Jericho cemeteries. Paul Lapp's important work at the Mirzbâneh cemetery between Kefr Mâlik and Mugheir on the eastern edge of the watershed ridge north-east of eṭ-Ṭaiyibeh has yielded a quantity of material from the M.B. I proper (twentieth-nineteenth centuries B.C.) which must probably be explained in much the same way as the great cemetery of M.B. II at near-by ʻAin es-Sâmiyeh. They both appear to reflect seasonal movements of semi-nomadic folk who spent their winters in the Jordan Valley and their summers on the edge of the hill-country above. Bâb edh-Dhrâʻ, where Paul Lapp has made extraordinarily important finds both in cemeteries and residential quarters from the third millennium B.C., appears to have come to an end just before this time, but we must await further work and publication of Lapp's results before drawing historical inferences. Whether the great site of Bâb edh-Dhrâʻ derived its importance chiefly from trade or had religious significance, is still quite uncertain—possibly both causes were operative. The total abandonment of the site, after long intermittent occupation and intensive settlement, towards the end of the third millennium, can be explained only by other causes—possibly by the natural cataclysm reflected in Gen. 14 and 19. For my

C. THE PATRIARCHAL MODE OF LIFE

Who were the Hebrew Patriarchs? This is a question which has been answered in many different ways during the past century of Biblical research. Some formerly held that the Patriarchs were really depotentized gods—in other words, gods who were transformed by legend into human beings and lost their divine characteristics. Others have thought that, in the course of many centuries of story-telling, the Hebrew Patriarchs came to reflect early ethnic movements. Thanks to our present evidence, it is certain today that the Patriarchs were indeed human beings who were the heroes of stories handed down from the Patriarchal Age. It is, however, quite true that there is a good deal of ethnic tradition intermingled with the Patriarchal narratives of Genesis, some of it very old, but mostly much later in date than the original stories of the Patriarchs. Even when the ethnic traditions are relatively late, few of them can have originated after the time of the JE recensions in the tenth–ninth centuries B.C. The so-called P material goes back ultimately to the same general period.[28]

About half a century ago, it began to be recognized by scholars that the traditions of Genesis reflect a semi-nomadic type of society in which tribesmen settled down much of the time but still moved about seasonally in search of pasturage, especially between summer and winter pastures (French *transhumance*). But there was still no explanation of what Abraham's 'Sitz im Leben' actually was. Ever since Israelite times it was supposed that the Patriarchs simply went wherever they pleased, in a country thought to have been relatively empty. The notion that the Patriarchs found little difficulty in pitching

previous work on the problem of Bâb edh-Dhrâ' see especially AASOR VI (1926), 53–66, and BASOR 95 (1944), 3–13.

[28] For references to the literature see Ch. I and n. 69 there.

camp and grazing flocks anywhere they wished is, however, in flat contradiction to the actual facts of life in all better-known periods of Palestinian history. Newcomers were not well received but were closely watched and were usually driven away. The life of wandering shepherds was anything but pleasant. People living in settled areas, as well as already accepted semi-nomads, bitterly resented any attempt on the part of outsiders to move in and take over their fields or pastures. In short, the semi-nomadic hypothesis was correct in some ways, but it failed to solve the problem of how the Patriarchs made their living and what their mode of life was. In the Bible we have many more data about the life and times of Abraham than we have about the circumstances of the later Patriarchs; these data have also been much more directly elucidated by archaeological discovery than traditions about the following ages of Isaac and Jacob.

Abraham is said to have come from Ur of the Chaldees and to have moved from Ur to Harran in north-western Mesopotamia.[29] It is no accident that Ur and Harran were two of the three greatest centres of trade in nineteenth-century Mesopotamia, and that the very name *Ḫarran* (*āl ḫarrānim*) meant 'Caravan City'. The two cities even shared the same cult—that of the Sumerian moon-god, Zuen (Sin). Abraham is said to have later adopted a citizen of Damascus.[30] This is indeed remarkable, since

[29] On Ur and Harran in this period, see the discussion and references in BASOR 163 (1961), 44 ff. On the close Patriarchal ties with the Harran region see most recently R. de Vaux, RB LXII (1965), 9 ff.

[30] Gen. 15:1–3. Damascus was capital of the land of Api (later Upi) (Hurrian Apina) in the Amarna period and, in view of its excellent location, was probably already capital of the district in the nineteenth century. According to the Saqqara Execration Texts published by G. Posener the land of Apum was ruled by a single prince. According to the eighteenth-century Mari economic tablets, it was ruled by kings (G. Dossin, *Syria* xx (1939), 109. In these texts it is called *māt Apim*, 'the land of Apum'. This land, with

this adoption almost certainly meant that Abraham followed a common practice of the day, well attested at Nuzi. By adopting the merchant, Abraham contracted to assign his property to the former in case of his own decease. This custom had doubtless originated at a time when real property was treated as inalienable, i.e., it was not allowed to be sold to an outsider. In this way he could obtain credit in order to buy donkeys, equipment and supplies for caravaneering or related activities.[31]

From Damascus Abraham is said to have gone south to Shechem, where he settled for a time. Shechem is mentioned in contemporary Egyptian texts of the early and late nineteenth century B.C., and pottery remains of that period have been found there by G. E. Wright. Farther south is Bethel, which also appears prominently in the story of Abraham. There we also find that the first important occupation after the late fourth millennium (so!)

---

its kings, is quite different from the land of Apum in the Khabur basin (A. Goetze, JCS VII, 1953, 65, 67), which was ruled by a chief and elders (G. Dossin, CRAI, 1958, 388 ff.). Obviously, these districts can scarcely be identified in any respect except in the name, which means 'Land of Reeds'. It is a pity that some scholars seem to have failed to note the radical difference in status between these two districts, which shared a common name.

[31] For the foregoing interpretation see my more detailed discussion in BASOR 163 (1961), 47. When I originally proposed this interpretation, E. A. Speiser was opposed because he refused to recognize any adoption in the Old Testament, apparently on the analogy of rabbinic law, which does not recognize it. In his *Genesis* (p. 112), however, Speiser accepts it in principle, though he bases his acceptance on a distinction between the *aplu* or direct heir and the *ewuru*, or indirect heir (in Hurrian family law). On the other hand, he does not even mention the formal contracts of adoption called *ṭuppī mārūti* which cover many cases in which a man of means was adopted as heir by another man who needed credit, but who had property collateral. In a still unpublished study, Dr. Seymour (Shalom) Paul has collected much indirect evidence for adoption in the Hebrew Bible. See also *mārūtu* in a forthcoming volume of CAD, and the already published article on *ewuru* and *ewurūtu*.

was precisely in the period of Middle Bronze I, during the twentieth and nineteenth centuries B.C. Hebron,[32] Beer-sheba and Gerar[33] are mentioned as places where Abraham established residence; outside Hebron he purchased the cave of Machpelah in order to bury his dead.

Above all, we have very important references to the desert of the Negeb. The 'Southland' in question is not the northern part of the Negeb, which is relatively well watered, but the arid desert between Kadesh-barnea and Shur (the Wall of the Prince, built by Amenemmes I, founder of the Twelfth Dynasty, in order to keep out the nomads). In Genesis 20:1 we are told, 'From there [i.e., from Mamre near Hebron] Abraham journeyed toward the Negeb and he spent his time[34] between Kadesh and Shur, while he was a foreign resident [*gēr*] in Gerar'. The area between Kadesh and Shur, which we have described, has always been a true desert in historical times, with only a few places where wells could be dug—although in ancient times, with somewhat more vegetation cover on the windward side of mountains, there were probably more wells than there are today. But the desert is virtually rainless, and it is almost incredible that Abraham could have spent his time there unless he was en-

[32] For the results of the Hebron excavation in 1964, see G. A. Larue in JBR XXXIII (1965), 337 ff. On Jebel er-Rumeideh, above the ancient site of the city proper, the Hammond expedition has found remains of both M.B. I and M.B. IIB (the Hyksos period).

[33] On Gerar = Tell Abu Ḥureira, see BASOR 163 (1961), 47 f. The site, which was much more extensive than the mound of the citadel in its centre, was also occupied in M.B. I and M.B. IIA (nineteenth–eighteenth centuries B.C.), dates which happen to suit (accidentally?) both the Abraham and the Isaac narratives.

[34] This translation of *way-yešeb* is attested elsewhere in Biblical Hebrew, but it may well be that there is a slight corruption in the text and that the original verb here was *way-yašŏr* (cf. Aramaic *šeyârâ*, 'caravan', Arabic *sayyāra*). The verb appears in Arabic *sāra*, *yasīru*, 'to travel, journey (of a caravan)'. It is tempting to emend the text to *wayyašŏr*, 'and he journeyed (with a caravan)', but this must remain hypothetical for the present.

gaged in caravan trade, leading donkey caravans back and forth between Palestine and Egypt.

The tradition preserved in Gen. 13:1–3 makes the nature of his occupations even clearer. We read there: 'And Abram went up from Egypt, he and his wife, with all his people,[35] including Lot, to the Negeb. And Abram was very rich in flocks, in silver and in gold. And his caravan journeyed by stages[36] from the south (Negeb) to Bethel.'

Such direct testimony is in full accord with what we hear elsewhere in the account of Abraham's life in Genesis; he not only spent time in Egypt, but kept up relations with the caravan centres at Harran and Nahor in Upper Mesopotamia.

A document fatal to the 'wandering "shepherd" hypothesis' has been preserved in Gen. 14. In 1961 I gave new explanations for several personalities and events mentioned in it, pointing out, for instance, that the hitherto mysterious Amraphel, king of Shinar (Babylonia), bears a name with the same consonants as Babylonian *Emudbal* (older *Yamud-balum* for *Yamud-pala*).[37] Our knowledge

[35] Note that this expression includes people as well as flocks and that *kōl* often means 'everyone' in Hebrew and Ugaritic.

[36] Note that the verb *hlk* is the same word as Old Assyr. *alāku*, 'to go (in a caravan)', from which are derived Acc. *ālik ḫarrāni*, 'caravaneer', as well as *aliktu*, later *alaktu*, 'caravan' = Heb. *halîkā*, 'caravan'; see Ch. I, § E, together with n. 104. Incidentally, note that these words refer in all early texts to donkey caravans in which the caravaneers walked behind the donkeys, whereas in camel caravans they ride the camels or walk at the head of their string of camels. Heb. *nasa'* means properly, as always recognized, 'to tear out tent-pegs', i.e., to travel in caravan stages. It has not always been recognized that *massa'* (found only in the Pentateuch in this sense), means 'caravan stage', that is, a normal day's journey for a caravan.

[37] For this explanation of the mysterious name 'Amraphel', see BASOR 163(1961), 49 f. and n. 67. In addition to what was said there, it should be noted that in many Old Babylonian names the second element appears in composition as *pala*. Judging from parallels, it is likely that the name was itself abbreviated (hypocoristic)

of the history of Emudbal has been greatly increased in recent years, and we know now from Mari that the people of Emudbal were actively engaged in caravan activities.[38] We also know that Emudbal was one of the most important states in all Babylonia and Susiana (Elam) during the century before the triumph of Hammurapi (c. 1697 B.C.).[39]

The campaign described in Gen. 14 thus has an historical foundation, however much it may have been shifted in the course of time. It stands to reason that the five kings of the Dead Sea Valley appear chiefly because their rôle in the episode was the primary interest of the narrator. Furthermore, the tradition centres on the very ancient north–south trade routes beyond Jordan and down the central ridge of Western Palestine which reached, according to the extant narrative, the very frontiers of Egypt. The campaign itself was presumably directed against the Egyptians. This again points to a date towards the end of the nineteenth or the beginning of the eighteenth century B.C. It is interesting to note that Abra-

---

and that the original was something like *Yamud-pala-Adad*, 'May the kingdom of Adad endure'. For the meaning 'endure', note also Ugaritic *'amd*, 'lasting' (G. R. Driver).

[38] See NMTRM 176 ff., 216 ff., 256 f. and *passim*.

[39] See D. O. Edzard's discussion of the chronology of the kings of Emudbal, ZZB 105 f., and Erika Reiner, JCS xv (1961), 121 ff., on the year-dates of the earliest king of the dynasty, Sumu-yamudbal. This king was contemporary with Sumulael, second king of the First Dynasty of Babylon (c. 1816–1781). This name is now known to belong to a group of names in which the second element is *sumu* and the third element is the name of a relative, god, or ethnic/territorial entity. The first element is usually either *yapi* or *yapa*, 'beautiful' or *yapi'*, 'glorious'; see BASOR 163 (1961), 52, n. 74; and BASOR 179 (1965), 39 f. Since it is perfectly possible that the name of this king was abbreviated to *Emudb/pal*, it may be that he is the original of 'Amraphel', especially since the chronology is approximately correct. It is safer, however, to treat the name as applying not to the founder of the dynasty but rather to the tribe or state to which he belonged.

ham's immediate retainers are called *ḥanîkîm*—a word which must be identified with the Egyptian *ḥnkw* used in the contemporary Execration Texts of the retainers of Palestinian chieftains, as well as with the *ḫanakû* of the Taanach letters, where they are the retainers of a local prince.[40]

At this stage in our discussion it is surely unnecessary to insist on the total absence of any evidence for the existence of camel caravans before the end of the Bronze Age (thirteenth century B.C.).[41] There are two main reasons why the caravan routes discovered by Aharoni and

[40] It is tempting to include further data on the archaisms in Gen. 14, but this is not the place for an extended discussion. Note my remarks at the end of Ch. I on the poetic survivals in vv. 19–20. There are also a number of other clear survivals of original poetry in vv. 6 and 10, as well as such linguistic archaisms as *miśśĕmôl*, 'north of' (cf. the *Banū-sim'al*, 'northerners' in the Mari texts). There are also very early place-names in the chapter, as we know both from Bronze-Age lists and from M.B. pottery on the sites in question. In this connexion the mysterious Hobah in v. 15 has hitherto not been explained. The identification with Upi of the Amarna tablets, which was written with *aleph* and *pe* (as we know from Egyptian transcriptions), is impossible. Equally impossible is the identification, proposed long ago by Wetzstein, with an Arabic *ḫôba*, 'barren land', since every original *ḫ* in Syro-Palestinian place-names had become *ḥ* before being taken over into Arabic. There is, however, an obvious identification which has never been pointed out hitherto. In v. 15 we have it in the phrase *'ad Ḥobah*. Remembering again that the longest known alphabetic inscriptions from the eighth century B.C. were all written without word-dividers, it is clear that the simplest kind of haplography (since *d* and *r* were written alike or nearly alike in several periods of Hebrew script) would yield this from *'ad Reḥobah* (for the use of both preposition and directive *he* in the same phrase, see numerous examples cited by Gesenius-Kautzsch, *Hebräische Grammatik*[28], pp. 260 f. This is naturally the Rehob which was on the southern border of Hamath (Num. 13:21; II Sam. 10:8; and I Sam. [GL] 14:47).

[41] On the question of the date of the introduction of the camel see BASOR 163 (1961), 38, n. 9, and HACH 158, n. 2. This point of view has been accepted by most independent students of the problem, and literature on the subject is swelling rapidly.

Rothenberg must have been used by donkey caravans. First, in the twentieth and nineteenth centuries we have much Egyptian information about donkey caravans in Sinai and Sudan, as well as a wealth of data from Asia Minor about donkey caravans connecting Cappadocia with Assyria along different routes in northern Mesopotamia and southern Armenia. Numerous Egyptian statements about the numbers of donkeys involved in Sinai and Sudan list up to 500, 600 and 1,000,[42] which is the

[42] See W. K. Simpson, *Expedition* (University of Pennsylvania) IV (1962), 39, with a photograph of the stela of the year 1927 B.C. on p. 38. The caravan in question had been sent in the fourth year of Amenemmes II in order to bring a particular kind of semi-precious stone from the region of Toshka. The thousand asses appear at the end of an enumeration of the components of the caravan, which included officials, lapidaries, stone-cutters, and 1,006 'labourers'. In the Sixth Dynasty a caravan of 300 donkeys was taken across the Nubian Desert by Harkhuf. Arkell estimates that the caravan in question would have to be divided three ways, roughly one-third of the donkeys carrying goods for trade, a third carrying food for men and asses, and a third carrying water for both. (Cited from Barbara Mertz, *Temples, Tombs and Hieroglyphs*, 1964, p. 110, after A. J. Arkell, *A History of the Sudan*, London, 1955, 2nd ed. 1961.) Naturally, in a better watered region the proportions might be altered drastically.

The expression *'my-'* (or *'my-'ȝ*; see H. Goedicke, JEA XLVI [1960], 62, n. 2), used as a title by two nobles of Elephantine, was explained by Sethe and Breasted as 'caravan leader'. This was rejected by Alan Gardiner, who rendered it 'interpreter'. We now have exhaustive studies, on the basis of much more extensive material, by Goedicke (JEA XLVI [1960], 60–4 and in a further unpublished article which he has kindly lent me), who explains the word as meaning 'commander of mercenary troops'. This must be approximately correct, but the precise meaning is made very difficult by the absence of any determinative for 'foreign lands' or 'troops'. In fact, the word never has any determinative of its own, though the context shows not infrequently that it means a group or body of men. The titles borne by Weni and Harkhuf in the Sixth Dynasty, designating them as *'my-'*(ȝ), 'who brings whatever is required from foreign lands to his lord', must therefore mean something like 'one who is in charge of caravaneers', 'caravan leader', just as maintained originally by Sethe and Breasted. The term

largest number so far mentioned in any of these stelae. In the Mari tablets there is a reference to 3,000 donkeys in a single caravan.[43]

Second, donkey caravans can be employed only where desert routes are sufficiently short or well-watered to make it possible for donkeys to reach the next supply of water and food within two or three days. Camels, on the other hand, which were not used until much later as caravan animals and which are never mentioned in any contemporary text before the end of the second millennium B.C., can get along where water and food are supplied

---

would then be a collective designating caravaneers without troubling to indicate their ethnic origin, whether Egyptian or foreign. When used of a number of men dressed in Egyptian garb and evidently in charge of captive oarsmen on ships of Sahure', the term merely suggests that they might serve in different capacities. At all events, the word '(ꜣ) appears in some such meaning in Egyptian texts in the Old and Middle Kingdoms—virtually always in regions where caravans were necessary. That the class in question is so anonymous is not surprising, since the dusty caravaneers were greatly despised by the Egyptians; see BASOR 163 (1961), 42, n. 28, on the *'mnw ḫt*, literally, 'the hidden ones of the rear(?)'. Note also the Story of Joseph (Gen. 42–4), with its numerous references to small donkey-caravans (not over 20 in a group) and its statement that the Egyptians were not permitted by their customs to eat with the *Hebrews*, i.e., the Asiatic donkey caravaneers.

[43] This caravan is mentioned in a letter partly published by Ch. F. Jean, *Semitica* 1 (1948), 21 f. In this first edition, quoted by Moshe Greenberg (*Ḫab.* 18), Jean completely misunderstood the context. The correct translation I owe to the kindness of Jean Bottéro, who wrote me 24 Nov. 1963, giving the correct reading and translation of the line, on both of which G. Dossin was in full agreement with him. There is no reference to the *'Apiru*, as supposed by Jean, but the context is now clear—which is far more important than another reference to *'Apiru*. The text actually reads, '3 *li-mi* (*ANŠE*pl) *ša* (*LÚ*)*Ḫa-na*(!) *re-qú-su-nu i-tu-ru-nim*', '3,000 donkeys belonging to the men of Ḫana have returned without loads'. In the preceding lines, Nusugga, king of Šinamu, is reported to have refused to sell grain or wool to the men of Ḫana (on the Euphrates north of Mari), so their 3,000 donkeys had to return unladen.

only once a week or so. These figures apply only to trained desert donkeys and camels, since untrained donkeys and camels living in well-watered areas are quite unable to carry loads so long without water or food. But the ratio between the needs of donkeys and those of camels remains roughly the same, so donkey caravaneers had to provide water by digging wells and building small storage reservoirs to hold the water for a few months.[44] The same is true of food; the caravaneers had to store food where possible; they also had to grow it along the caravan routes in the Negeb and Sinai. In the same period (M.B. I) we find basins for collecting water and walled terraces where grain could be grown. Even when it could not mature, it was available as green fodder and unripe ears.

D. HEBREW AND ʿAPIRU

The problem of the identification of the Hebrews with the ʿApiru has become more and more complex in recent years. In 1954 and 1955, two excellent studies were published; the first edited and partially written by Jean Bottéro, and the second written by Moshe Greenberg.[45] But during the subsequent decade there has been such expansion of our knowledge that we can see patterns much more clearly. After analysing all the material now available as objectively as possible, I have been able to reach quite definite conclusions. One must fight shy of predictive 'models' in this area, for we must remember

[44] We must remember again that before the development of the art of digging or building cisterns and lining them with watertight plaster (made with slaked lime), no large cistern would hold water long, and only small pits lined with clay or 'hydraulic' lime plaster (i.e. made with unslaked lime) were available. Some of these pits would undoubtedly hold water for a few weeks or possibly months.

[45] See the list of abbreviations, s.v. 'PḪ' and 'Ḫab'.

that models are no more reliable than the statistical or stochastic (hypothetical) foundations on which they are built. Whenever there are serious gaps in our knowledge we cannot safely use such models in social or historical studies.[46]

Two cuneiform terms are used of the Hebrews: one is the Sumerian logogram SA.GAZ, the exact pronunciation of which is unfortunately doubtful; the other is *Ḫa-BI-ru*. That the latter was indeed the normal equivalent in Semitic of Sumerian SA.GAZ we know from the regular correspondence of the two in Hittite treaties, the Amarna tablets, Ugaritic lists, and elsewhere. This interchange of Sumerian logogram and Semitic translation, together with the close relationship of societal function between SA.GAZ and 'Ḫabiru' in groups of documents where there is no direct proof that the expressions were synonymous, leaves no room for doubt that the two must be equated. Cuneiform *Ḫa-BI-ru* used to be put into English as 'Khabiru', but since the middle sign could in that age be read *pi* as well as *bi*, and since *'ayin* (which had long been lost in cuneiform) was regularly transcribed as ḫ, it came as no surprise to specialists when it turned up in Egyptian as *'pr* or *'A-pi-ru* and in Ugaritic as *'pr*. The cuneiform name appears in the twelfth and eleventh centuries as *Ḫa-bir*-A.A = *Ḫabirāyu*, which shows an unmistakable *b*.

It has been pointed out by Edouard Dhorme and

[46] An essay in this direction has been undertaken by G. E. Mendenhall, 'The Hebrew Conquest of Palestine' (BA xxv, 1962, 66–87). For an attempt to describe the function of models in scientific and other disciplines (including social studies and even ethics), see Marshall Walker, *The Nature of Scientific Thought* (Prentice-Hall, 1963), 143–65. Meanwhile the use of 'model' has gone so far that theologians are using it as a normal part of their vocabulary to designate almost any speculative hypothesis (cf. Ian T. Ramsey, *Models and Mystery*, London, 1964). For the use of historical analogy in biblical history, see my Rockwell Lectures on *Archaeology, Historical Analogy, and Early Biblical Tradition* (Louisiana State University Press, 1966).

Riekele Borger[47] that in normal West Semitic this word can mean only 'dusty'; the original word, *'apiru* (with two short vowels), belongs to a very well-known Hebrew family of adjectives referring to a temporary condition, such as 'hungry', 'thirsty', 'barefoot', etc., and the word came down into Syriac, with well-known phonetic shifts, as *'afîr* or *'appîr*, 'dusty'. The use of the word to describe a caravaneer is a perfectly normal semantic development, like the Sumerian expression 'dusty man' (LÚ.SAḪARA), meaning 'groom' or 'chariot attendant'.[48] Similarly, in the Middle Ages the Old French term *pied-poudre*, meaning originally 'dusty foot', passed into English law as 'pie-powder' (pedlar). It was perfectly natural to call all of these people, whether they were caravaneers, grooms or pedlars, by the term 'dusty' or 'dusty foot'.[49]

The term SA.GAZ first appears in Sumerian tablets about 2500 B.C.; it is then found in texts of the Accad

[47] See *Revue historique* CCXI (1954), 261, and ZDPV LXXIV (1958), 126 ff. It should be added that the word cannot functionally be a passive participle, as suggested by Borger. On the other hand we should remember that the passive *qŭtĭla* and intransitive *qătĭla* fell together in Imperial Aramaic, both becoming *qĕtîl*. The doubling is just as secondary as in *qaddîš* and *ṣaddîq*, both replacing original *qădĭš* and *ṣădĭq*.

[48] Generally written LÚ.IŠ. In no case does the word ever seem to mean 'charioteer' as sometimes rendered.

[49] A curious additional example is Mandaean (Zimmern, *Akkadische Fremdwörter*, Leipzig, 1915, p. 47) *arqabirgal*, a contemptuous term for 'lowly person', literally '(one with) earth on (his) foot'. I am indebted to Dr. M. Gertner of London for a reference to Gen. 18:27, where Abraham is quoted as saying to God, 'I am (only) dirt and fine dust'. This expression was long ago connected by Hugo Winckler with the Amarna *ep(i)ru/'aparu ša šēpêka* 'I am the dust/dirt of thy feet', etc., used by a grovelling vassal in addressing Pharaoh. Accadian *ep(i)ru*, dust, dirt, is derived from earlier *'aparu* and was borrowed by Canaanite in the sense 'fine dust, ashes', Hebrew *'efer*. As pointed out by R. Borger, ZDPV LXXIV (1958), 128 ff., I had missed the sense of North-west Semitic personal names like *'pr-B'l*, etc., which means 'Dust (on Which) Baal (Treads)', not 'Fosterling of Baal'.

period (twenty-fourth to twenty-second centuries B.C.) and often in Ur III (c. 2060–1955 B.C.).[50] In this early period, it is certain that the word had both a good and a bad connotation. We find, for instance, tablets of the eighteenth century B.C. containing lists of rations given to the SA.GAZ, and a little later the 'canonical' vocabularies list SA.GAZ as an agricultural worker (harvest hand).[51] The term thus has a good sense, since obviously robbers would not be receiving regular rations of sheep and clothing—even in prison, of which there is no hint at all. The bad sense is illustrated by the listing of SA.GAZ in the sense of 'robber' in two vocabularies as well as in omen texts.[52]

In the Sumerian literary texts from the end of the third millennium, preserved in copies dating a few centuries later, there are quite a number of occurrences of the word. For example, in the Curse of Accad we read[53]

From the watch-towers the watch has fled,
On the caravan road the SA.GAZ lie in wait,[54]
In the gate of the land the door moves in the wind.[55]

[50] I wish to thank Robert D. Biggs for kindly furnishing me information about LÚ-SA.GAZ in early Sumerian tablets. For the Dynasty of Accad see F. R. Kraus in BiOr XV (1958), 77 f. For the Dynasty of Ur see especially PḪ, 3 ff.; Ḫab, 1 f.

[51] See CAD, as well as AHW, s.v. *ḫabātu* and derivatives. A good deal has been written on the subject, but most of it is inconclusive. For my own position, see my remarks, CAH[2], II, ch. XX, 16.

[52] For the omen texts, see PḪ, 136–41.

[53] On the Curse of Accad see S. N. Kramer, *The Sumerians* (1963), 64. For the text cf. especially S. N. Kramer and Inez Bernhardt, SLTN, No. 33 on pl. 76, lines 12 ff. See also E. Chiera, *Sumerian Texts of Varied Contents* (Chicago, 1934), 94, lines 13–14.

[54] For the translation 'lie in wait' (Sumerian ba-e-DÚR) cf. A. K. Grayson, *Studies Presented to A. Leo Oppenheim* (Chicago, 1964), 90 ff., where he deals with Accadian *šubtu* and *šūšubātu*, 'ambush'.

[55] This translation of KÁ-GAL-kalam-ma-ka IG im-ma ba-e-GIN is much more likely than 'the doors of the gates of the land turned

This describes the desolation which has settled over the old capital city Accad after its destruction by the northern barbarians following an impious act of king Naram-Sin. After the destruction of Accad the old caravan trade came to an end, and the donkey caravaneers returned to their alternative 'occupation' as bandits. We also have a model letter from the reign of Shulgi, the second king of Ur III in the late twenty-first century B.C.[56] This contains an interesting description of the SA.GAZ which runs as follows:

> The unruly ones,[57] the SA.GAZ people,
> Their green plain[58] (is) devastated (by locusts?);
> As for their men and their women—
> Their men go where they please,
> Their women carry spindle and spinning bowl,[59]
>
> Their encampments are wherever they pitch them,
>
> The decrees of Shulgi, my king, they do not obey.

In other words, the SA.GAZ were semi-nomadic, but not true nomads, since the women who travelled with them used their spare time manufacturing woollen textiles.[60] Besides, their rebelliousness does not prove that

---

to clay'. In the first place, the massive wood-and-bronze doors of a city-gate could scarcely turn to clay, but doors in recently abandoned gateways can swing on their sockets in the wind.

[56] For the text see S. Langdon, BE XXXI, No. 54 on Pl. 45, corrected by S. N. Kramer, JAOS LX (1940), 253. For the translation see A. Falkenstein, ZA (NF), XIX (1959), 286, n. 32, supplemented by valuable suggestions in a letter of 13 Oct. 1963, from Th. Jacobsen.

[57] Read lú-la-ga with Jacobsen.

[58] If Sum. edin meant only 'desert', this obvious rendering of sisiga (=sig-sig-ga, 'yellow, green, of growing vegetation') would not be possible, but it refers also to the broad plains of Mesopotamia and eastern Syria, which were covered with grass in spring.

[59] See CAH² I, ch. XX, 16, n. 8 and T. Dothan, IEJ XIII (1963), 97 ff.

[60] See below, n. 76.

they were not eager for employment whenever they could find it, as we shall see later. With this description of the SA.GAZ we may contrast the description of the true Beduin in the Martu Epic, which is probably earlier.[61] Here we learn that the western nomads, that is, the nomads of the Syrian Desert, lived in tents, had no houses, ate their food raw, left their dead unburied, raised small cattle but no grain, and in general behaved like savages. All through this period, a clear distinction is made between the SA.GAZ or ʻApiru on the one hand, and the Sutû or other true nomads on the other.[62]

In the Lipit-Ishtar Code (c. 1870 B.C.) we have an obvious translation of a Semitic case-law into Sumerian. It runs as follows: 'If a man has rented a ship and has sent it on a trading expedition under contract, but bad luck has attended that trading expedition, where the crew that mans the ship gives itself to SA.GAZ activity, the man who has rented the ship must pay compensation for the ship (to its owner).'[63] We clearly have in this law a reference to smuggling or similar activities, including possible piracy. At all events, since the river boat had fallen into the hands of a lawless crew, it was lost to the lessor, and had to be replaced by the lessee.

The Mari letters from the late eighteenth century B.C. provide us with a mass of pertinent material which has

[61] For the description of the Amurrû Beduin, see S. N. Kramer in *Genava* VIII (1960), 281.

[62] On the relation of (LÚ)SA.GAZ and Sutû, see NMTRM, *passim*, and Kupper's additional communication in RA LV (1961), 197–200.

[63] See for the text F. R. Steele, AJA LII (1948), 435 f. and ArOr XVIII (1950), 490 ff. My translation has been worked out in collaboration with W. G. Lambert and Th. Jacobsen (letter of 13 Oct. 1963). The text is an obvious translation into Sumerian from Accadian. The translation is based on the following restoration: tuku[m-bi] lú-ù má in-ḫun kaskal KA-KÉŠ-DU-a in-na-an-gar [na]m-[ḫu]l kaskal-⌜bi⌝-[a](?) ki-erén-ma⌜u⌝$_5$-[da](?) sa-gaza-šê ba-ak[a] lú má i[n-ḫun-gá] má ìb-[sú-sú].

only recently been clarified. In 1964, André Finet pointed out for the first time that the northernmost of two groups called 'Sons of the South' and 'Sons of the North' (literally 'Sons of the Right' and 'Sons of the Left') is clearly identical with the SA.GAZ or 'Apiru, in tablets which deal with the extreme north-west of Mesopotamia.[64] It had already been noted by others that there are parallels between the Banū-yamīna or 'Children of the South' and the biblical Hebrews of the Patriarchal Age.[65] For example, the same name is given to a tribe of Israel known as Benjamin, which also means 'Son of the Right Hand', that is, 'Son of the South'. The Benjaminites seem, therefore, to have inherited the name 'Southerners'. The 'Northerners' (Banū-sim'al) do not appear to have left any specific imprint in Hebrew tradition, though this may be only because we do not yet know the names of their tribes. On the other hand, we know that the Banū-yamīna were divided into at least four or five tribes, two of which apparently bear the same names as two extinct clans of Judah mentioned in Genesis. Er and Onan died without leaving any offspring and so may safely be identified with extinct clans of the tribe of Judah. The name *'Ônān* (LXX: *Aunan*) has already been compared by Kupper with the best-known tribe of the Banū-yamīna, the Awnanum (Babylonian Amnānum).[66] The second most important tribe, the Yaḫrurum or Yaḫurrum,[67] is certainly to be identified with the Yauri (i.e. *Ya'urru*) of the inscriptions of Adad-nirari I, about 1290 B.C.; they are mentioned together with the Akhlamu and Sutû as a lead-

[64] See André Finet, 'Yawi-Ila, Roi de Talḫayum', *Syria* XLI (1964), 117–42, especially pp. 139 ff.

[65] Cf. G. Dossin in the *Mélanges Dussaud* II, 981–96, and NMTRM, 47–81. The Banū-yamīna tribe of Yariḫû has recently been identified with Jericho, but this is impossible (except that both names include the same element, *yariḫ*, 'moon'). The reading *Mārū-yamīna* is incredible.

[66] NMTRM, 50, n. 1.

[67] NMTRM, 49 ff., 75 ff.

ing nomadic or semi-nomadic people of Mesopotamia.[68] Since the two spellings show that the first consonant of the root would be *ʿayin*, not *ḥet*, in Hebrew, it is probable that *ʿEr* stands for older *ʿIrru* or *ʿUrru* (hypocoristicon of an original **Yaʿrur-El*〉 **Yaʿur-El*).[69] There is a striking additional case: the name of the third most important tribe of the Banū-yamīna, Ubrapi'û or Ubrapû, is derived from a personal name *Ub-rapi'*,[70] the normal hypocoristicon of which would be *Rāfē'* in Hebrew. But this is the actual name of an extinct clan of Benjamin (*Raphē* in LXX). Such a triple coincidence seems too close to be accidental, especially since all three became extinct in pre-Israelite days.

In 1963 A. Falkenstein pointed out that the kings of the Awnanum tribe at Erech were related to the Hammurapi dynasty, which supported Sin-kâshid and sent troops of the Awnanum and Yaḫrurum tribes (settled at Sippar north of Babylon) to aid him.[71] In April, 1965,

[68] In Adad-nirari's historical introduction to his inscriptions (AOB I, xxii ff., 62 f., lines 22 f.) he calls his father, Arik-den-ili (c. 1307–1296) 'Conqueror of the land of Kutmuḫ and all of its helpers, the "whole" of the Aḫlamû, Sutû, Ia'ur(r)u and their lands'. The supposed Ya'uri Mountains of Luckenbill, AR II, §§ 164, 171, do not exist; we must read in the inscriptions of Tukulti-Ninurta I (Weidner, TN XXVI, No. 16, line 30 and XXX, line 45) *ana libbi mātiya lūrā*, 'I brought (the Hittite captives) into the midst of my land!'. The word *gunnu* does not mean 'elite troops' (CAD), but simply 'whole', 'lot', etc.; it is derived from Sumerian gu(n), 'totality' (with AHW).

[69] Such highly reduced abbreviations of personal names are common in Hebrew and should not cause any difficulty.

[70] See BASOR 163 (1961), 45, n. 44 for the divinity 'Ub/'Eb; see also Ch. III, § c. The name of the god appears both as *'Eb* or *'Ub* (Heb. *'ōb*, 'spirit of the dead') and as *'El'eb*, like *Wer* and *Ilwer*. It refers to the ancestral divinities (*manes*), either in the plural or in the person of a single great deity, perhaps later Graeco-Syrian *Ōp*, 'the very great god'; see R. Mouterde, *Mélanges Dussaud*, I (1939), 391 ff.

[71] See *Baghdader Mitteilungen*, II, 23 ff., as well as F. R. Kraus in BiOr XXII (1965), 292.

J. J. Finkelstein presented a paper at the Chicago meeting of the American Oriental Society, in which he discussed a tablet from the British Museum describing the funeral of 'Ammiṣaduqa. It contains a list of his ancestors, including the first nine kings of Babylon I and before them, a long list of their precursors, divided into two dynasties.[72] The names of these ancestors are very mixed —mostly Semitic but some non-Semitic; among them are the eponymous founders of the tribes of Awnanum and Yaḫrurum. Two other lists containing the same names in more fragmentary form celebrate the ancestry of Samsuiluna son of Hammurapi, as well as of the latter's older contemporary Shamshi-Adad I of Assyria.[73]

These exciting new tablets cannot be discussed more fully in advance of publication, but they appear to prove that the ancestral Hebrews founded the First Dynasty of Babylon, and that they exercised some sort of hegemony in northern Mesopotamia after the end of the Qutû (Guti) rule, i.e. in the twentieth and nineteenth centuries B.C.[74] They were, in this case, most certainly of mixed blood, just as has often been deduced from names like Arphaxad and Nahor, neither of which is Hurrian.

[72] I wish to thank Professor Finkelstein for writing me on 30 April 1965, and enclosing a transcription of the text. [See now JCS XX (1966), 95–118.]

[73] I wish to thank Prof. Benno Landsberger for this information, which he kindly gave me in November, 1965. Meanwhile the valuable pertinent study by F. R. Kraus, *Könige, die in Zelten wohnten* (Amsterdam, Netherlands Academy, 1965) has reached me.

[74] There is a badly broken reference to the SA.GAZ in the hymn of Ishme-Dagan of Isin, predecessor of Lipit-Ishtar in the early nineteenth century, which has been recently discussed in great detail by W. H. Ph. Römer in DMOA XIII (1965), 50 f. and n. 384 on p. 72. In lines 224 ff. we read: 'I have verily broken the SA.GAZ . . . with the pick-axe; on his neck (?) I have verily imposed the yoke (?).' This attempt to suppress the restless energy of the 'Apiru does not seem to have been very successful; within half a century they had occupied extensive tracts of Babylonia proper.

In Semitic tribal genealogies, there is nearly always much shifting of periods and relationships. A once important tribe might decrease drastically in number or might be divided into splinter groups. A group might develop from a small family into a large clan or tribe in the course of a few centuries. A tribe might be split into clans which joined different tribes, or it might retain its identity of name and tradition after being separated by considerable distances from its original habitat. Examples of such situations are found in vast numbers in Arab tribal history, and there are many illustrations in genealogies of tribes and clans in the Bible as well as in the Ostraca of Samaria (eighth century B.C.).

There is a very interesting analogy between the tribal situation in Palestine after the Hebrew tribes had settled down and the similar situation in Palestine after the Crusades. The hill-country of central western Palestine (Ephraim, Benjamin and northern Judah), left largely depopulated by the Muslim reconquest, was repeopled by tribes from Arabia, whose occupation areas were still well defined in the third quarter of the nineteenth century A.D. when the Survey of Western Palestine was being made, as well as forty years ago when I was collecting historical traditions among the Arabs. The most important of these tribes in Palestine were the Beni 'Âmir, Beni Ḥasan, Beni Ḥârith, Beni Mâlik, Beni Murrah, Beni Sâlim, Beni Zeid.[75] The same tribes are still found in different parts of Arabia: in Yemen, 'Asîr, Ḥejâz, Nejd, 'Omân, el-Ḥasa, etc., as well as occasionally in more remote parts of the Arab world. There can be no doubt that the separation of the Arab tribes into segments which remained in their original home or migrated into new lands, goes back a millennium or more in some cases. In

[75] On the distribution of these tribes and clans in Arabia, see especially the index to the Admiralty *Handbook of Arabia* I (1920); see also M. von Oppenheim, *Die Beduinen-Stämme* (1939–52), *passim.*

other words, the period of a few centuries involved in early Hebrew displacements is short by comparison.

From the Mari documents we learn that the Banū-yamīna were semi-nomadic, living in villages (*kaprātum*) as well as in pastoral camps (*nawûm*). They were sheep-herders, building sheep-folds (*ḫaṣirātum*) and raiding the sheep of others. They also sowed wheat and barley, spending their time at the threshing floors during harvest. The women usually travelled with their men, but were left with settled friends when the men went on raids. Again, just as in the Shulgi letter cited above, we note that the women specialized in manufacture of woollen cloth; in a Mari letter we read that 300 garments were to be made for the court by the Banū-yamīna, apparently at very short notice.[76]

We may be surprised that the 'Apiru of the Mari letters are seldom specifically connected with donkey caravans, but we must remember the changing conditions at the time. It was precisely in the Mari period, about 1700 B.C., that the Hyksos first occupied Egypt, and completely disrupted land and sea trade between Egypt and Syria. Shortly before, the Assyrian trading settlements in Cappadocia had been abandoned for good. Thus we have no direct references to trade with Egypt[77] and scarcely any to commerce with Asia Minor; no objects of clear Egyptian origin have been reported from Zimri-Lim's palace

[76] Cf. the paintings representing the group of donkey-nomads headed by 'Absha' from Beni Ḥasan (early nineteenth century B.C.), showing the gaily woven (or embroidered) garments worn by men and women who brought stibium to the nomarch Khnum-ḥotpe.

[77] Egypt was called *Makan*, i.e., *Makkan*, at Mari (the simpler spelling is characteristic of Old Accadian and Old and Middle Assyrian). I have been promising a paper on this subject for years and hope to find time to publish it before long. The same spelling is found regularly in the inscriptions of Tukulti-Ninurta I in the late thirteenth century B.C., to designate Egypt and its Asiatic empire.

at Mari. On the other hand, there was active overseas trade with Cyprus and Crete. That the 'Apiru were engaged in caravaneering whenever the opportunity offered, is made probable by references to them as Sutû or as men of Yamudbal: as pointed out by most scholars today, they were members of a class, not properly of an ethnic group. We also have clear references to their concealing raids on caravans by pretending to go out with their own caravans.

Two of the chief caravan cities of north-western Mesopotamia, Harran and Nahor,[78] both mentioned in the Patriarchal narratives, appear also in connexion with the Banū-yamīna. The latter are reported to have 'killed a young donkey', i.e., to have made a treaty, with the kings of Zalmaqum in the temple of the moon-god Sin at Harran.[79] Frequent references in Old Babylonian texts to the two suburbs of Sippar, Sippar-Awnanum and Sippar-Yaḫrurum (see above, on the tribes of the Banū-yamīna), remind one of the suburb of Aleppo called *Ḫlb-'prm* in the Ugaritic lists as well as of the *kārum Kaneš*, a settlement outside the walled city of Kanesh in Cappadocia, where Assyrian merchants and caravaneers had been installed during the preceding two centuries.

We may safely suppose that in the heyday of donkey caravaneering in the early second millennium, the 'Apiru were usually employed, but as they increased in numbers and as opportunities for caravan trade became fewer with the breakdown of international commerce in the late eighteenth century and subsequently, they had to resort to other activities. Banditry was only one of a number of possible alternatives, and probably not the most remunerative. Their usual course was to become either mercenaries or slave troops, as in Syria and Anatolia (see below), or to sell themselves into slavery as at Nuzi and

[78] Mentioned by name, Gen. 24:10, where it is explicitly called *'îr*, 'city'.

[79] See n. 65 above.

elsewhere. Slavery was by no means as unpleasant a condition of life in those days as it became later, since the slave was protected by his owner and enjoyed more or less regular shelter, food and clothing, whereas the unemployed free man often had neither protection nor livelihood.[80] Since it was quite easy for a slave to escape in a milieu where there was little, if any, difference in colour and general appearance, it was much wiser for a master to treat his slaves well and keep them in his service than to treat them badly and drive them to escape.

Turning to the Old-Hittite texts from about the sixteenth century B.C., we now have an extremely interesting tablet recently published by H. Otten, and dated by H. G. Güterbock in the Old Empire.[81] In this tablet three special groups of 'mercenaries' are listed, with pledges given for their good treatment in the Hittite forces. These three groups are the desert tribes (*Lîm-ṣêri*), literally, 'tribes of the desert', like the *Le'ummîm* of Gen. 25:3.[82] After the men of the desert tribes we have the grooms, that is, men who took care of the chariots and horses; they are designated by the Sumerian logogram for 'dusty men' (LÚ^{pl}-SAḪARA). Third come the SA.GAZ men, who were, accordingly, neither light-armed desert scouts nor grooms, so they must have been the men who handled the transport and baggage of the army. In other words,

[80] A good illustration of the poverty of the common caravaneer (*ālik ḫarrāni*, Heb. *hōlek 'oraḥ*) is the fact that there is no evidence that he carried any foreign pottery or other imported objects with him. The pottery found in the caravan stations of southern Palestine is always local Palestinian ware. The same is true of the Assyrian colonies in Cappadocia, where no Assyrian pottery has yet been reported and practically all objects found in the *kârum* of Kanish are also of local Anatolian provenience.

[81] See ZA LII (1957), 216–23 and JAOS LXXXIV (1964), 109, n. 19.

[82] See my paper in *Geschichte und Altes Testament* (Alt *Festschrift*, Tübingen 1953), 10, n. 3, and note also that the Sutû are called *ṣāb ṣēri* in the texts of Sargon (NMTRM, 106).

they were caravaneers who filled the same transport function in the Hittite army as they normally did when employed in civil life. We have already noted that the word 'dusty' was applied to grooms in Sumerian, just as it was applied to caravaneers in Semitic.

Later in Hittite texts we find the 'Apiru (SA.GAZ, *Ḫabiru*) and the Lulaḫḫi listed together; the gods of these two peoples appear together in the lists of deities called on to sanction Hittite treaties. From other sources we know who the Lulaḫḫi were.[83] Called *Lullu* or *Lulubi* by the Mesopotamians, they were mountaineers from the Zagros, who may or may not have been related to the modern Lurs of Luristan, but like the Lurs, who leave the mountains to find work in Iraq, the Lullu found jobs as caravaneers in the Hittite empire.

Late-Bronze Syria-Palestine yields a wealth of information about the *'Apiru-'Abiru.*[84] We know from texts of Ugarit and Alalakh that they were scattered through northern Syria and that they were responsible to the kings of these Syrian cities for service, in return for which they received land and rations. They had their own somewhat irregular organization. In the early fifteenth century Idrimi had to flee from Alalakh in order to escape from his older brothers, and found refuge with the 'Apiru. We read in the tablets of Ugarit that escaped slaves had been accustomed to find asylum with the 'Apiru, preferably on the other side of the border between the Hittite empire proper and the vassal state of Ugarit. This practice was

[83] See Landsberger, 'Ḫabiru and Lulaḫḫu', *Kleinasiatische Forschungen* I (1929), 321–34.

[84] See my discussion, CAH[2] II, ch. XX (1966), 14 ff. Note that it is never possible to determine from occurrences of the name *Ḫa-BI-ru* in Old or Middle Babylonian whether the middle consonant is *p* or *b*; it is only in Middle Assyrian texts that we can be sure of the spelling with *b*. We can therefore not say just when the consonantal assimilation with concomitant popular etymology changing *'Apiru* to *'Abiru*, 'one from beyond (the river)', first came into use.

explicitly forbidden and runaway slaves had to be extradited.

We find constant complaints in the Amarna tablets about ʿApiru raids in both Syria and Palestine, as well as about intrigues of Canaanite rulers with the ʿApiru. A Palestinian ruler distinguishes clearly between three groups: ʿApiru, robbers (*ḫabbātu*) and Beduin (*Sutû*). Biryawaza, prince of the Damascene, refers to his ʿApiru and his Sutû. A triumphal inscription of Amenophis II (c. 1430 B.C.) lists among captives, 3600 ʿApiru, 15,200 Shasu (= Sutû), 36,300 Hurrians, and 15,070 men of Nuḫashshe (between Hamath and Aleppo).[85] In other words, a clear distinction was drawn in this period, at least in Palestine and Syria, between ʿApiru and Beduin on one hand, and robber bands on the other. The ʿApiru might rob, and so might the Beduin; on the other hand, robbery was usually sporadic among the ʿApiru and they were much less nomadic than the Beduin.[86] We learn from Hittite sources that in Syria, Tette, king of Nuḫashshe, was grandson of an ʿApiru chieftain whom the Hittites had placed on the throne. Tette seems to bear an abbreviated Hurrian name. The Amarna tablets insist on the close relation between Abdi-Ashirta and his son Aziru, on the one hand, and the ʿApiru on the other; it is possible that they were themselves of ʿApiru origin, which might

[85] See John Wilson in ANET, 245 ff., and B. Maisler (Mazar), BASOR 102 (1946), 9.

[86] CAH² II, ch. XX (1966), 15. A sidelight on the type of country which was preferred by the ʿApiru towards the end of the fourteenth century B.C. comes from the first Beth-shan stele of this king; see my study of it, BASOR 125 (1952), 24–32, where I first abandoned my long-standing attitude of 'cautious neutrality' towards the equation *Ḫa-BI-ru* = Hebrew. The Egyptians were called in to stop an attack which had been launched against the Asiatic nomads of Ruhma by the ʿApiru warriors and the Tayaru. So far as it goes this text confirms the view of M. B. Rowton that the later ʿApiru preferred wooded and scrub country for security (*Studies B. Landsberger*, Chicago, 1965, 375–87).

throw light on their grandiloquent assumption of the ancient Babylonian title, 'king of Amurru'.

The most interesting 'Apiru personality was Lab'ayu ('Lion Man') in central Palestine. Lab'ayu first appears as a chieftain against whom the Canaanite princes of both southern and northern Palestine were fighting.[87] As usual, we hear of much alleged duplicity and changing of sides, and it is often hard to tell just what facts underlie widely divergent reports. The same anomalous situation appears in nearly every Palestinian letter referring to specific events in which the 'Apiru are involved. Later, after Lab'ayu's death, we are told that his sons continued his policy of infiltration and aggression. In one letter we hear of 'Lab'ayu and [his sons who] have given the land of Shechem to the 'Apiru people'.[88] This may be one of the early crises in the history of Shechem which led to its being occupied by a dominantly Hebrew population in the time of Joshua, as we gather from the Book of Joshua, which nowhere mentions a Hebrew conquest of Shechem, though it became the focus of the Israelite confederacy in Joshua's own time. In the Pentateuch, on the other hand, we have specific references to the capture of Shechem by the Hebrews in the time of Jacob.[89]

We have an interesting hieratic story dealing with events of the early fifteenth century B.C. which relates how an Egyptian officer succeeded in capturing the town of Joppa by a ruse which reminds one both of the Trojan horse and of Ali Baba. In this story the officer stopped at the town on his way north, and was hospitably received by the local Canaanite prince. The prince tells his guest that one of the grooms[90] can take care of the chariot

[87] CAH² II, ch. XX, 18 f.

[88] *Ibid.*, 20.

[89] See BPAE, 32.

[90] Erman was undoubtedly right in supplying Egyptian *ma-ru-'i*, 'groom' in this passage; see now the A. M. Blackman–W. K. Simpson ed. (Harper Torch Book, 1966), 167. Alan Gardiner's substi-

horses, but if no groom is available, he will simply stop a passing 'Apiru and assign him the task. This presupposes that the 'Apiru, as one of the donkey caravaneers who by this time had long been used to mules as well as to donkeys, was able to take care of a horse perfectly well, and could do so without losing caste—he already belonged to the lowest caste in Palestinian society. In the thirteenth and twelfth centuries, during the reigns of Ramesses II and III, large numbers of 'Apiru were still being used by the Egyptians as transport labourers to bring stone from the quarries.[91]

But the 'Apiru/'Abiru must have been turning increasingly from caravaneering as well as from brigandage to more peaceful activities, such as trade[92] and cattle-

---

tute *maryan* is perhaps equally possible from the standpoint of hieratic traces, but is intrinsically impossible because the *maryannu* were nobles and could not be sent out to perform such menial services, whereas it was a groom's business to take care of horses and chariots. (In PḪ, 168 f., C. Posener follows Gardiner.)

91 See PḪ, 169 ff.

92 I continue to hold that the Hebrew verb *sḥr* (originally, *sẖr*) as well as its derivatives in the Patriarchal narratives (*as handed down to us*) refers to trade; see BASOR 163 (1961), 44 ff., and against this interpretation E. A. Speiser, BASOR 164 (1961), 23 ff., together with my brief rejoinder, *ibid.*, p. 28 (cf. also R. de Vaux, RB LXII, 17 ff.). In my opinion the evidence of the versions is alone decisive in favour of my position, which agrees only in part with that of C. H. Gordon, JNES XVII (1958), 28 ff. There is, however, a clear additional piece of evidence to which J. A. Fitzmyer, S.J., has called to my attention (letter of 27 March 1962). In a Sefîre treaty the words *mlky' zy sḥrty* (Stele III, lines 7 f.) are translated provisionally by Father Fitzmyer 'all the kings of my trading area' (i.e., 'all the kings who trade with me'). Later in the same line we have *lkl ḥpṣy*, 'for any business of mine'. See also J. J. Rabinowitz, *Biblica* XXXIX (1958), 40. Speiser is, of course, quite right in doubting that the 'Apiru were merchants, but merchants and caravaneers were by no means in the same class. A. F. Rainey in his paper, 'Business Agents at Ugarit', IEJ XIII (1963), 313–21, has some good observations on the words for 'merchant' (*mkr*) and 'agent, broker' (*bdl*) at Ugarit. His objections to my interpretation of the 'Apiru

raising.[93] The most interesting of these occupations were probably viniculture and viticulture. In Egypt during the early fifteenth century B.C., 'Apiru appear as vintagers, probably in the north-eastern Delta, though the north-western Delta is also possible.[94] In the thirteenth century B.C. there is much evidence for Semitic and other Asiatic vintagers in the north-western and the north-eastern Delta, biblical Goshen.[95] When the 'Apiru were forced by the decline of donkey caravaneering to find other means of livelihood, growing vines and making wine would be one of the most natural occupations for them both in Palestine and in Goshen. We have a vivid illustration of this fact in the archaic blessing of Judah found in Gen. 49:11.

> He tethered his donkey to a vine,
> To a grape-vine his young donkey;
> While he washed out his garment with wine,
> His robe with the blood of grapes.

---

as properly donkey drivers are not relevant and he has wholly misconceived the rôle of the donkey driver in comparing him to the *šamallūm* of the Code of Hammurapi, §§ 99–107. In these laws the merchant (*tamkārum*) is described as advancing money or goods to an apprentice merchant (*šamallūm* = Babylonian Aramaic *šəwalyâ*) in order to represent him in a caravan and make a profit for him if possible. The apprentice merchant had every hope of becoming a journeyman merchant, i.e., a full member of the merchants' guild (*mārū tamkārim*). It would be most surprising if the despised donkey drivers should be mentioned at all in the Code.

93 Especially, of course, sheep-herding. In the light of our present much broader evidence for the background of the 'Apiru in Mesopotamia and Syria, we may have to return to the old explanation of *bĕnê Lē'āh* and *bĕnê Rāḥēl* as *originally* cattle-raisers and sheep-herders.

94 PH, 166 f.

95 Called 'the land of Rameses' (Gen. 47:11) and 'plain of Tanis' (Ps. 78:12, 43), probably from the late tenth century B.C. As is well known today, Tanis and Rameses either were identical, or were adjacent precincts.

The first bicolon contains three words which appear at Mari in connexion with a donkey sacrifice, celebrated in the temple of the moon-god at Harran in order to seal the above-mentioned treaty between the 'Apiru and kings of north-western Mesopotamia; they even appear in the same order in the Bible and at Mari.[96]

E. MESOPOTAMIAN COSMOGONY IN GENESIS

While there is no evidence that the Hebrews brought any special material culture with them from Mesopotamia to Palestine, it is now quite certain that they did keep a considerable part of their ancestral higher culture. Much of the early higher culture of the Hebrews as preserved in the books of Genesis and Exodus (rarely elsewhere), contains elements brought from Mesopotamia during the time of the Patriarchs, that is, no later than the sixteenth century B.C.

First we must list the cosmogonic stories. Among them we note particularly the accounts of Creation in Genesis 1–2 and the Garden of Eden in Genesis 4 and 5, the accounts of the Great Deluge of Noah (Genesis 6–8) and the Tower of Babel (Genesis 11). The account of Creation in Genesis 1 follows the ancient Sumerian cosmogonic pattern ud . . . udbi(a) 'when . . . then', literally 'the day of . . . that day', which was kept in Accadian translation but has not hitherto been found in North-west

[96] Cf. BPAE 12, and for the Mari material see G. Dossin, *Mélanges Dussaud* II (1940), 981 ff.; for the complete formula see ARM II (1950), 82, No. 37:11, *'ayaram mār atānim* (=Heb. *'air ben 'ātôn*) . . . *ušaqtil.* In this connexion I wish to express my regret for having overlooked the statement of Eduard Nielsen in the *Studia Orientalia Ioanni Pedersen* (1953), p. 274: 'No wonder that the ass in the Abraham and Joseph traditions plays an important rôle: the wanderings of Abraham reflect in reality the ancient trade-routes with a centre in Haran.'

Semitic texts outside of Hebrew.[97] It also appears in both the comogonic passages Gen. 2:4 and 5:1.

Genesis 1, though going back to early times in its original poetic form, received its present form in the seventh century B.C. ('P'), and is probably a specifically Israelite synthesis of elements from Babylonia, Egypt and Canaan (Phoenicia), largely obscured by Israelite demythologizing.[98] On the other hand, the account of creation in Genesis 2 is very definitely Mesopotamian in origin, as shown by mention of the Primordial River (Hebrew *'ēd*). This is transparently Sumerian id, 'river', which was taken over as the proper name (*Id*) of the River-god, especially in the valleys of the upper Euphrates (Mari) and Tigris (Assyria).[99]

97 See for example JBL XLIV (1925), 363 ff., OTMS, 38, and E. A. Speiser, *Genesis* (1964), 3 ff., 12 f.

98 See my treatment of Gen. 1 in my forthcoming *Experience on the Road to Reason: Phoenicia, Israel and Ionia* (vol. II of the McGraw-Hill series).

99 For data available up to 1939, see JBL LVIII, 102 f. The identification was originally made by P. Dhorme, RB, 1907, 274. It is certain from many references that the Sumerian pronunciation was *id*, which was also the name of the river-god, written ^{d}(ÍD)*i-id*, in the Assyrian law code (e.g., Col. III, 93). There does not seem to be any real proof that the Semitic name of the divinity was ever *nāru*, since most of the names which have been explained in this way have nothing to do with it. The most important of these was *Narru*, a name of the Sumerian god of music, Dunga (^{d}NAR). There was also a Sumerian Nari mentioned in the Creation Epic, and a Hurrian Nara, consort of Namshara. Id was certainly one of the chief gods of Mari in the third and early second millennia B.C. A cuneiform ritual text (L. W. King, *The Seven Tablets of Creation* [London, 1902], pp. 128, 200) includes a cosmogonic passage in which the River-god (variant: goddess) is said to have created everything. The new evidence for the cosmogonic rôle of the river deity, given below, should be decisive. E. A. Speiser (*Genesis*, 16 and the material there cited) defends an identification with the Accadian word *edû*, which means 'tide', 'river-flood', etc. Phonetically and semantically this identification is possible, but it totally lacks the mythological and historical attestation that we have in the case of the river divinity.

We may render Gen. 2:4b–7a as follows: 'When[100] Yahweh-Elohim made Earth and Heaven,—before any vegetation had yet come into being in the earth and before any herbage had yet sprouted, for Yahweh-Elohim had not yet caused rain to fall on the earth and mankind was not there to till the soil—(then) he caused the primordial river to rise from the earth, irrigating all surface soil. Then Yahweh-Elohim formed mankind of (loose) earth from the soil and breathed living breath into his nostrils.'

In spite of the completely monotheistic character of the passage, its background in pagan cosmogony is clear. It is also clear that this particular text is only the introduction to the story of Eden, also derived from North-Mesopotamian mythological sources. A remarkable illustration of its crude background in the mixed Hurrian and Sumero-Accadian civilization of northern Mesopotamia appears in the cosmogonic text published by W. G. Lambert and A. R. Millard.[101] This extraordinary myth is preserved in a damaged Late-Babylonian tablet in the British Museum, which is expressly attributed in the colophon to an original from Assur (destroyed in 614 B.C.). The first three lines are badly damaged; then we read (lines 4 ff.):

> Furrowing [with] their plough(s), they caused
> (Nether) Sea[102] to produce offspring

[100] The Hebrew *bĕ-yôm* is etymologically identical with Accadian *inūmi, inūma*, but is normally used in Hebrew and Ugaritic with a following noun or infinitive in the meaning 'when' before a verbal clause.

[101] See CTBT XLVI (1965), pl. 39, as well as W. G. Lambert and Peter Walcot, *Kadmos* IV (1965), 64–72.

[102] *Tāmtu* refers in Accadian to either a salt sea or lake, but its original meaning, as shown by Hebrew and Ugaritic, was 'the subterranean fresh-water sea', Sumerian abzu (Acc. *apsû*). In this case it is obvious that the sea in question must be the nether (fresh-water) sea, in keeping with the original meaning.

[ ] By themselves[103] they gave birth to Amakandu[104]
For his [sp]ort (?)[105] they built Dunnu-of-Both-Sources[106]
[Ḫaḫ]arni[107] laid claim for himself to lordship over Dunnu.
[Earth] raised her face to her son Amakandu
"Come, let me make love to you," she said to him.
Amakandu took his mother (as mistress) and
Ḫaḫar[ni], his [father] he killed,
In Dunnu, which he loved, they laid (him) to rest.
And Amakandu took over his father's lordship [and]
(Nether) Sea, his sister, [ ] he took (as wife).
Laḫar, son of Amakandu, came [and]
Amakandu he killed, and in Dunnu,
In the [coffin?] of his father he caused him to rest.
[(Nether) S]ea, his mother, he took (as wife),
And (Nether) Sea confined (?)[108] Earth, her mother.

[103] Text *i-na ra-ma-n*[*i*]*-šu-n*[*u*]. The expression sounds odd in this context; one suspects that the divinities in question created Amakandu by normal sexual intercourse.

[104] For this name, which is a variant of the Sumerian name which usually appears in Accadian as Šakkan, see Lambert, *op. cit.*, p. 67.

[105] Read almost certainly [*a-na me-l*]*u-ul-ti-šú.*

[106] The text has *ālDu-un-nu*[ ]*ṣa-a-tú ki-lal-la.* Read in the broken space probably [*š*]*á*, rather than ⌜*a*⌝. The word *ṣa-a-tú* is obviously the plural of *ṣîtu*, and is to be transcribed either *ṣâtu* or *ṣa'ātu.* It appears in the inscriptions of Shalmaneser III in the phrase *ṣît naqabiša*, literally the egress of the (tunnel) source (of the Tigris); cf. CAD XVI, 218a. The expression is identical with Sumerian id-ka-min-na, 'the source of both rivers' (Accadian *pî nārāti kilallê*); see AJSL XXXV (1919), 163, 172 f. Note that the early Mesopotamians believed that the Tigris and Euphrates shared a common source in the far north.

[107] This is surely the same name as the *dḪa-ḫar-ni* of line 37, where his descendant (*ṣiḫir*) is mentioned. In lines 7 and 11 the text is broken, with the beginning missing in the former and the end missing in the latter. It seems clear that the late cuneiform copies reflect an original *Ḫa-ḫar-ni.* In any case, the reading *Ḫain* is unattested elsewhere.

[108] Read perhaps *ta-ni*[*-i'*] rather than *ta-ni*[*-ir*] (as Lambert seems to restore). It does seem a bit late in the myth for Earth to

(20) On the 16th of the month Chislev, he took over lordship and kingship.
[X] son of Laḫar, took River (*dId-da*), his own sister (as wife), and
[Laḫar, (his) fa]ther and (Nether) Sea, his mother, he kil[led and]
[ ] laid them to rest . . . (?).

The dreary tale goes on: Y, son of Laḫar's son X, took his sister U'ayum[109] as wife (line 25), after which he killed (his father and) mother, River (line 30). Then Z son of Y married his sister, Ningeshtinna[110] and killed his father Y and mother, U'ayum. . . .

The account of the Garden of Eden is not necessarily Mesopotamian in its extant form, but it is certainly of Mesopotamian origin, since it deals with the division of a single cosmic source into four great rivers, including the Tigris, Euphrates, and two mythical streams.[111] In Babylonia we have many representations of and references to the two cosmic streams which spout from a vase held by the god of the subterranean fresh-water ocean, Enki or Ea, and these two sometimes appear as four rivers in representations where two gods hold vases, each of which has two streams spouting from it. The finest illustration of the four-river scene comes from the famous fresco

---

be murdered, and we should certainly expect the usual *dāku*. It may seem a little surprising to have Nether Sea limiting the movements of Earth, whereas the opposite is generally true. The idea of Earth's putting a limit to Sea's encroachment is familiar in ancient literature (cf. Job 38:8–11).

109 Read simply *dU-a-a-am*. This might then be an old accusative of Sumerian u'a = GANÁM. It would not be surprising in such syncretistic myths to find both equivalents of (d)GANÁM, Laḫar and U'a, separated into two divinities.

110 This is phonetically a shortened form of the full Sumerian Nin-geštin-anna, 'Lady of the Vine of Heaven', consort of Tammuz.

111 See my study, 'The Location of the Garden of Eden', AJSL XXIX (1922), 15–31. For an important modification in the supposed geography of Eden (*ibid.*, p. 29) see the text below.

painting found by André Parrot in the palace of Zimri-Lim at Mari, from the late eighteenth century B.C.[112]

Returning to the cosmogonic myth translated above, attention should be called to the fact that we have here a classical description of the inheritance by sororate marriage which has been discovered by P. Koschaker and E. A. Speiser in the cultures of the mountaineers of the second millennium B.C. Koschaker first pointed it out in the case of Ḫayasha (in Armenia Major), where its existence is known from Hittite sources, and extended it to the Hurrians and Elamites.[113] E. A. Speiser has further confirmed its existence among the Hurrians.[114] We have a clue to the original location of this myth in line 41, where the colophon refers to the city of *Šu-pa-at* [ ]. This is obviously Shubat-Enlil, modern Chagar Bazar, in the upper basin of the Ḫabur river. The same spelling,

112 For previously known representations of the flowing streams, see my paper 'The Mouth of the Rivers', AJSL XXXV (1919), 161–95. The motif is very common in Mesopotamian monumental and glyptic art. For the example found by A. Parrot in the palace of Zimri-Lim at Mari see Parrot, *Syria* XVIII (1937), 335 ff. and M.-Th. Barrelet, *Studia Mariana* (1950), 9 ff. There can be little doubt that the Mari representation from the latter part of the eighteenth century B.C. does reflect mythological motifs which have in part survived in the story of the Garden of Eden; note especially the two female divinities standing opposite each other in the central panel, each holding a vase with four flowing streams spouting from it. On either side of the central panel are three registers of apotropaeic figures with two ferocious mountain bisons facing each other at the bottom and two pairs of bearded cherubim facing one another in the second and third registers from below. In front of the apotropaeic figures are two tall flanking trees of obscure identity. Behind the figures are two other flanking trees which may easily be identified as date palms. All this reminds one strikingly of the symbolism in the story of Eden.

113 See P. Koschaker, ZA XLI (1933), 1–89.

114 See *Studies and Texts: I, Biblical and Other Studies,* ed. Alexander Altmann (Harvard University Press, 1963), pp. 15–28, where he discusses 'The Wife-Sister Motif in the Patriarchal Narratives'.

Šupat-Enlil, appears in a text cited by A. Goetze.[115] The town was very ancient and became one of the royal residences of Shamshi-Adad I, whose ancestors may well have lived in the area at one time (see above). Unhappily we do not know the origin of the name *Ḫaḫarni*, but W. G. Lambert has pointed out that it does occur in cuneiform texts together with that of another god, Ḫayashu (*Ḫa'ašu*).[116] It may well be that the name is connected with that of the country Ḫayasha, which lay directly north of it in the Armenian mountains. The North-Mesopotamian character of our text is demonstrated by the mixture of Sumerian, Accadian, and other non-Semitic cosmic names. It is particularly interesting to find the feminine order of fertility given as *Tāmtu* = *Tehôm*, the subterranean fresh-water ocean followed by *id* = *'ēd*, the primordial river (which can, of course, be either masculine or feminine). This is obviously a secondary development in which two separate myths have been fused.

The Dunnu-of-Both-Sources, which the two primordial divinities Ḫaḫarni and Earth built for Amakandu, Sumero-Accadian god of animal husbandry, strongly suggests the later Garden in Eden of the biblical narrative, which was also at the source of the rivers. Strangely enough, it does not seem to have been noticed by anyone—least of all by the writer—that the obscure *miqqedem* after 'And Yahweh Elohim planted a garden in Eden' means 'in primeval times', as so often in the Hebrew Bible, and not 'from the east'.[117]

The two lists of antediluvian patriarchs in chapters 4 and 5 of Genesis are most instructive, since they vary in number from seven (or eight) to ten in our lists. We have the same variations in number in Sumerian lists of the kings of Babylonia before the Great Flood; we have simi-

[115] See A. Goetze, JCS VII (1953), 58. On the identification of Shubat-Enlil with Chagar Bazar, see especially NMTRM, 2–8.

[116] See W. G. Lambert, *op. cit.*, 67.

[117] See n. 111, above.

lar reduction of ages before and after the Flood, though the ages are very much higher in all Babylonian lists.[118] While the names in Genesis are quite different from the Babylonian names, and no similarity has been found at any point, the variations in numbers and ages prove some sort of connexion—though not through written tradition. Incidentally, it may be remarked that Lamech, the last of the descendants of Cain in Genesis 4 and father of Noah in 5, may now be considered as a shortened form (hypocoristicon) of names like *Lamki-Mari*, which belonged to a king of Mari about the middle of the third millennium B.C.; cf. Old Accadian *Lamkīyum.*[119]

The story of the Flood in Genesis is so close to the various Sumerian and Accadian accounts of the Great Deluge that a close relationship is certain.[120] It is quite impossible, however, to assume that the story of the Flood is derived from any of the extant Sumerian or Accadian versions. They are all different in detail, and the Hebrew story shows archaic features which must have been derived from a form of the Mesopotamian myth earlier than any preserved in cuneiform sources. It is very difficult

[118] See SKL for the evidence up to 1939. Since then more such material has been discovered, but the picture has not been radically changed; see most recently J. van Dijk, *XVIII. vorläufiger Bericht über . . . Uruk-Warka* (1962), 44–52.

[119] I noted this equivalence several years ago, but have not published it. Meanwhile Stanley Gevirtz has (PEPI, 26) independently made the same identifications. In addition to the suggestions for explanation of antediluvian names which I included in my discussion, JBL LVIII (1939), 95 ff., it may be added that Adam may possibly be the Adamu listed among the early ancestors of Shamshi-Adad I, described as living in tents, and Jabal (Gen. 4:20) may be the god Yabal, whose name occurs in such composite names as Mut-iabal. I am still very sceptical about the identification of Cain as the eponym of the Kenites or of Seth as the eponym of Sutû-Shutu.

[120] On their relationship see A. Heidel in *The Gilgamesh Epic and Old Testament Parallels* (Phoenix ed., Chicago, 1963), 224 ff., and E. A. Speiser, *Genesis* (1964), 54 ff.

to separate a myth found all over the world, even as far away as pre-Columbian South America, from the tremendous floods which must have accompanied successive retreats of the glaciers in the closing phases of the Pleistocene Age. In other words, the Flood story presumably goes back, in one form or another, at least ten or twelve thousand years and, for all we know, much further. Now it is certain, thanks to recent prehistoric discoveries, that European man was much further advanced culturally in Middle and Upper Palaeolithic than had been supposed. There can, therefore, no longer be any serious difficulty in tracing some of the cosmogonic narratives of Genesis back ultimately to stories first told over ten or even twenty thousand years ago. So far no trace of a true Flood story has been found in Egypt and no such myth is yet known from Phoenicia proper, either at Ugarit or in Sanchuniathon.

Finally we have the account of the Tower of Babel, which is transparently Babylonian in origin. I do not, however, believe for a moment that the origin of the story has anything to do with the temple-tower (*ziqquratu*) of the First Dynasty of Babylon, Etemenanki, in the precinct of Esagila, though it is perfectly possible that the existence of a new tower after the early seventeenth century B.C. may have had something to do with the persistence of the story. Babylon is said by native historiographers to have been built 'opposite Accad'[121] by Sargon I, who founded the first great empire in south-western Asia. We now know that Accad was itself on the Euphrates near Babylon and quite possibly within the walls of the Greater Babylon of Nebuchadnezzar II. It was destroyed by the Guti between c. 2200 and 2150, as described in the often-mentioned Sumerian 'Curse of Accad'.

[121] An analysis of the Babylonian tradition about the foundation of Babylon was prepared years ago but was never finished, since new data kept coming to light from cuneiform sources. I hope to deal with this evidence elsewhere.

The Euphrates then flowed *east* of Babylon, and Accad lay presumably deep under the present water-table, south-east of the Esagila complex, across the ancient river bed from it. The 'Gate of God' (*Bāb-El*), Sumerian Kadingirra(k), may have been the original name of the temple-tower of Accad. The temple-tower seems to have been introduced into Babylonian architecture precisely in the Accad Dynasty, since it was unknown before, but was already normal in Ur III.[122]

It is highly probable, therefore, that the story goes back not to the time of Hammurapi or later, but rather to a time shortly after the downfall of Accad in the twenty-second century B.C. It may also be observed that the word *šem* does not mean here 'name, fame' as commonly supposed, but 'an (inscribed) monument'.[123] It was, therefore, as a tremendous monument to its builders that the Tower of Babel was intended.

It is not necessary to suppose that all these stories were first brought to Palestine at the same time; presumably successive waves of 'Apiru moved westward from before Abraham's time down to the sixteenth century B.C. (see below). Some of the apparently incongruous features may perhaps be explained not so much by the growth of tradition in later times, as by differences between successive forms of the ancient stories before they were brought to the West.

122 For a clear representation of a temple-tower of the Accad period, see Edith Porada, *Iraq* XXII (1960), 120 and pl. 15. For the underlying symbolism of the mountain summit (also called *ziqurratu*), cf. the Naram-Sin Stele of Susa (e.g., ANEP 100, No. 309). For the 'Gate of God', see the remarks of W. Andrae, *Das Gotteshaus und die Urformen des Bauens im Alten Orient* (Berlin, 1930), especially pp. 16 f. on the temple as gateway; Andrae's discussion does not refer, even indirectly, to the name Babylon.

123 For lack of space I refer again to a forthcoming study of analogous material (e.g., Acc. *šiṭir šumiya*, 'monument bearing my name').

F. MESOPOTAMIAN LAW IN HEBREW TRADITION

When we turn to the laws and customs of the early Hebrews, we find extraordinarily pertinent evidence for Mesopotamian origin of the customary laws known accidentally from Nuzi, about 150 miles north of Baghdad. The southern ʿApiru (Banū-yamīna) were chiefly found in Upper Mesopotamia, south of the hill-country, while the northern ʿApiru (Banū-sim'al) were to be found in the more mountainous region to the north.[124] It is not at all surprising that the mixed Hurrian and Semitic population of the two Patriarchal cities of Harran and Nahor in the eighteenth century B.C. exhibited a pattern of customary law similar to what we find at Nuzi in the fifteenth century. In the broad plains of northern Mesopotamia a distance of two or three hundred miles was unimportant, given semi-nomadic mobility and similar racial mixture. E. A. Speiser has collected a score of striking parallels between customary law at Nuzi and in Genesis; we have seen above that the resemblance in the case of adoption is even closer than he supposed.[125] These laws were presumably brought to the West by the migrating ʿApiru donkey caravaneers of early Patriarchal times.

On the other hand, there is a still better attested type of case-law which must have been brought to the West from Babylonia in late Patriarchal times, perhaps in the sixteenth century B.C. I am referring to Exodus 21–3, where we have the torso of a considerably longer code of case-laws following ancient Sumero-Accadian patterns established no later than the late third millennium B.C. For comparison we now have either the whole or extensive fragments of at least six codes of cuneiform case-law,

[124] See n. 64 above for a reference to André Finet's work.

[125] See above, n. 31. R. de Vaux's cautions in his review of Speiser's *Genesis* in JBL LXXXIV (1965), 75, are not really valid in the ethno-cultural situation described in this chapter.

all dating from between c. 2100 and 1500 B.C.; three of these are Sumerian, two are Accadian and one is Hittite. It was formerly thought that the Hittite laws belonged to the Late-Hittite Empire; now, however, we know that they were already written down in the Old-Hittite Empire.[126] They contain remains of two successive periods of previous legislation. In addition to these six cuneiform codes, we have a seventh, Middle-Assyrian, code from the palace of Tiglath-pileser I and clearly written about 1100 B.C. It is generally thought that the content of this code may be substantially earlier, but this is increasingly doubtful. In any case, the Assyrian law-code reflects a later, harsher, phase of law-enforcement, and may be omitted from consideration here.

By far the closest in content to the 'Book of the Covenant' are the Code of Eshnunna and the famous Code of Hammurapi, which date before c. 1725 and c. 1690 B.C., respectively, in our low chronology. The structure of these case-laws is identical with that of the Book of the Covenant; all begin with 'if' (*kî*), proceed with stipulations introduced by 'provided that' (*'im*), and end with a statement of the legal penalty. Similarly all laws begin in Sumerian with *tukumbi*, in Accadian with *šumma* and in Hittite with *takku*. In several cases we have identical laws in Hebrew and in one or both cuneiform codes; I shall limit myself to two examples which show how we can reconstruct the original form of the Hebrew laws in Exodus 21–3 on the basis of the two Babylonian law codes with the aid of textual variants in the Greek translation of the Pentateuch from the early third century B.C., a thousand years before the earliest Hebrew texts known until 1948. In Ex. 21:29, the Authorized Version reads: 'But if the ox were wont to push with his horns in time

[126] See H. G. Güterbock, JCS XV (1961), 64 f.; XVI (1962), 17 ff.; and JAOS LXXXIV (1964), 109.

past, and it hath been testified to his owner, and he hath not kept him in, but he hath killed a man or a woman; the ox shall be stoned and his owner shall also be put to death.' By following the two Babylonian case-laws and recognizing that there are two simple corruptions in the Hebrew text, we may render the verse: 'If the ox has habitually gored in the past, and his owner has been officially informed (by the authorities) and yet has not dehorned it, and it shall kill a man or a woman, the ox shall be stoned and its owner also shall be executed.'[127]

Another case is more complex; but we can draw on the Greek Bible, which must go back to an old Hebrew recension differing from the Masoretic text. In the light of the Code of Hammurapi (§ 266) we can select the more correct reading from the two divergent recensions and can supply a missing word. This law deals with the loss of a domestic animal which has been put into the care of another person. The Authorized Version follows the Masoretic Hebrew text and reads: 'If it be torn in pieces, (then) let him bring it (for) witness (and) he shall not make good that which is torn' (Ex. 22:12). Restored in the light of the Babylonian code and the Greek translation of another Hebrew recension of Exodus over 1400 years later, it reads: 'If it is torn by wild beasts, he shall bring it (to its owner) and ⟨shall swear⟩ an oath; he

[127] On Eshnunna Code, § 53, and the parallel law in the Code of Hammurapi, § 251, see A. Goetze, *The Laws of Eshnunna* (AASOR XXXI, 1956). In the Eshnunna Code one can scarcely read *p[a]-ši-ir*, corresponding in meaning to CḪ, *ušarrim*; I suggest reading *i[b]-ši-ir*. The word does not seem to appear in Accadian so far, but would be equivalent to Arabic *bšr*, 'to remove something from a human body, tree, or ground, by shaving, scraping, or otherwise denuding the surface'. The Accadian synonym *šrm* corresponds by the normal sibilant shift to Arabic *srm*, 'to cut or lop off'. As Goetze has seen, we should read in the Hebrew text *yšrmnw* for the *textus receptus yišmĕrennu*, and for the preceding *we-hūʿad* read *we-hūdaʿ*.

shall not pay compensation for the torn animal.'[128] This is exactly what the Babylonian code stipulates.

There are also quite a number of interesting archaisms in the Book of the Covenant which confirm the impression made by the structural identity in formulation. In Ex. 21:22 there is a reference to 'judges' (*pelîlîm*). This word is found only in three archaic or archaistic passages in the Old Testament, and its use was abandoned early. The verb appears, however, in the Assyrian letters from Cappadocia dating from the nineteenth century B.C., in the same sense of 'arbitrate' as we have in the Book of the Covenant.[129]

Samuel Iwry has recently discovered that Hebrew *nimṣā'*, found several times in the Book of the Covenant and mistranslated 'be found', actually means 'be caught (in the act)', in accord with the parallels in the Babylonian and Hittite laws. Interestingly enough, this correct original use of the word was not recognized until noted by Iwry in a Qumran variant of the First Isaiah Scroll!

Another curious expression which has always been misunderstood by later tradition is found in a law (Ex. 23:5) dealing with what one should do when one finds an enemy's ox or ass going astray or falling under a burden. At the end of the verse we are told, in the translation of the Authorized Version, '. . . thou shalt help with him'. In the Ugaritic epics we find the very same word employed in the sense 'adjusting the load of the donkey', which means that we should read '. . . thou shalt adjust his load'.[130] While this is a small point, it well illustrates the

[128] The Greek rendering presupposes an original *'ad* instead of *'ēd*, i.e., *'âd*, 'oath, pact', before which we should perhaps insert *yā'îd*, which would disappear by haplography. On the word, see W. F. Albright and D. R. Hillers, '*'Âd*, *'Êdût*, "Covenant", and Related Words in Hebrew', expected to appear soon as a separate monograph.

[129] See E. A. Speiser, *Landsberger Festschrift* (1965), 389 f.

[130] This verb, Hebrew *'zb*, appears in Ugaritic as *'db* for *'ḏb*. Its pertinence to this passage was first pointed out by U. Cassuto.

fact that in many cases where we would not suspect a wrong translation or an erroneous use of a word, we must yet beware. Especially significant is the archaic use of *'elôhîm*, 'gods', referring to oaths by pagan divinities (several passages).

Even more important is the archaic use of the term 'Hebrew' in Ex. 21:2. We are told that if a Hebrew slave has served six years he shall be allowed to go free. In other words, a native Hebrew slave was actually an indentured servant and could not be subjected to life-long slavery like ordinary slaves of foreign origin.[131] How shall we explain the fact that the Book of the Covenant contains such archaic material, going back long before the time of Moses? There is only one likely explanation—that the case-laws of early Israel were already in use among the Hebrews before the Mosaic period and had probably been brought from Mesopotamia by later Hebrew immigrants, presumably after a considerable body of Hebrews had already settled in the West. Historically, this movement is most likely to have taken place during the troubled times in the sixteenth century B.C., when the Cossaeans occupied much of Mesopotamia, and many of the semi-nomadic Hebrews presumably fled to the West. Though we cannot say just when or how the modified Babylonian case-laws came to the West, it is clear from Ex. 21:2 that they were already used by the Hebrews in pre-Mosaic times. In any case, it was these laws which formed the basis for Mosaic jurisprudence.[132] Again we have an example of the fact that the antiquity of Hebrew

[131] See especially A. Alt, KSGVI I (1953), 291 ff. Note also that in archaic legal terminology *'Ibrî* was still occasionally used in Deuteronomy and Jeremiah, though naturally in a somewhat different sense.

[132] See below, Ch. III. Note that W. G. Lambert has suggested that the *lex talionis*, which occasionally appears in the Code of Hammurapi, but has not yet been found elsewhere in Babylonian legislation, may have been taken into the Code of Hammurapi from the customary laws of the Amorites; see JTS XVI (1965), 289.

tradition is much greater than commonly thought. It is entirely unnecessary to suppose that the case-laws were brought to the West in written form, since customary laws are everywhere handed down orally before being put into writing.

We are rapidly learning about another branch of early Hebrew law not so closely connected with Mesopotamia, which includes making agreements, contracts and treaties —'covenants' in biblical English. There are two old words for covenant in Hebrew: *bĕrît*, which has now been found in extra-biblical sources from pre-Mosaic times;[133] and *'êdût*, a term hitherto rendered 'testimony' but which is undoubtedly a synonym of *bĕrît*.[134] In the course of time, however, the term *bĕrît* came to have other meanings such as 'contract labour' and the like,[135] whereas *'êdût* was originally the plural of a word meaning 'oath', which came into use in Assyria and among the Aramaeans in the sense of 'treaty' no later than the beginning of the first millennium B.C., and which had probably been employed for several centuries previously.[136] Thanks to

[133] See especially BASOR 121 (1951), 21 f., where we have the expression 'to cut a *berītu*'. The two tablets in question are ration lists for payment to ERIN^{pl} *A-ša-[an]-nu*. The Ašannu also appear as a class at Alalakh. These Qatna tablets may be dated about 1400 B.C. In Egyptian texts from the twelfth century B.C. we find a similar Semitic loan word *birta*; see below, n. 135.

[134] See above, n. 128.

[135] In view of the different nominal forms mentioned in n. 133, *berītu* and *birtu*, one might look for different meanings, but they both seem to be used in the same sense, which is not the ordinary sense of Heb. *bĕrît*. In my opinion, an etymological identification of the form *berītu* with Acc. *birītu* 'fetter' still remains highly probable; its relation to the form *birtu* would be something like that of Heb. *qiryā* and Phoen. *qart* for **qirtu*, 'town'.

[136] Assyr. *ādê* seems to appear first in our texts about the middle of the eighth century B.C., but the reason for its apparent absence in earlier texts of the first millennium may easily be that we have no treaties or specific references to treaties in royal inscriptions before this time. In Aramaic the plural *'âdayyâ*, lit. 'oaths', appears as the

the research of G. E. Mendenhall and others, we now know that the structure of the suzerainty treaty between Israel and Yahweh was almost identical with that of second-millennium treaties preserved in Anatolian and Syrian archives from the fifteenth–thirteenth centuries B.C.[137] Some elements of the patterns were still in use with little change in Assyrian and Aramaic treaties of the eighth and seventh centuries B.C., but there are important modifications in the structure as a whole. These facts point to a high antiquity for the pattern which appears most fully in Joshua 24. Characteristic of these early covenants between God and the Hebrew, Israelite, or Jewish ethno-political unit is their archaism and their religious purpose. The covenant between Yahweh and Abram in Gen. 15 is strikingly archaic; it is preserved in our oldest documentary source 'J'.[138] Hitherto no clear parallel has been found anywhere outside of the Bible.

It is scarcely surprising that these covenants are so basic to biblical religious history, because of the long prehistory of covenants among the Hebrews. Being prevailingly caravaneers and so ethno-political intruders in the West, the early Hebrews were in constant need of contractual and treaty protection. To illustrate, when the Hebrews started on an expedition they had to make contracts with suppliers of beasts and equipment, as well as of food for man and beast; they had to make contracts with the merchants and business agents who owned

---

word for 'treaty' throughout the Sefîre treaties from c. 750 B.C. The Assyrian singular was undoubtedly **ādu*, from older **'ahdu*. Since an Accadian origin is precluded by the vocalization, it was probably borrowed from North-west Semitic.

137 See especially G. E. Mendenhall, BA XVII (1954), 26–46, 49–76, reprinted in *Law and Covenant in Israel and the Ancient Near East* (Pittsburgh, 1955). See most recently H. B. Huffmon, 'The Treaty Background of Hebrew *Yāda'*', BASOR 181 (1966), 31–7.

138 On Gen. 15 see Speiser, *Genesis* (1964), 110 ff., and for a striking chronological archaism in it see BASOR 162 (1961), 50 f.

goods and often accompanied the caravans; they had to make treaties with the states and tribes from whose territories they started, through whose territories they travelled and to whose territories they were going. Contracts had to be made between the chief caravaneers and the men who drove and cared for the donkeys, besides performing other stipulated duties. We must remember that caravans were constantly threatened by raiders, so it was necessary for all the caravaneers to carry arms and to be ready to fight at a moment's notice. This is undoubtedly one of the chief reasons why the *'Apiru* not only raided other caravans (as in the Mari letters) but also became attached as mercenaries or slave troops to the forces of many big and little states of south-western Asia. We now possess copies of such an agreement between the Hittite king and his 'Apiru troops from the sixteenth century B.C. (see above). Contracts and treaties were common everywhere, but only the Hebrews, so far as we know, made covenants with their gods or God.[139]

The paternal god of the Patriarchs, Shadday,[140] is now paralleled in similar ancient caravaneering societies, especially among the early Assyrian merchants of the nine-

139 Note that this statement is provisional and that a new discovery may at any time partially disprove it.

140 See my basic discussion, JBL LIV (1935), 173–93; M. Weippert, ZDMG CXI (1961), 41–62; F. M. Cross, Jr., HTR LV (1962), 244–50. It must be added that objections made by Weippert and others to an original vocalization *šaddāy* are not valid, since the formation in question is attested not only in Accadian, where it is very common, but also in North-west Semitic. The best example in the latter is *rabbāyū*, used of an important nomadic tribe or group of tribes in the Mari texts (NMTRM, *passim*). The name means transparently 'archer(s)', and is a form like *šaddāy* and numerous Accadian parallels, from the North-west Semitic stem *rby*, 'to shoot an arrow'. Incidentally, the singular *rabbāyum*, *rabbû* is naturally the direct source of Heb. *rabbîm*, 'archers'. As I pointed out, *ibid.*, p. 184, n. 36, the same word survived in Assyrian as *šaddā'û*. Of course the word does not mean simply 'mountaineer', but properly 'one who inhabits the mountain(s)'.

teenth and eighteenth centuries B.C., as well as among the Nabataeans and other North-Arabian caravaneers in the first centuries A.D. Among these groups it was customary for a man to worship one particular god, namely, his paternal or ancestral deity (Greek *theos patrōos*).[141] The paternal god or ancestral deity also played an unusually important rôle among the Hebrews of the Patriarchal and Mosaic ages. From this so-called 'monolatry' to a true, though perhaps implicit, monotheism, only a single long step was required. As we shall see, just such a step was taken by Moses. Because of the inevitable differences in emphasis, we can understand the survival of conflicting traditions: the Patriarchs are said to have worshipped 'other gods' in Mesopotamia and Egypt (Joshua 24) and yet a strong monotheistic spirit pervades Genesis. I formerly held that the religious traditions of Genesis were, in general, retrojections from post-Mosaic times, but I have now changed my mind, since there is no reason to single out religious traditions as relatively late while accepting the antiquity of Patriarchal customary law and historical tradition in general. Thanks to the work of E. A. Speiser and Frank M. Cross, Jr., it has become clear that early Hebrew religious traditions rest on pre-Mosaic foundations, since the divine names and forms of cult are different from anything in the later theology and cultic legislation of the Pentateuch.[142] We must, therefore, go back to Patriarchal times in order to understand the nature of specifically Israelite religious institutions once thought by most critical scholars to have developed only under the Monarchy (c. 1000–600 B.C.).

141 See A. Alt, KSGVI I, 1–78; F. M. Cross, Jr., HTR LV (1962), 225 ff.

142 See especially *Genesis* and HTR LV (1962), 225–59. On the Mosaic contribution, see below, Ch. IV.

III

Canaanite Religion in the Bronze Age

A. THE ETHNIC AND CULTURAL BACKGROUND OF THE CANAANITES

Syria and Palestine form a land bridge which has been utilized from the very earliest times by peoples and armies moving between the continents of Asia and Africa.[1] Natural routes are relatively narrow and sharply defined by sea, lakes and mountains in the west and desert in the east. It was possible for groups to maintain their identity without being seriously disturbed by the passing of traders and other migrants or by the march of hostile armies, since they could simply retire into the mountains or to the fringe of the desert while awaiting a more favourable time to resume a normal mode of life. We must, however, remember that, because of the commerce which we have described in Chapter II, Palestine and Syria were never really isolated, but were always being traversed in season by trading caravans and visited in season by ships from different parts of the Mediterranean. Though Palestine was generally a poor country, Syria, on the other hand, was naturally wealthy. Because of their location between the rich foci of power in Egypt and Asia, both Syria and Palestine were considered very important prizes in the world politics of the third as well as the second millennium B.C.

Today it is clear that the ethnic identity of the people later known as 'Canaanites' was already established no

[1] For a succinct account with special reference to antiquity, see my survey in *Historia Mundi* II (1953), 330–5 and pertinent observations on pp. 335–76.

later than the end of the fourth millennium B.C. This statement might have been rash a few years ago, but the situation has changed radically. In the first place, we now know of a considerably larger number of towns with good Semitic names which were first occupied before the end of the fourth millennium B.C. In the second place, the material culture of Palestine and south-western Syria had since that time been generally different from that of northern and eastern Syria with its cultural hinterlands. In such periods as Early Bronze II (c. twenty-ninth–twenty-sixth centuries B.C.) and Middle Bronze–Late Bronze, the civilization of Phoenicia, southern Syria and Palestine was quite homogeneous. It is true that some scholars have insisted on the non-Semitic origin of a number of early Palestinian and south Syrian place-names, but the evidence for their assertions is exceedingly weak.[2] For example, to insist that Mount Tabor has a non-Semitic name which may be connected with that of Atabyrion[3] on Rhodes or of Mount Tibar in the Zagros region is quite superfluous, since there is a perfectly good Semitic etymology.[4] To hold that names like 'Jordan', original *Yordân*,[5] 'Jabbok' (*Yabbōq*), and *Yarmûk* are

[2] On the other hand, we have some good recent studies on Semitic place-names in the ancient Near East as well as on Israelite and pre-Israelite place-names in Palestine, by B. S. J. Isserlin in *Proc. Leeds Philos. Soc.* VIII (1956), 83–110 and PEQ, 1957, 133–44.

[3] The fact that Tabor is called *Atabyrion* by Polybius means no more than that *Taḥpanḥes* was called *Daphnē* in Greek or *Tēpe* was called *Thēbai*.

[4] Ugaritic *tbrrt*, presumably pronounced *tabrurtu* from a masculine **tabruru-*taburru*, 'brightness, purity'.

[5] The combination of *Yordân* with Greek *Iardanos* is irrelevant. The oldest form of the name was probably **Yurdân*; *Yordân* is the original form which was kept in 'Amorite'; in Canaanite proper the form in the thirteenth century B.C. was spelled *Ya-ar-du-na* = *Yardôn*, which is the normal dissimilated form. Later Heb. *Yardēn* is an Aramaizing development from Canaanite-Hebrew; see VESO 36, IV, 6 for an analysis of these forms, with references.

non-Semitic overlooks the fact that they all have good Semitic forms and, in the case of the first two, obvious meanings. None of the characteristic Sumerian, 'Subarian', Hurrian, South Anatolian, or other recognizably non-Semitic place-names appear at all in Palestine—or, for that matter, anywhere in southern Syria and Phoenicia. Towns such as Beth-yeraḥ, Megiddo, Jericho, and Arad, which were first occupied before 3000 B.C., have good Semitic names which cannot belong to any other recognizable linguistic stock. When the Sumero-Accadians called the people of Palestine-Syria as well as their own nomads of western origin 'Westerners' (*Amurrium*, later *Amurrû*), the designation was applied to people bearing personal names of North-west Semitic type. When the Egyptians, no later than the early Pyramid Age, borrowed North-west Semitic *karmu* in the sense of 'vineyard'[6] and *qamḥu* in the sense of 'wheat flour', they were already employing typical North-west Semitic words, which were still used in Hebrew and cognate dialects millennia later. In the Execration Texts of the late twentieth and nineteenth centuries B.C., all hitherto identified personal names from Palestine and southern Syria were not only Semitic but nearly always specifically North-west Semitic.[7] At that time there is no evidence of non-Semitic populations in this region. There were, however, undoubtedly many historical movements of non-Semitic peoples into southern Syria and Palestine. For instance, there must have been an irruption from the north-west about 2500 B.C. when the so-called Khirbet Kerak pottery suddenly, though for a short time, flooded into Syria and

[6] For this word see JPOS VIII, 231, n. 1 and VESO 8, n. 21.

[7] See especially JPOS VIII (1928), 223–56 and BASOR 81 (1941), 16–21 and 83 (1941), 30–6. I am not citing other scholars here, since the few who know both Egyptian and the Semitic languages of the early second millennium B.C. and who also possess the necessary familiarity with comparative linguistics and historical phonology, have so far contributed only individual observations.

Palestine from Asia Minor. In a case like this, our principal reason for explaining the change of pottery styles as due to the sudden irruption of invaders is that the new style appeared first in Anatolia, spread to Syria, and inundated northern Palestine, occupying only part of the country and then vanishing with apparently equal rapidity. This pottery style is rare in central Palestine and scarcely appears at all in the south. It is impossible to say whether any specific linguistic stock was involved in the movement. We do not even know whether it affected Phoenicia and the coast of Palestine at all.

This 'Khirbet Kerak invasion' was followed by a strong cultural movement from Mesopotamia, illustrated by the caliciform ware of Syria[8] between the twenty-third and twentieth centuries B.C. and the debased pottery of the same origin which spread over Palestine in the twentieth–nineteenth centuries. As pointed out in Chapter II, this ware is useful for the chronology of the Patriarchal Age, though it was not brought into the country by the caravaneers, as far as we know.

During the twenty-third–twentieth centuries B.C. under Accad and Ur III, there was a very great increase of Mesopotamian influence in Syria. From this time on we can trace strong—though superficial—Mesopotamian influence on Syro-Palestinian culture. During the period of the Third Dynasty of Ur, about 2060 to 1955 B.C., this influence reached its height; at least one prince of Byblos was an acknowledged vassal of the king of Ur, receiving the title *ensi*, 'viceroy', about 2000 B.C.[9] To Ur III belongs also the earliest cuneiform tablet yet found in Palestine or Phoenicia. This is a very interesting phonetically arranged vocabulary of cuneiform characters from Byblos, proving that the Byblians were already trying to master

[8] See BASOR 168 (1962), 36–42; 184 (1966), 26–35.

[9] See E. Sollberger, AfO XIX (1960), 120 ff. and BASOR 163 (1961), 45.

the difficult cuneiform script by use of methods not yet attested in Mesopotamia![10]

During the following centuries the North-western Semites governed most of the city-states of Mesopotamia as well as of Syria and Palestine, sharing common personal names as well as a common language and undoubtedly many common customs. There is no reason to suppose that the Hebrews had yet achieved any degree of ethno-political solidarity; they were still semi-nomadic donkey caravaneers of chiefly North-west Semitic stock (see Chapter II).

During the Hyksos period, in the seventeenth and sixteenth centuries B.C., there was a series of invasions and migrations from the north-east and north, which brought the Hurrians (biblical Horites) down from northern Syria as far as the southern edge of Palestine. They were largely under the leadership of Indo-Aryan (Manda) chieftains, nearly a hundred of whose names have been identified as good early Indic (Vedic) forms.[11] It is quite probable that Anatolian (Luvian) elements entered Syria about the same time, since a good many Syrian names (especially at Ugarit and Alalakh) appear to belong to this stock. Other peoples may have come in with them, and it may well be that some of the non-Semitic groups whose names are found in the lists in the Bible, such as the Hittites, Hivites, Perizzites, Girgashites, etc., came in at this time.

In the Middle and Late Bronze Ages, between about 1700 and 1200 B.C., we find a surprisingly uniform devel-

[10] BASOR 163 (1961), 45, n. 46.

[11] For the latest survey of the field, which limits itself to identifications of Indo-Aryan names which appear to be certain and does not include many probable identifications, see the valuable survey by M. Mayrhofer, *Indogermanische Forschungen* LXX (1965), 146–63. The most difficult problem in making these identifications is that cuneiform phonology (itself a very complex subject) is just as important for a given equation as Indo-Aryan onomastics and historical phonology.

opment of material civilization extending from Ugarit, on the Syrian coast opposite the northern tip of Cyprus, to southern Palestine, and from the sea to the desert. This culture can be illustrated by artifacts of everyday use, such as pottery, tools, weapons, as well as by objects of art, plans of temples and other buildings, types of fortifications, etc. There is a no less striking similarity in the North-west Semitic personal names, the same names recurring from Hebron to Ugarit and from Gaza to Damascus. Their language was also very similar: while we know of several distinct dialects and of numerous local variations, the differences between them were relatively slight. We cannot, in fact, delimit any of these dialects precisely, and in them we find recurring phenomena which appear odd at first sight to students of classical Hebrew or Aramaic. There is not the slightest reason, then, to doubt the existence of a uniform higher culture throughout western and southern Syria as well as Palestine, during this whole period.

The chief dialects known to us from inscriptions of the fifteenth–thirteenth centuries are North Canaanite (Ugaritic),[12] South Canaanite (Amarna, etc.),[13] and Egyptian Canaanite (Proto-Sinaitic).[14]

B. THE NATURE OF CANAANITE RELIGION: THE EPIC PANTHEON

The religion of the Canaanites is incomparably better known now than it was twenty-five years ago, thanks to

[12] The best Ugaritic grammar is C. H. Gordon's *Ugaritic Textbook* (Rome, 1965). See below, n. 16, for the local dialect of Ugarit.

[13] Our manuals of Amarna Canaanite are quite out of date and have not been replaced by any systematic study, though a great deal of detailed work has been done in recent years, on which see W. L. Moran, in BANE, 54–72.

[14] See *The Proto-Sinaitic Inscriptions and Their Decipherment* (Cambridge, Mass., 1966), by the present author.

the discoveries at Ugarit. It is not clear to what extent Ugarit was considered a part of Canaan, though there are passages which seem to distinguish sharply between Ugarit and Canaan.[15] In some passages it seems, however, to be simply another Canaanite city, and it certainly shared a common Canaanite culture and language. Furthermore, the religion of the epics which have been recovered from Ugarit is virtually identical, so far as we can see, with the religion of the North-western Semites throughout Palestine and Syria. Differences are mostly due to admixture of linguistic elements—Hurrian, Accadian, etc.—and foreign myths.

The language of the epics is certainly not the contemporary tongue of Ugarit, which is represented by an increasingly large number of letters and documents dating mostly from the thirteenth century B.C.[16] The generalized epic dialect found at Ugarit and probably in some early

[15] Cf. A. F. Rainey, IEJ XIII (1963), 43–5 and BA XXVIII (1965), 105 ff. This approach is decidedly misleading, since 'language' and 'nationality' are both fluctuating terms. For example, it would obviously be absurd to say that the Austrians and Swiss do not speak German because their countries are not part of Germany. Arabic was until recently the chief language of all parts of Palestine and Syria, but this fact had little to do with the national divisions of the area. The fact is that 'Canaan' was never, so far as we know, a national unit. The geographical extension of this term undoubtedly fluctuated, and we cannot attribute the same borders to it when we find it mentioned in different periods and literatures. Between 1250 and 1150 B.C., for instance, the territory of 'Canaan' shrank enormously. I have always preferred to call Ugaritic 'North Canaanite', and since we now know that the dialects of North-west Semitic were very similar from north-western Syria to northern Egypt, it is going much too far to refuse the designation 'Canaanite' to any of them, as long as we explain what kind of 'Canaanite' we are talking about. In any case, as we shall see, the epics of Ugarit are written in a generalized epic language and its gods were worshipped all over Palestine and Syria, as well as in Egypt.

[16] See BASOR 150 (1958), 36–8, and Mario Liverani, 'Elementi Innovativi nell' Ugaritico non Letterario', *Atti della Accademia Nazionale dei Lincei* (1964), 1–19.

Hebrew verse (see above, Chapter I) differs no more from any one of these dialects than Homeric Greek does from the Mycenaean Greek of the Linear B tablets deciphered by Ventris and Chadwick in 1953. These Mycenaean texts come chiefly from Knossos, Pylos and Mycenae; all exhibit virtually the same speech, which has much in common with the language of Homer, but is different in detail. The relation between the Mycenaean *Koinē*, the generalized epic dialect of Homer, and later dialects such as Cypriote, Aeolic, Ionic, Boeotian, Attic, Doric, etc., is similar to the situation appearing in the hymnal-epic language of early Babylonian poetry, where we also have a blend of different dialects. This tendency to generalize is partly due to the composite sources of epic verse, but chiefly to the need for a common vehicle through which it can be understood by speakers of different dialects. Of course the language of the Ugaritic epics has been modernized in certain respects to accord with the grammatical development of Canaanite between c. 1700 and 1400 B.C. By this time the characteristics of Middle Bronze North-west Semitic had changed. For example, mimation had certainly been abandoned. Such modernizing of earlier linguistic forms is a common characteristic of most oral transmission. In no case can the absence of mimation be used to argue for a relatively late date of origin.

Thanks to the place-names mentioned in the Ugaritic epics, we can locate the chief source of their dialect quite precisely in Phoenicia and the hinterland. Places specifically mentioned include Tyre and Sidon, and apparently Byblos; they also include such inland sites as the source of the Adonis river north-east of Byblos and *Hrnm* = Hermel at the source of the Orontes in the Biqâ‘ east of Byblos.[17] Among mountains we have Lebanon and An-

[17] For the last two identifications, see M. H. Pope, *El in the Ugaritic Texts* (Leiden, 1955), pp. 72–81 and my remarks in BASOR 130 (1953), 26f.

tilibanus, and especially Casius north of Ugarit in the far north. This was the holy mountain of the Canaanites, Mount Ṣaphon, modern Jebel el-Aqra‘, just north of Ras Shamra, which recurs several times in biblical verse of Canaanite origin. The marshy districts of the Ghâb on the middle Orontes and Ḥûleh in the northern Jordan valley are also probably mentioned.[18]

In the Baal and Keret epics we find quite a mixture of ethnic backgrounds, including non-Semitic names of Anatolian type in the former, and very clear Hurrian and Indo-Aryan elements in the Keret epic. The latter, undoubtedly the latest of the great Ugaritic epics, mentions horses and chariots; it definitely goes back to a Hurrian prototype of some kind, though it has been quite thoroughly semitized in style and vocabulary. The hero, *Krt*, is probably the *Kirta* who was the ancestor of the reigning dynasty of Mitanni; he bears a good Indo-Aryan name.[19] The myths of the Baal epic are specifically Canaanite and do not reflect either a Mesopotamian or a Hurrian background, although there are, of course, parallels from all neighbouring regions, including Asia Minor, Egypt and the Aegean, as we should expect because of the movements of population and culture described above.

The gods of the epics are just as generalized as their language and style. In other words, there is no local pantheon, any more than there is in the Homeric epics.

[18] For the Ghâb, see BASOR 91 (1943), 42, n. 33, and for the sea or marsh of *Šmk* (Aram. *Yam Simko*), see IV AB, ii:9.

[19] As pointed out to me by P. E. Dumont. For the reading *Kirta*, see also my remarks in *Interpretation* XVIII (1964), 196. The name was first read on the *Saushshatar* seal. At fifteenth-century Alalakh the same name appears, spelled *Ki-ir-ta*. This is the name of the Mitannian king who was apparently founder of the dynasty of Shuttarna about 1500 B.C. or earlier, and whose name was formerly read *I-di-ir-ta* instead of the correct *mār Ki-ir-ta*. That *Krt* was the putative founder of a dynasty was pointed out long ago by Johannes Pedersen.

Instead we find a selection of important and interesting deities, most of the details which would tie them down locally being omitted. And just as the language of the epics differs from the current dialect of Ugarit, so the gods named and described in the epics differ from the divinities of the city as they appear (usually in a fixed order) in the official pantheon of Ugarit (see below) and in sacrificial lists. The discovery of Babylonian cuneiform lists which parallel fragments already known in alphabetic cuneiform makes the identities of the divinities certain almost throughout. The divine names in question frequently recur in theophorous personal names in the Ugaritic texts. From Mari (c. 1700 B.C.) we also have an official pantheon differing widely in detail from the list of divinities which can be put together from personal names in the Mari tablets (G. Dossin in *Studia Mariana* [Leiden, 1950], pp. 41 ff.). It has been urged by some classical scholars that the striking differences between the local pantheons of Pylos and Knossos and the pantheon of Homer proves that Homer must be much later than Mycenae. This is not, however, a valid objection to an early date for Homer, since we find an exactly comparable situation in the texts of Ugarit. In other words, both early Greek and Ugaritic texts exhibit a similar contrast between generalized epic and local pantheons.

Turning now to the gods and goddesses mentioned in the epics, I will limit myself to discussing some outstanding figures. In this case most of the material comes from the Baal epic, and somewhat less from Aqhat. In Keret we have significant information only about minor divinities. The head of the epic pantheon is the god El.[20] El

[20] See Pope's book, referred to in n. 17, as well as O. Eissfeldt's *El im Ugaritischen Pantheon* (Leipzig Academy, 98 [1951], 4). In general, for the latest discussions of the gods and goddesses of Ugarit, see especially M. H. Pope and W. Röllig in WM I (1965), 219–312, which deals with Syria in general and Ugarit and Phoenicia in particular. An earlier but very useful survey is that of

had probably declined in relative prominence during the second half of the third and the first half of the second millennium (judging from theophorous names of Semitic origin on cuneiform tablets ranging in date from the twenty-sixth century on). Yet he remained the active head of some local pantheons, and his name still appeared as the first component of such divine names as *El-ʿelyôn* and *El-ʿôlām.*[21] But by the time of the composition of the epics he had become otiose. In this respect he resembled the Greek deity Kronos (with whom he was regularly identified in later times) as well as the Egyptian Rēʿ and the Babylonian Anu. In the epics El appears as the father of mankind and as creator, but seldom figures actively in mythology. He is also called 'the Bull, El'. The name El meant originally 'the strong one', or 'the leader'. Thus 'the Bull' was an appropriate designation, since among wild cattle, horses, etc., strength and precedence are almost synonymous, the leader being the bull or stallion strong enough to vanquish all rivals. That the name *'el* is also borne by any and every god means only that the chief god is the god *par excellence.*

In order to visit El, the gods have to journey to the region known as the 'source of the two rivers, the fountain of the two deeps',[22] which is described as being very remote. Marvin Pope has made it probable that this region was originally in the heart of Canaanite territory, namely at Aphaca, later the site of an important sanctuary of Adonis. The name originally meant simply 'fountain'.[23] The nearness of Aphaca and the remoteness of its location in the epic need not disturb us at all, since such ambivalence is common in all mythology, e.g., Casius and Olympus were both homes of the gods, but the gods also dwelt

---

M. J. Dahood in ADS (1958), 65–94. See also the discussion by John Gray in LC², especially pp. 152–92.

21 See F. M. Cross, Jr., HTR LV (1962), 236–44.

22 For this rendering of the passage, see ARI 72, 194.

23 See above, n. 17, for Pope's discussion.

in heaven. Later the earthly mountains were considered as terrestrial counterparts of the celestial abode. We have no idea, of course, how far it was supposed to be between the terrestrial entrance to the subterranean home of El and the actual abode itself. In any event, El was not thought to communicate with gods or men except through visits or visions, respectively.

His consort, Asherah, has a name which was originally part of a longer appellation, which appears in Ugaritic as *Rabbatu 'athiratu yammi*, meaning either 'The Lady Who Traverses the Sea',[24] or 'The Lady Who Treads on the Sea (Dragon)'. Just as El was called *Bâniyu binawāti*, 'Begetter of Creatures', so Asherah also has the appellation *Qâniyatu 'elîma*, 'She Who Gives Birth[25] to the Gods'. In some earlier myth she was presumably thought to have destroyed the Sea Dragon, thus making it possible for El to create the earth. Later Baal or his sister Anath displaced Asherah as the dragon slayer.[26] (We must always remember that it is not possible to make either the myths or the figures of Canaanite mythology fit into a logical framework.) One of Asherah's most common appellations was 'Holiness' (Canaanite *Qudšu*). The 'holiness of Asherah' is a term with many ancient parallels,[27] even in Rabbinic literature, where 'the Holiness' is a designation of God. In contemporary Egypt the name *Qdš* (*Qudšu*) is attached to a nude goddess shown *en face*, with spirally curled locks and with raised hands

24 See ARI 77 f. It has also been plausibly suggested that Yam was the sea-dragon rather than the literal sea. Both explanations are perhaps equally tenable. Yahweh also appears as 'treading on the back of Yam' (Job 9:8).

25 For this appellation see most recently BASOR 173 (1964), 52.

26 BASOR 84 (1941), 14–17.

27 On the rendering 'holiness', see ARI 78 and 196, n. 17 and MSD I, 118, n. 2. This translation has been accepted by H. L. Ginsberg in all his subsequent writings. Note also that in Jewish Aramaic the same word for 'holiness', *qudšâ*, is used of God.

holding lilies and serpents.[28] Often she stands on her sacred animal—a lion. In Palestine and Syria many plaques showing the same goddess without the lion have been found in sites ranging from c. 1700 to 1200 B.C. There are indications that the absence of Asherah's lion in Asiatic representations is accidental. For instance, the 'Mistress of the Lions' is mentioned in an Amarna letter from Zaphon in the middle Jordan Valley (probably Tell es-Sa'īdîyeh today).[29]

In the Baal Epic Asherah appears many times, usually as the sworn foe of Baal and his sister Anath. She appears as a bricklayer (builder) and as the patronness of diviners,[30] just as in a fifteenth-century letter found at Ta-

[28] See especially the illustrations in ANEP, 471–4.

[29] Cf. BASOR 89 (1943), 15–17. The existence of the town of Zaphon is well established from the Late Bronze Age to the period of the Maccabees, whereas I have long been identifying it with Tell es-Sa'īdîyeh (see already *Annual* VI [1926], 46). On the other hand, there is little evidence for the existence of a town named Zarethan. It was, in any event, north of the area of Tell es-Sa'īdîyeh. Incidentally, the princess of Ṣapuna (Zaphon) called 'Lady of the Lions' lived a good century before the princess whose rich burial was recently discovered by J. B. Pritchard at Sa'īdîyeh.

[30] See II AB iv–v, lines 58 ff. In my opinion the passage should be rendered:

And the Kindly One, God of Mercy, replied,
'Not a slave am I, A play-boy of Athirat;
Not a slave am I, An apprentice carpenter;
If Maid Athirat Will mould bricks,
A house will be built for Baal.'
[The metre seems to be 2 + 2/2 + 2/2 + 2 + 3.]

Details of this translation will be discussed elsewhere; note meanwhile that *'nn 'Aṯrt* is related both to the Canaanite word *'anni* or *'anini* of reciting (Eg. *ḏd*) to music (*'nn*) and Heb. *'ônēn* 'to recite charms'. Ug. *'aḫd 'ulṯ* may be compared to Acc. *āḫizu*, 'learner', and the foreign loanword *'Ilš*, name of the carpenter (*ngr*) god in Ugaritic. 'Maid' (*'amt*) is a common designation of Athirat herself. Note that on a Phoenician coin of the reign of Gordian III (A.D. 238–44), published in IEJ IV (1954), 208, 224 (No. 138), and pl. 21, we have a scene showing a goddess engaged in building

anach in Palestine.[31] How complex her figure was may be seen from the early Babylonian description of her once as 'bride of Anu' (god of heaven and also the equivalent of West Semitic El) and again as 'wife of Anu'.

Two very interesting Asherah myths appear in Late Bronze sources outside the epics. In one myth, preserved in a Late Hittite tablet,[32] we read that Asherah (*Ašertum*) tried to seduce the storm-god (Baal), who rejected her advances. Asherah then went to El-Creator-of-the-Earth (*El-qônê-erṣi*, written *El-ku-ni-ir-ša*, pronounced *Elkoners*) and complained about Baal's treatment, presumably alleging (like Potiphar's wife) that it was actually Baal who had insulted her. El tells Asherah to deal with the storm-god as she pleases, but the latter's friend 'Ishtar' (Astarte or more probably Anath) listens to the conversation and apparently goes to her friend's aid.

Another myth may be roughly inferred from a three-story altar-house from Bethshan (twelfth century B.C.).[33] The latter shows the naked goddess Asherah seated on the window sill of the third story, while two gods seem to be stepping out of two doors in the second story as they fight over her. Around the corner of the terrace the lion of Asherah walks towards them, while her serpent emerges from a window of the first story towards the feet of the god on the left, presumably in order to bite him.

---

with the Greek inscription *Didō* and the Phoenician 'LT ṢR, 'goddess of Tyre'. Since this goddess of Tyre is presumably Asherah, the question of possible identification with Dido comes up, but need not be discussed here, where we are interested in the goddess as builder.

[31] See BASOR 94 (1944), 18.

[32] See H. Otten, MDOG 85 (1953), 30 ff.; MIOF 1 (1953), 125 ff.; E. von Schuler in WM 1 (1965), 159; cf. also my remarks in the Mowinckel *Festschrift* (1956), 7 f., where I omit the conjectural part of the restored plot.

[33] See FCTBS, pls. xvii:2 and lvi A:1 and 3. This house altar must not be confused with the somewhat similar one published as plates xvii:1, lvi A:2, lvii A:1 and 2.

No reconstruction of the myth would be worth while, but the situation speaks for itself.

But the most important active figure of the Canaanite pantheon was Baal.[34] Baal is called 'son of Dagan', (*Dăgăn*, later Hebrew *Dāgōn*, Phoenician *Dăgōn*). The god Dagan makes no other appearance in Canaanite mythology so far as we know, except that the name was employed in Hebrew (*dāgān*) and Phoenician for 'grain'. Dagan was originally a god of fertility who was worshipped from the earliest times in the Euphrates Valley. Recently discovered Ugaritic texts identify him specifically with the chief god of Tuttul, perhaps Tell el-Biya' near the confluence of the Euphrates and the Balikh rivers.[35] At Tuttul Sargon of Accad had paid homage to the god Dagan in the twenty-third century B.C.

Baal's personal name was usually *Hădăd*, which appears in many different spellings and in various shortened forms. Just when the appellation 'lord' (which is the proper meaning of *Ba'al*) became applied to Hadad as a personal name we do not know. It scarcely ever appears in the Mari texts[36] and never in Egyptian transcriptions from c. 1900 to 1700, but it was certainly common from the fifteenth century on. There is good reason to believe that *Ba'al* was coming into use as a personal name of the god during the Hyksos period (seventeenth to sixteenth centuries B.C.), when Hadad was identified with the Egyptian storm-god, Seth.[37] Baal is not only storm-god,

[34] See ARI 73 ff.; ADS 75 ff.; WM I, 253 ff.; and LC², *passim*.

[35] See BASOR 20 (1925), 13 ff. The site has scarcely been mentioned in recent literature, but was exceedingly important in the late third millennium.

[36] APNMT, pp. 100, 174 f. The number of clear examples at Mari where *ba'lu*, *ba'al* is a proper name rather than an appellation, 'lord', was still very small. The feminine form *ba'altu*, *ba'alat* came into use as a proper name as well as an appellative at an earlier date; see JAOS LXXIV (1954), 231.

[37] See J. Zandee, ZÄS XC (1963), 144–56. The Egyptian material seems to be rather exhaustively collected, but the author does not,

but is also king of heaven and earth. He is thus the Canaanite equivalent of Greek Zeus and also of Babylonian Marduk in so far as the latter was considered to be the active head of the pantheon. His terrestrial home was on Mount Casius or Ṣaphôn (Zaphon or Zephon) and, because of this association, he was called Baal-zephon (*Ba'al-ṣaphôn*).[38] Among Baal's favourite titles in the epic are 'Triumphant (*'Al'iyan*) Baal', 'Cloud-Rider' (*rākibu 'arapāti*), and 'Majesty, Lord of the Earth' (*zubūlu ba'alu 'arṣi*). Baal is said to have destroyed a monster of chaos, who is called '(his) Majesty, the Sea' and 'Judge River'. The figures of Sea and River were originally distinct (see Chapter II), and have obviously been conflated in this cosmogonic myth.

Baal also had a struggle with the god of death, which ended when Môt, 'Death', conquered him and took him

---

for instance, realize that *Sūtaḫ* is only the older form of the later *Sēth* in which the final consonant is strongly aspirated and is not a spirant at all. The references to Seth as storm-god in early texts do not seem to have any relation at all to the Canaanite storm-god Hadad or Baal.

[38] On this divinity see especially O. Eissfeldt, *Baal Zaphon, Zeus Kasios und der Durchzug der Israeliten durchs Meer* (Halle, 1932), and my supplementary study, 'Baal-zephon', in the *Festschrift* for Alfred Bertholet (Tübingen, 1950). For the primacy of this god at Ugarit see O. Eissfeldt, FF XXXVI (1960), 338 ff., where he correctly read *B'*[*l*]*-ṣpn* in PRU II (1957), No. 18. The original form was not *Ṣăpŭn*, as I once thought, but *Ṣapân*. In a letter published in 1956 by J. Nougayrol (PRU IV, 132), we should actually read (see BASOR 146 [1957], 35): *ilānu*^{pl} [*ša māt āl*] *U-ga-ri-it* ^{d}*IM* [*ša* (*ḪUR.SAG*) *Ṣa-*] *pá-ni* ^{d}*Pí-id-ra-i* [*û puḫur*] *ilāni liṣṣurū-ka*, 'May all the gods of Ugarit, [Baal-ze]phon, Pidrai, and all the gods keep thee'. In 1957 I also saw that Pidrai (*Pdry*) was, of course, the daughter and consort of Baal. This passage proves that the original vocalization of the name was indeed *Ba'al-ṣapân*, which later became (as in the Assyrian spelling *ṣapun-* for both mountain and god) *ṣaphôn*. Baal-zephon is simply the conventional English transcription of the Masoretic Hebrew text. WM I, 258 is doubtless right in deriving the name from the stem *ṣpy*, meaning 'to watch', as 'lookout'.

down to the underworld, from which his sister and sometime consort Anath freed him by destroying Môt after a violent conflict. As in most such myths there is a pronounced ambivalence. In mythology an event which is recurrent in actual life or cultic practice may be treated as occurring once for all. In the Baal epic it is recorded that at the beginning there was a victory of Death over Baal, which was later followed by a triumph of Baal over Death, at the end of which the sad refrain,

> Truly I know that Triumphant Baal is dead,
> That the Lord of the Earth has perished

is changed to

> Truly I know that Triumphant Baal lives,
> That the Lord of the Earth exists.

It is not easy to say just what this means. At first it was considered by all scholars that the Adonis myth in general refers to summer death of vegetation (or farther north, his death in winter). More recently it has been urged by C. H. Gordon and others that this is a mistake and that the god was not killed and brought to life again more than once. But we must bear in mind that an actual ecological situation must be presupposed. The god or goddess of fertility comes to life with the growth of vegetation. He or she dies when vegetation dies, either because of winter frosts or, in Mediterranean climate, because of summer drought. In irrigated regions the god or goddess of vegetation is brought to life by annual or seasonal flooding. In the Near East the concept that the vegetation god dies because of cold weather and comes to life again with warm is rare, but it inevitably enters the picture because many of its peoples originally occupied or still inhabited mountain regions or high plateau areas in which there is snow in winter. The plateau of Asia Minor and the mountains of Armenia and the Zagros were almost impassable during this season. It is the death, for one reason or another, of grain or other vegetation that is the common factor. A given myth may gather a considerable variety of motifs from different ecological sources. Traces of these only confirm the identification of the birth and death of a divinity with that of the vegetation he or she represents. The error of those who deny this lies in their attempt to apply our post-Aristotelian logic to pre-Aristotelian thought patterns—an attempt which obscures, rather than clarifies, these patterns. The fact that Death (Môt) was eventually destroyed and completely reduced to powder, which was then scattered to the wind and devoured by birds, does not in any way indicate that he died once for all. There is no solid basis for the idea that the myth of Baal and Death involves a seven-year famine or seven years of plenty. There is, however, ample proof that there was annual weeping for Tammuz, for Adonis at Byblos, and for Hadad-Rimmon (the Aramaic form of Hadad) at Megiddo. Whatever the 'original' motif may have been, the decease of the god of fertility came to be celebrated annually.[39]

As we have seen, the principal form of Baal at Ugarit was Baal-ṣaphôn. While his terrestrial home was on Mount Ṣaphôn, he had a palace or temple in heaven, just as the Greek gods occupied Olympus as their terrestrial home, it being understood at the same time that their home was also in heaven. Baal-ṣaphôn was not only Lord of the North, but also lord of the northern storms.[40] Hadad was himself in a general way the storm-god, but Baal-ṣaphôn was the marine storm-god *par excellence*, like Greek Poseidon. As such, he was also the protector

[39] Since writing these lines I have received a short paper from S. N. Kramer [BASOR 183 (1966), 31], in which he accepts A. Falkenstein's correction of the key passage in the Sumerian myth of Inanna's Descent to the Underworld (BiOr XXII, p. 281). Now we know that both Tammuz and his sister-consort Inanna (Ishtar) were to spend half of every year in the Underworld.

[40] Cf. p. 9 of my paper mentioned in n. 38.

of mariners against storms. In his honour temples were built and ports were named along the Mediterranean littoral as far as Egypt, where we find Baal-zephon worshipped at Tahpanhes (Daphne) and Memphis. In later times he was succeeded by Zeus Casius, after Mount Casius, the hellenized Anatolian name (*Ḫazzi*) of *Ṣaphôn*. The consort of Baal-zephon in the treaties between Ugarit and its Hittite suzerains, as well as in an Aramaic text in demotic characters written nearly a thousand years later,[41] was *Pidraya*,[42] named first in the list of Baal's three daughters in our epic. The name may be derived from Ugar. *pdr*, synonym of *'r*, 'town'; it may then mean 'She of the Underworld'.[43] In fixing relationships we must remember that both in Egypt and Canaan the notion of incest scarcely existed. In fact, Phoenicia and Egypt shared a general tendency to use 'sister' and 'wife' synonymously. Such kings as Akhenaten and Ramesses II married one or more of their own daughters as late as the fourteenth and thirteenth centuries B.C.

Baal was closely associated with two other goddesses. The relations between him and the goddesses Anath and Astarte were very complex. For example, Anath was not only Baal's virgin (*batultu*) sister, but also his consort. While she was in the form of a heifer, he raped her in an epic myth '77—even 88 times'.[44] The figure of Anath can

[41] See my articles in the Bertholet volume (see n. 38), pp. 9 ff., and the Mowinckel volume (see n. 32), pp. 6 f.

[42] See above, n. 38.

[43] An additional parallel would be the appellation of the Tyrian Baal, *Milk-qart*, Melcarth, which I have shown elsewhere to mean almost certainly 'King of the Underworld City'. This Baal was probably an original Resheph (= Nergal); see below.

[44] I* AB v, 17 ff., where the animal is called *'glt*, 'a female calf' and *prt*, 'a heifer'. For the corresponding Egyptian designation of Anath as a heifer (with the determinative for 'cow' attached), see A. Massart, *The Leiden Magical Papyrus* (Leiden, 1954), pp. 71, 73, where other occurrences are listed. The word *'amraya* presumably meant 'heifer from 'Amr', or the like, referring to a highly regarded Asiatic breed.

be better understood in the light of several Egyptian accounts of the goddess, unquestionably translated from an original Canaanite myth, to judge from words and idiomatic expressions.

Extensive mythological material of Canaanite origin is to be found in the great Egyptian magical collections from the Nineteenth Dynasty.[45] The most striking of the Canaanite myths of Anath preserved in Egyptian dress runs as follows: Anath was bathing on the shore of the sea, at Ḥamkat. Baal (Seth) went for a walk and raped her, 'leaping her as the sacred ram (of Amun) leaps, forcing her[46] as a . . . forces . . .' Baal fell ill because of this, but Anath came unexpectedly to his rescue: 'Anath the Victorious, a man-like woman, dressed as a man but girded as a woman, went to the sun-god, her father.' Re replied at some length, stressing Baal's folly and ending, 'It is punishment for his folly, since he . . . had intercourse with her in fire and raped her with a chisel.' The chisel of Anath appears in another magical text.[47] On Roman coins the divinity of Ascalon named *Phanebal(os)*, 'Presence of Baal', has long been recognized as a man-like goddess, with slender uncurved body in female dress but fully armed.[48] Another Egyptian magical

[45] For a complete collection see BAeV, 494 ff.

[46] On the meaning of the Semitic loanword *'mq* see ARI, 197, n. 39. Contrast BAeV, 494.

[47] BAeV, 495, after the Leiden Papyrus (A. Massart, p. 36, line 6).

[48] G. F. Hill, *Catalogue of the Greek Coins in the British Museum; Palestine* (1914), pp. lix–lxi, 115–39, *passim*, describes the coins of Ascalon which represent a war divinity, labelled specifically *Phanēbal(os)* on second-century pieces. The coins in question (pls. xiii–xiv) extend from Augustus (A.D. 6/7) to Severus Alexander (230/31): 'The figure on the coins of Ascalon has generally been described as male . . . in spite of the curiously feminine appearance . . . on some coins, which show a long skirt and broad hips.' However, the 'broad hips' seem to indicate a robe caught up at the hips, not the hips themselves. Since there is sometimes a

text says that 'the mouth of the wombs of Anath and Astarte, the two great goddesses, was closed by the god Horus (Canaanite *Ḥôrân* or *Ḥaurôn*), so they could become pregnant but could not bear, and was opened by Seth (Baal)'.

It cannot be accidental that this late form of Anath at Ascalon was also called *Derketō* = *darkatu*, 'dominion, rule'.[49] Among Anath's titles as queen of heaven in a recently described Ugaritic tablet[50] are *Ba'latu mulki*, *ba'latu darkati*, and *Ba'latu šamêm(i) râmêm(i)*, 'Mistress of Kingship, Mistress of Dominion, and Mistress of the High Heavens', respectively. Below we will show that the Carthaginian appellation of the goddess Anath, *Tennît-panê-Ba'al* means 'Radiance of the Presence of Baal', or the like. Tennît was often identified with Juno Caelestis, Juno as queen of heaven, or as Virgo Caelestis, 'the Heavenly Virgin' (cf. the standing appellation at Ugarit, *batultu 'Anat*, 'the Virgin Anath'). At the same time Anath could be consort and wet-nurse, as we know from passages in the epic literature. Such apparent contradictions meant nothing in a prelogical world of thinking, as soon as they were transposed to a dimension over which man could normally exercise no control.

Anath was, not surprisingly, an extraordinarily cruel goddess, represented as having slaughtered mankind from 'the rising of the sun' to 'the shore of the sea'. Apparently the slaughter delighted her, since 'her heart rejoiced and her liver exulted' over the massacre.

> Beneath her were heads like balls,
> Above her were hands like locusts.

'Tanit' symbol beside the figure, the divinity of Ascalon is evidently related to the chief goddess of Carthage; see below.

49 This I first suggested in JPOS XIV (1934), 130, n. 53; cf. JBL LXIII (1944), 219, n. 82. In connexion with *drkt-darkatu* see further M. Dahood, ThSt XV (1954), 627 ff., and *Biblica* XLV (1964), 404.

50 Ch. Virolleaud, CRAI, 1962, 109.

She plunged her knees into the blood of warriors,
Her thighs into the blood of youths.

It has been pointed out by Marvin Pope that there are many traits which Anath shares in common with the Indic goddess Kali or Durga.[51] In fact, the respective figures are in some ways so similar that coincidence can scarcely be the only explanation. It may be that major common traits spring from a substratum extending from the Mediterranean to India before the intrusion of the Sumerians (no later than the fourth millennium B.C.) and that minor resemblances are the result of secondary pseudomorphism. Both goddesses are represented as protecting and destroying, their beneficent and destructive aspects complementing each other in a way that startles and shocks a Westerner, but which undoubtedly does reflect the reactions of primitive man to the sharp contrasts of his environment.

When Anath found the dead body of Baal, we read in a recently published tablet:[52]

While Anath walked along, lamenting (?)[53]
The beauty[54] of her brother ⟨–how fair!⟩[55]

[51] In several papers presented before learned societies, as well as in printed comments; his eagerly awaited monograph has not yet appeared.

[52] Ch. Virolleaud, CRAI, 1960, 182 ff. For details see also M. Astour, RHR CLXIV (1963), 4 ff. [I have since become acquainted with the paper by E. Lipiński, *Syria* XLII (1965), 45–73, which gives valuable additional suggestions, though I cannot agree with his interpretation of this passage as a whole.]

[53] The abrupt introduction of Anath's name and the strange word-order demand that we begin the sentence in the lost (?) preceding line.—Read *hlkt* for *tlkt* (presumably a scribal error).—My rendering of the verb *šnw* is conjectural; cf. Eth. and Arab. *snw*, 'to irrigate', etc. Here it would refer to the flow of tears.

[54] I cannot accept the rendering 'tambourine', though this meaning for *tp* is well attested in Ugaritic. Translate rather 'beauty', from *wpy*, assuming a form *tôpê* for **tawpay* like Ug. *tsm* (*tôsamu*),

The charm of her brother—how seemly!
She devoured his flesh without a knife
And drank his blood without a cup.

Apparently she was carrying her gruesome burden as she devoured it. The clear parallel between this episode and well-known Dionysiac myths and rites has been pointed out by M. Astour.[56] The practice of *omophagia*, eating sacrifices raw, is well known. Legend pointed to Zagreus, a form of Dionysus, who was torn to pieces and devoured by the Titans. The Bacchantes tore Pentheus to pieces and a band of their sisters treated Orpheus in the same way. (It must be remembered that cannibalism is said in early Hittite historical inscriptions to have been practised in Armenia about the sixteenth century B.C.)

Anath's ferocity could, however, be combined with tenderness as, when she attacked Death in order to rescue Baal from the underworld, we read,

Like the longing (heart) of a wild cow[57] for her calf,
Like the longing of a wild ewe for her lamb,
So was the longing of Anath for Baal.
She seized Death, son of El;
With the sword she split him open.

The figure of 'Athtart/Astarte appears very rarely in the epics, where her *Doppelgängerin*, Anath, steals the show.

'charm', from *wsm; note the perfect parallel in Cant. 7:7 [and the remarks of Lipiński].

55 This phrase is needed for the metre; it was presumably lost by vertical haplography. For the idiom, see the material from Hebrew and Ugaritic collected in my paper *Mélanges bibliques . . . André Robert* (Paris, 1957), pp. 22–6.

56 See Astour (cited in n. 52).

57 It must be emphasized that *'arḫ* means '*wild* cow' in Ugaritic, just as in Accadian; similarly, *ṯa't* means '*wild* ewe'. Anyone who is accustomed to the reaction of female wild animals with young, will understand how much stronger the comparison is than the usual one with a 'cow' and a 'ewe'. Note that both words appear also in Proto-Sinaitic inscriptions as designations of sacrificial animals (PSID 38, 44). At Serābîṭ they would have to be wild.

In Phoenicia and Palestine Astarte grew in importance, while Anath became hidden under various other appellations. Still later, as Aramaean influence spread, both goddesses were fused into a new conflate figure, Atargatis.[58] We know from the evidence of names, and especially from Egyptian sources, that Astarte was already very popular in the Late Bronze Age.

The Egyptian story of 'Astarte and the Sea (*Yam*)' is obviously a variant form of the Ugaritic epic myth of Baal and Sea (*Yam*), to which we have referred above. In both, Sea intimidates the gods, who pay tribute to him and finally offer him Baal (in the Ugaritic text) or Astarte (in the Egyptian version). In both, Baal (Seth) takes the initiative against Sea, and in both Astarte plays an important rôle (as central figure in the Egyptian version, and as supporting figure in the Ugaritic myth). Astarte is called 'daughter of Ptaḥ' in the hieratic text, but we do not know which of the alternative identifications of Ptaḥ, with El or Koshar, is involved here.

More information about Astarte comes from New Kingdom Egypt. Especially significant are numerous representations of Astarte (spelled *'Astar(a)ta* and rarely *'Asita*[?]) as a naked girl, with immature breasts, astride[59] a galloping stallion.[60] She is armed either with bow and arrows or with shield and javelin. These representations

[58] On the origin of the name *Atargatis*, see my studies in AJSL XLI (1925), 73 ff., 283 ff., and XLIII, 233 ff. While these are antiquated, the explanation of the name as a fusion of Aram. *'Attar* (for *'Aṯtar*) and *'Attah* has long since been accepted by all competent scholars. The reduction of the doubling is a normal phenomenon in early Aramaic.

[59] While both of the rider's legs can sometimes be seen, this phenomenon may much more easily be explained by the conceptual approach (in H. Schäfer's sense) of much Egyptian art, rather than by supposing that she actually rode sideways, 'à l'Amazone'.

[60] On this whole subject see J. Leclant, 'Astarté à cheval', *Syria* XXXVII (1960), 1–67. [In the Ugaritic text 18.39 (PRU V [1965], 189 f.) *both* 'the horse of Astarte and the horse of Anath' appear.]

are obviously no earlier than the seventeenth century, when the horse first came into general military use. Between the seventeenth and the twelfth centuries B.C. horsemen do not ordinarily appear in combat, where chariots were supreme. In Syria and Palestine it was not until the ninth century, after the first Assyrian victories, that cavalry replaced chariotry in warfare. Astarte's appearance on horseback is, therefore, a glorification of the young divinity as goddess of war, like Ishtar and Shulmânîtu before her.

Astarte's full name as war-goddess was *ʻAštart-šem-Baʻal*, 'Splendour of the name of Baal', attested as far back as the Ugaritic epics, and appearing occasionally in late texts, down into Persian times. 'Splendour' is not the usual translation of the name *ʻAthtart*, but it must be emphasized that all suggested cognates or derivatives which are found in the other Semitic languages, such as Arab. *ʻāṯūr* and *ʻaṯarīy*, are doubtful and at best quite secondary to the fully developed figure of the goddess. The name *ʻAthtart* was always connected with the evening star, just as *ʻAthtar* (the corresponding masculine name) was the morning star all over the West Semitic world from Syria to South Arabia. The ancients early became aware of the fact that the evening and morning star were simply different manifestations of the same entity—since they saw that the two have the same magnitude and never appear together, yet always in related positions in the heavens. The word may originally have belonged to a stem meaning something like 'sparkle, of a star',[61] yielding the substantive appellation, 'splendour', which became ultimately the abbreviated form of the full name.

Similarly the name *ʻAnat* is probably an abbreviation

[61] Like the words for 'sparrow/bird' in Semitic, Heb. *ṣippōr*, Acc. *iṣṣūru*, Arab *ʻuṣfūr* (note also *ṣpr*, 'to sing, of a bird'), the quadrilateral *ʻAṯtar* may be a congeneric assimilation (*Mischbildung*) from such stems as *ʻṯ* and *ʻṯr*; cf. Arab. *ʻaṯṯa*, 'to beat, of heart, pulse'; *ʻaṯara*, 'to vibrate, of sound, to trill'.

of an original *'Anat-panê-Ba'al*, meaning something like 'Turning of Baal's Face', that is, 'Wrath of Baal'. The word *pānîm*, 'face, presence', connotes both favour and disfavour in the Hebrew Bible, where it must sometimes be rendered 'wrath', depending on the context.[62] In Hebrew it was also hypostatized as a designation of Yahweh: 'The Presence'. The same designation, *panê Ba'al*, was also applied to the Carthaginian Tennit (*tennît-panê-Ba'al*, properly 'Glory[63] of the Face of Baal') as well as to the chief goddess of Ascalon (see above). Also like Tennit, who was regularly called by the Romans *Juno Caelestis*, Anath, in a recently described cuneiform text from Ugarit, is called 'Mistress of the Lofty Heavens' (see above).

The coexistence of the three goddesses, Asherah, consort of El, Anath, and Astarte, apparently both sisters and wives of Baal, not unnaturally confused the Egyptians, used to a more highly crystallized hierarchy of gods. In late Ramesside times (twelfth century) they identified all three, as we know from a painted limestone relief published by I. E. S. Edwards.[64]

One of the most interesting figures of the epic pantheon is Kôshar, patron of all forms of craftsmanship, from con-

[62] I owe some valuable hints in this connexion to Dr. M. Gertner, of the University of London. The evidence is far more extensive than might be supposed; for example, in very old Samaritan tradition *fanûta* for older *panûtā* means 'the Period of Divine Wrath'.

[63] For the pronunciation *Tennît* see A. Berthier and R. Charlier, *Le sanctuaire punique d'El-Hofra à Constantine* (Paris, 1955), pp. 167, 169 and pl. xxviii, A and C (ΘΙΝΙΘΦΑΝΕΒΑΛ, ΘΕΝΝΕΙΘ ΦΕΝΗ[ΒΑ]Λ). For the meaning of the first element see above, Ch. I, n. 86. Note that the unassimilated form *tmnt*, used of God in Num. 12:8, is rendered both in Greek and in Syriac by words meaning 'glory'. For the original form *tabnît*〉*tamnît*〉 *tennît*, see also Ch. I, n. 86. My former explanation of the word in question as the infinitive construct of the word 'to give' (*tnt*, which actually appears in Proto-Sinaitic) is no longer possible after the Ḥofra transcriptions.

[64] JNES xiv (1955), 49–51.

struction through metallurgy to magic and music. Here again the name appears in a variety of dialectal forms, the original of which was *Kauṯar*, Syriac *Kauṯar*, Arabic (Quranic) *Kauṯar*, Ugaritic *Kôthar* (pronounced *Kôsar*, *Ku-šar* in Accadian transcriptions).[65] In Phoenician times the name was pronounced *Kûšōr* (Gr. *Chūsōr*). In the Bible the name appears in the feminine plural *kôšārôt*, 'birth pains' (literally, divine midwives)[66] and dissimilated as *kîšōr*, 'skill' (Prov. 31:19).[67] In fifth-century Ecclesiastes the verb and its derivatives regularly mean 'be skillful, skill'. This god was identified at Ugarit with Babylonian Ae ('Ea'), god of wisdom (both practical and esoteric); he was the inventor and contriver of new constructions and instruments, such as the composite bow. His full name in the epics was Kôthar-and-Khasis, 'the

[65] On the various forms of the name cf. my treatment in JAOS LX (1940), 296 f. (which has now appeared in revised form in HACH, 170 f.). See most recently J. P. Brown, 'Kothar, Kinyras and Kythereia', JSS x (1965), 197–219, whose discussion of Kothar and Kinyras is good, but whose treatment of the name of the island of Kythera and the derived appellation of Aphrodite, *Kythereia*, is spoiled by his lack of linguistic training. *Kythera* (with a strong aspirate in the middle) cannot reflect *Kôṯar* ('*Kôthar*'), because the latter was pronounced **Kausar* in Canaanite and *Kaušar* in 'Amorite' during the Bronze Age, as early as the Sethe Execration Texts, c. 1900 B.C., where Kaušar is a chieftain of the 'Amorite' 'Shutu' mentioned between a 'Job' and a 'Zebulun'. Note that original *ṯ* normally became *š* in 'Amorite'. In other words, we should have to go back to the third millennium to make such a derivation possible. The initial Greek κ instead of usual Greek χ (a strong aspirate) = Semitic *k* could be a normal dissimilation, since Greek did not tolerate an aspirate before another aspirate.

[66] See below, n. 86.

[67] Heb. *kîšōr* in Prov. 31:19 does not mean 'spindle' but 'skill' (Pešiṭta *kaššîrûṯâ*, Targ. *kušrâ*). All these Aramaic words are ultimately derived from Canaanite; Aram. *ktr*, 'await, remain', was originally *ktr*, not *kṯr*. It should be added that all derivatives of *kšr* in Ecclesiastes refer to 'skill', and that 'utility' is quite secondary; this applies also to the meaning 'useful purposes' given by the Greek in Prov. 31:19.

Very Skillful and Intelligent One'.[68] Wholly unexpected is the discovery that in the epic literature Kôshar was believed to be particularly fond of Memphis and Crete. This is sometimes denied, but if we remember how often in our Ugaritic epic texts we find words, phrases and lines omitted in one of two occurrences of passages repeated in prospective and narrative form, it is easy to restore the complete text here too. If we take the chief passages in the Baal and Aqhat epics together, the following picture emerges. In both passages the divine craftsman Koshar is the central figure, to whom a special messenger is sent and who is honoured by a special banquet. Koshar is called explicitly (by filling an omission in one from the other):

b'l Ḥkpt 'el klh
Kptr ks'u ṯbth
Ḥkpt 'rṣ nḥlth

Lord of the Memphis-of-Ptaḥ[69]—it is truly his,[70]
Kaptara (Crete), the throne on which he sits,
Ḥekupta (Egypt), the land of his heritage.

The admission that the arts and crafts came to Canaan from Egypt and Crete probably goes back to the Middle Bronze Age, when the cultural influence of both was at its height.

68 It should be pointed out here again that the original *Kauṯăr* was an augmentative (the opposite of diminutives like Arabic *fu'ail*⟩ *fu'êl*), with the same meaning as Acc. *Watar-ḫasīsim* or *Watram-ḫasīs* ('Atraḫasis').

69 The identification of Ug. *Ḥkpt* with Amarna *Ḫikuptaḫ*, for Eg. *Ḥ(t)-kȝ-Ptḥ* (pronounced *Ḥekuptaḥ*) is perfectly satisfactory (contrary to many contemporary assertions). Two successive occurrences of *ḥ* in the same word are virtually always dissimilated in Semitic. Nor does the meaning offer any difficulty, since Amarna *Ḫikuptaḫ* refers to Memphis, while Homer's *Aiguptos* means 'Egypt'. Ptaḥ and Chusor are closely linked in the Phoenician cosmogony handed down under the name of Mochus; see Ch. V.

70 Read *kî-lahu.* The adverb *kî* is a strong asseverative; see above, n. 55.

As we shall see below, the feminine counterpart of Kôshar, Kôshart(u), was the goddess of childbirth, and the seven Kôsharôt are the divine midwives.

Another important god, whose name was originally *Ḥaurân*, appears as *Ḥôrân* in Ugaritic, *Ḥôrôn* in South Canaanite and *Ḥaurôn* (Gr. *Aurōnas*) later in southern Palestine.[71] This divinity was identified with Sumero-Accadian Ninurta, the Assyrian war-god, as we know from personal and place-names where Ninurta appears as the second element in some texts, while Ḥaurôn appears as the second element in others. Thus the *Bît Ninurta*, which the prince of Jerusalem mentions in the Amarna tablets, is not Bethlehem, as suggested by O. Schroeder, but undoubtedly Beth-horon the Nether,[72] which was claimed as part of his territory by 'Abdi-Kheba of Jerusalem (c. 1360 B.C.). In the Baal epic Ḥaurôn appears only rarely, and then together with Astarte as the military champion of Baal. From later texts it is certain that Ḥaurôn was a form of the god Baal.[73] In Egyptian texts

[71] On this god see ARI, 80 f.; ADS, 82 f.; LC^2, 178 ff.

[72] On this site see EM II, cols. 73 ff., s.v. *Bêt Ḥôrôn*. Beit 'Ûr et-Taḥtā was occupied in the Late Bronze, and its location about equidistant (in a straight line) from Jerusalem and Gezer fits the indications in EA 290.

[73] See especially BASOR 76 (1939), 8, and T. H. Gaster, Or XI (1942), 44. I should translate the relevant lines of the Arslan Tash incantation as 'By the incantation of the wife of Ḥûrûn, whose word is true, and her seven co-wives and the eight wives of Baal [?]'. Neither I nor Gaster saw the picture quite correctly, though he was undoubtedly right in referring 'whose word is true' to the wife of Ḥûrûn (the late Phoenician pronunciation of Ḥaurôn). He was, however, wrong in the very natural identification of the goddess in question with Ereshkigal. This follows partly from an item preserved by Eusebius from Philo Byblius mentioning *Ūrūmbēlos* and his consort *Thūrō* (= *Tĕwūre*, later *Thŏēris*), name of the Egyptian goddess of child-birth, wife of Seth (= Baal). Since the latter was expressly identified by Philo with *Chūsarthis* (= *Kûšart*, singular of the word which appears in Hebrew as *Kôšārôt*), there can be no reasonable doubt that the hitherto mysterious COYPMOYBHΛOS

of the New Kingdom he was, however, identified with Horus, especially in the form of Harmachis, god of war.[74]

A god who became very popular as a war-god in Egypt and who appears as the angel of death in the Bible, is Resheph (Hab. 3:5), identified with Apollo in Cyprus. In the Mari texts his name is spelled (following Amorite pronunciation) as *Rasap*, but in Phoenician it was pronounced *Rašōp* (modern Arsûf = Apollonia). All these names go back to an original appellation *Rašpu*, probably 'He Who Burns', and his sacred emblem was the head of a gazelle. Since 1926 (cf. ARI 79) I have insisted on treating him as a Nergal figure, that is, as a god of the underworld, a god of pestilence and destruction, of death and war. At the time he was considered by all to be a storm deity, so my identification was rejected, in spite of arguments which retain their validity. Discovery after discovery has confirmed the correctness of this identification, until, finally, the recent discovery of two equivalent official lists of the Ugaritic pantheon, one in Ugaritic, the other in Accadian, has shown that *Ršp* was directly equated with Nergal. In the texts of Ugarit Resheph appears only rarely, but as the sender of pestilence, like Nergal. He also appears at Ugarit as the 'Lord of Good Fortune' (*b'l ḥẓ*), just as, in Phoenician inscriptions from Cyprus a thousand years later, he is called 'Resheph of Good Fortune' (*ḥṣ*).[75] In New Kingdom Egypt Resheph appears again and again as a redoubtable war-god who brings death to the foe; he is regularly represented with a gazelle's head projecting from his helmet, just above his

of Philo is indeed a deformation of OYPOYMBHΛOS (for details see Vol. II of my McGraw-Hill series, now in preparation).

[74] See the discussion of the plaques of Amenophis II in BASOR 84 (1941), 7 ff., and the further discussions by G. Posener and K. C. Seele, JNES IV (1945), 240–44.

[75] The usual translation 'Resheph-of-the-Arrow' is naturally wrong; see Samuel Iwry, JAOS LXXXI (1961), 27–34.

forehead. The gazelle was also particularly sacred to Nergal, for reasons which also escape us.

Thanks to the Egyptian magical texts we know that the consort of Resheph was named *'A-tu-m*, which can be normalized either as *Atum* or as *Adum*. Fortunately, the name is preserved in the Bible as that of a Canaanite convert to Yahwism, which we must vocalize as *'Abd-'adōm* ('Obed-edom'), following the LXX. The meaning of the name was wholly obscure until M. Dahood demonstrated convincingly that there is a Hebrew word *'dm*, to be vocalized *'ādōm*, literally 'the red (earth)' which means 'earth' like the feminine *'adāmāh*. Resheph's wife was thus an underworld divinity, just as 'Arṣay, daughter of Baal, is identified in the Pantheon of Ugarit (see below) with Allatu, consort of Nergal. On the other hand, the name *Šamš-'at/dum*, given in the lists of Tuthmosis III (c. 1468 B.C.) to a town in northern Galilee or south-central Syria, can scarcely have anything to do with the goddess.[76]

C. THE PANTHEON OF UGARIT

As we have observed, the pantheon of Ugarit is quite different in detail from that of the epic texts and is, in fact, derived from different ethnic and linguistic sources. In 1929 M. Schaeffer discovered a broken alphabetic text (No. 17) among the first lot of tablets found at Ugarit; it was not considered important until the excavation of an Accadian tablet of similar content in the 1956 campaign (20.24). J. Nougayrol identified the two lists of gods, calling the alphabetic tablet 'B' and the Accadian 'A'; the former is clearly more original than the latter. B:1 (only

[76] For the Leiden Magical Papyrus V, 7, see A. Massart's edition (above, n. 44), pl. II and pp. 17, 65 f. For Hebrew *'ādōm* (MT *'ādām* or *'ĕdōm*), 'earth, underworld', see M. Dahood, CBQ XXV (1963), 123 f., with our joint observations in *Biblica* XLIV (1963), 292.

in the alphabetic text) begins with a heading: 'Gods of Mount Casius' (*'el ṣpn*). Then follows a long list of divinities, which we will summarize, stressing figures with which we have not dealt so far.[77]

First comes *'El['e]b*, whose name is translated into Accadian as 'the god of the father'. This is a remarkably accurate translation, though the element *'eb* has nothing directly to do with *abu*, 'father'. As pointed out independently by A. Goetze and me, 'El'eb is the patron of ancestor worship, and in the plural the word seems to mean the *manes*, dead spirits of ancestors. In the Aqhat epic we find the plural used in the following passage:

> *nṣb skn 'el'ebh*
> *b-qdš ztr 'mh*
>
> Who sets up the stelae of his ancestral spirits,
> In the holy place the guardians (?) of his family.[78]

Etymologically *'Eb* and *'El'eb* are analogous to *Wêr* (*Mêr*), *Iluwêr*,[79] *Elwêr* in the stele of Zakir, king of Hamath (eighth century B.C.); *'El'eb* appears as a divine element in a seal from Palestine, mentioning the personal name *'Abd-El'eb*.[80] The frequent replacement of *'Eb* by

[77] See CRAI XVIII (1957), 82 f.; AfO XVIII (1957), 170.

[78] My translation (BASOR 94, 35) has been adopted by H. L. Ginsberg, ANET 150.

[79] The name appears as an element in *Tukultī-Mēr*, name of an early Assyrian ruler, and often a *I-lu-me-er, I-lu-we-er*, etc.; intervocalic *m* in Babylonian orthography was pronounced *w*. The North-Mesopotamian divinity is identified either with Adad or with Shamash.

[80] The word *'Ib* probably appears in the meaning 'ghost' in Is. 14:19, where the reading of MT, *yôrĕdê*, may be corrected to *yûrĕdû* by 1QIs$_1$ (middle of second century B.C.), in keeping with 14:11 and 14:15, where we also have the *hof'al* of *yrd*. This poem teems with mythological allusions; for the same idiom, see the Ug. Baal Epic and Psalm 88:5. Read probably:

> *yūrĕdû⟨šĕ'ōlāh⟩ 'el'ĕbê bôr*
> Let them be brought down ⟨to Sheol⟩,
> O ghosts of the Nether World!

'El'eb probably has two immediate reasons: (1) *'eb* alone is homonymous with *'eb* (Heb. *'ôyēb*), 'enemy'; (2) *'eb* in the sense of 'ghost' is too easy to confuse with the god by the same name. The short form *Ib*, *Eb* also appears in two names, *Ib-dâdî*, *Ib-addî* from Byblos about 2000 B.C.,[81] as well as (in the labialized form *Ub*[82]) in the early tribal name *Ub-rapi'* (see Chapter II). The labialized *'ub* is, of course, the source of Heb. *'ōb*, 'ancestral spirit, ghost'.[83] Cf. especially Isa. 29:4, where the expression *'ōb mē-'ereṣ* should probably be read *'ōb-m 'ereṣ* and rendered 'ghost of the underworld', in keeping with the context.[84] Most interesting is a hitherto unexplained passage in Job 8:8, where our *'ōb* has been discovered by J. A. Fitzmyer, S.J.:

> Be sure to enquire from men of past ages,
> Set about to examine their ghosts.[85]

It is more than likely that the same god continued to be worshipped in Roman Syria as the 'very great god' (*theos megistos*) Op (*ōp*), whose name is found in two inscriptions from Syria; the god is represented in the Mashtala stele as standing on a lion (*not* a bull) under whom are two large serpents. Op is clearly a god of the underworld

81 Published by E. Sollberger, AfO XIX (1960), 120 ff. For the explanation of the names see BASOR 163 (1961), 45, n. 44.

82 Such labialized vowels were very common in North-west Semitic; cf. Heb. *lĕ'ummîm* = Ug. *l'emm* and Ug. *'um* = Heb. *'ēm* (for **'imm*).

83 The basic meaning is probably like French *revenant*, 'ghost, apparition' (cf. Arab. *'āba*, 'return'), as pointed out long ago. In other words, the original intransitive participle *'ib* was used as a noun in different senses: 'foe' and 'ghost'. One can easily imagine possible semantic developments to explain the facts.

84 For the enclitic *m* in archaic construct chains see Ch. I, § D and n. 88.

85 Communicated to me orally. There is no need to change the transmitted Hebrew consonantal text; read probably *dôrê* instead of *dôr*, 'age' (see BASOR 163, 1961, 49 f.) and clearly *'ōbôtām* for *'ăbôtām*.

like Nergal; no such Sumerian divinity as the suggested Ub is known.[86]

Next comes El, who was the head of the pantheon in the epics. He is followed by Dagan, the grain god (father of Baal in the epics). Then come seven different storm-gods (*B'lm*, corresponding to the Hebrew plural *Bĕʿālîm*, 'the Baals'), headed by Baal-zephon (in Accadian Adad of Mt. Casius). Among the names which follow is Accadian *Šasurātum*, '(divine) midwives'. These midwife goddesses were actually called in Ugaritic, as well as in Canaanite generally, the *Kôsharôt* (see above). According to the epic of Aqhat, there were seven *Kôsharôt*, and Philo Byblius gives the same number of divine midwives, called by him the Artemides or Titanides, Greek names for divine midwives.[87]

Of the other names of divinities, some are Canaanite, some are Accadian, some are Hurrian, reflecting the ethnic mixture of northern Syria. Preserved are: the moon-god Sīn (probably *Yaraḫ*), Mt. Casius itself (*Ḫazzi*, Ugaritic and Hebrew Ṣaphôn), Ae ('Ea' = Kôthar), the Hurrian divinities Ḫebat and Aštabi, the Canaanite goddesses (in Accadian transcription) Ašratum, Anatum, the sun-goddess 'Šamaš' (Ugar. Šapaš), the underworld goddess Allatum (= 'Arṣay, daughter of Baal), and the Accadian goddess Išḫara (['*I*]*šḫr*), Ishtar-the-Hurrian (['*A*]*ṯtart*).[88] Next we have the 'Auxiliaries of Baal',[89] Nergal (= *Ra-*

[86] For Greek ΩΠ see R. Mouterde, *Mélanges . . . Dussaud*, 391–7.

[87] I owe this combination to Delbert Hillers. Note that we may have one, seven, and fourteen birth-goddesses; a similar wide variation in their number is found in Egypt. [On the Acc. name (explained by W. G. Lambert) see M. Astour, JAOS LXXXVI, 280.]

[88] This is, of course, the '*Astar-Ḫuru* of Egyptian texts and Ishtar of Nineveh. Nineveh was a Hurrian city before c. 1350. For the name see VESO 37, V.A.8.

[89] The '*ḏr B'l* (cf. Heb. '*ôzĕrê Rhb*, 'auxiliaries of Rahab', the primordial dragon of chaos, Job 9:13) may either be rendered in

šap), the Hurrian god Dadmiš, the 'Council of the Gods' (*pḫr 'elm*), the Sea-god Tāmtu (Yam), the divine incense burner (*'Uṯḫt*[90]), Kinnâr,[91] (the divine lyre), and Salimu (*Šalim*).[92]

The divine incense burner, if correct, is very interesting, since it reminds us forcibly of the chief god of Carthage, Ba'al-ḥammôn. He was the active head of the Punic pantheon, whereas El, Latin Saturnus, was relatively inactive. The name Ba'al-ḥammôn meant 'Lord of the Incense Burner'.[93] The view that Cinyras, king of Paphos, the mythical father of Adonis, bears a name going back to a god of the lyre is also substantiated (see above).

The third daughter of Baal, Arṣay, now appears in the pantheon of Ugarit as equivalent to Babylonian Allatum,

---

this way, or as 'warriors of Baal', since the word *'ôzer*, 'helper', was borrowed in Egyptian as *'u-ḏi-ir*, 'warrior' (VESO 38, V.C.1).

90 I provisionally accept J. Nougayrol's translation of *'Uṯḫt*, which he compares with Accad. *šēḫtu*. The latter means 'high incense burner', i.e., an incense burner on a pole (cf. BASOR 85, 1942, 18–27), from Accad. *šēḫu*, 'grow, be high'. (For this word see Müller, *Das assyrische Ritual* [MVAG XLI:3, p. 21].) But the first syllable would remain unexplained, so we may have to identify the name with Accad. *ašūḫu*, Jewish-Aramaic *'ašûḥâ*, said to mean 'female (!) cedar'. It may be that *'Uṯḫt* was a tree-goddess like Eg. *nūhe*, 'Sycomore', a solution which might explain the idea that the cedar is unisexual. Note that a vocalization *'ušúḫatu* would suggest original **'ašuḫatu*, just as Ug. *'urbt*, 'lattice' = Heb. *'arubbāh*, stands for **'arúbatu*.

91 Spelled *Ki-na-ru*(*m*). On the name and its feminine counterpart Kinnartu (Chinnereth) see A. Jirku, FF XXXVII (1963), 211. Note, however, that the Ugaritic vocalization reflects the ancestral vocalization of Heb. *kinnôr*, 'lyre' (Eg. *kennur*, VESO 47, IX.C.6). In later Phoenician the final vowel became *û*, yielding *kin*(*n*)*ûr* = Κινυρας.

92 This is presumably the *Šalim* of the liturgy for Šaḥar and Šalim, 'Dawn and Dusk'.

93 See my detailed treatment in ARI 215 f., following H. Ingholt in *Mélanges . . . Dussaud* II (1940). 'Lord of the Brazier' would probably be more correct; see below, Ch. V, § C.

consort of Nergal, goddess of the underworld, Greek Persephone. We may then include among the divinities of the pantheon Pidray of the cuneiform treaties from Ugarit, who is the first daughter of Baal in the epic; in the treaties she is the consort of Baal-zephon, and a millennium later she still appears in the Aramaic magical text in Egyptian demotic script to be published by R. A. Bowman. It is highly probable that she is also the *Peraia* (for **Pedraia*) of Philo Byblius.[94] Pidray was the first of the three daughters of Baal, and, of course, a daughter could also be a consort, as we have seen. The second daughter, *Ṭly* of the epic, is not yet known outside of the epic.

D. SOME OTHER PHOENICIAN PANTHEONS

But what of the Bronze Age pantheons of Byblos, Tyre and Sidon? These pantheons were remarkably tenacious, and yet by no means static, since new gods and identifications of deities seem to have made their appearance at regular intervals in all of them, so that we are frequently hard put to define the exact nature of the basic pantheons. Only at Ugarit do we have a complete pantheon in any period.

The chief god of Tyre in later times was Baal Melcarth; the appellation *Milk-qart*, 'King of the City', refers to the city of the underworld, as in the case of various Sumerian divinities of the Nether World.[95] In Hebrew

[94] See above, and n. 38. A false etymology is presumably responsible for the omission of *delta*.

[95] See ARI[4], 156 f., 219, 226 f., 227 for discussion and references. The most important direct contribution is J. M. Solá Solé's proof that *Ršp* (in the form *'ršp*) was identified with Melcarth in Punic Spain (*Sefarad* XVI [1956], 341–55), as well as H. Seyrig's demonstration that Melcarth was still identified with Nergal in the Roman period (*Syria* XXIV, 1947, 62–80). On the pantheon of Tyre see also R. du Mesnil du Buisson, RHR CLXIV (1963), 133 ff. A valuable study of the Melcarth of Gades (Cadiz) has been published

tradition Baal and Asherah (I Kings 16:33, 18:19) were heads of the Tyrian pantheon, and the rôle of Asherah at Tyre is confirmed by the Keret Epic, centuries earlier. (On the pantheon of Tyre see also below, Chapter V, § c.)

The basic pantheon of Tyre is probably represented in Egyptian art, including particularly a beautiful stele in the British Museum, which shows a triad with 'Holiness' (Qudshu) in the centre.[96] She is standing stark naked on a lion, with a spiral headdress which came originally from Babylonia and was then developed in Twelfth-Dynasty Egypt. Since the Palestinian plaques showing Qudshu with the spiral locks are in many cases indistinguishable from contemporary plaques found in Babylonia, there is good reason to believe that the representation spread westward from Babylonia to Egypt and not north from Egypt.[97] The lion appears elsewhere as her special favourite. In her right hand she holds lotus blossoms, and in her left stylized serpents (not onions!). At her right is El, represented, because of the great stress laid in Canaanite mythology on his virility, as the ithyphallic Min or Ptaḥ. At her left is the young god, Resheph, with a gazelle head projecting from his forehead and with a spear in his right hand. Since Melcarth was later identified with Nergal, the Babylonian god of the Nether World,[98] and since Rašap was equated with Nergal in the pantheon of Ugarit, there is no difficulty in the identification (see above, n. 95).

At Byblos the situation is less transparent. The earliest pantheon, dating from the eighteenth century B.C., consists of a native deity, who is reflected by the Egyptian sun-god, incarnated in Pharaoh; of a mother-goddess, who

---

by A. García y Bellido, *Archivo Español de Arqueología* XXXVI (1964), 70–153. See further below, Ch. V, § c.

[96] See above, and n. 28.

[97] See *Mélanges . . . Dussaud* I, 114 ff.

[98] See above, n. 95.

is called the 'Lady of Byblos'—*Ba'lat* for short—represented by the Egyptian cow-goddess, Ḥatḥor; and of the Egyptian patron of the forests of Lebanon, Kha'y-taw.[99] This last god is probably Phoenician Koshar (see above). It is likely that the Damu mentioned in the Amarna tablets from Byblos is the Damu of the Sumerian Tammuz litanies from the early second millennium B.C. where it is the short form of the name of the latter.[100] The name *Tammuz* was originally Sumerian *Damu(Dumu)-zid-abzu*, meaning something like 'the faithful son of the subterranean fresh-water ocean'. This probably means that Koshar was later identified with Tammuz and that the Byblian figure of the dying god Adonis (literally *'adōnî*, 'my lord') was identical with Koshar. That the cutting down of the coniferous trees of Lebanon should become a symbol of the god who dies but is always reborn, is not surprising. With this was combined the annual death of Adonis when the waters of the River Adonis (Nahr Ibrahim) are coloured blood-red after the first heavy winter rains bring down mud stained with the ferrous oxide of the *terra rossa*.[101]

According to Greek tradition, derived from Paphos in Cyprus, Adonis was the son of the Cyprian king Cinyras, who must be identified with Phoenician Kinnûr, god of the lyre (see above on the new Ugaritic pantheon), and of a mother called *Myrrha* or *Smyrna*, both variant Greek dialect forms of the word for 'myrrh' or 'incense'.[102] Syr-

[99] See BASOR 176 (1964), 44 f., n. 25, and for the name in general see P. Montet, *Byblos et l'Égypte* (Paris, 1928), pp. 64 ff.

[100] See O. Schroeder, OLZ XVIII (1915), 291, on EA 84:31–35, written by Rib-Addi of Byblos to Pharaoh. These lines should be rendered: 'And let my lord send men in order to take the property of my god Damu (Adonis) to my lord, but let not that dog (Abdi-Aširta) take any property of thy gods.'

[101] W. W. Baudissin, *Adonis und Esmun* (1911), pp. 65–202, especially pp. 71 ff.

[102] It is at least a striking coincidence that *'Uṯḫt* and *Knr* are mentioned together, possibly as the two parents of Adonis. The

iac tradition reports that Tammuz was son of Kautar (the later Aramaic form of the original *Kauthar* (= *Kôshar*). In view of the fact that *Tammuz* stands for Sumerian 'son of the *abzu*', which is the home of the god Ea, it is curious indeed that the Canaanite god identified explicitly with Ea appears as father of Tammuz. Two such cases are scarcely coincidences; we are probably faced with different forms of the common mythological replacement of a father by a son with similar attributes. The historical cause of such replacements may be that when the cults of two different divinities clash because the latter are not similar enough to be identified, an easy way out is to make the newer arrival son of the older one.

At Sidon the situation is at least equally complex. In 1931 I published an article in which I proposed to identify the chief Iron Age deity of Sidon, Eshmûn, the god of healing, with the Bronze Age Shulmân.[103] This proposal seemed somewhat adventurous to many scholars at the time. But it is remarkable that there is no mention of Eshmûn in that form in the Ugaritic literature. One instance is the minor goddess Thatmânîtu[104] (or the like).

---

incense in question must have been derived from resin of the cedars and pines of Lebanon, regardless of the etymology (on which see n. 90); for the importance of the fragrant resin and resinous oil from the forests of Lebanon in the twenty-third century see BASOR 168 (1962), 40 f., and for an Egyptian view in the eighteenth century B.C. see BASOR 179 (1965), 41.

103 AfO VII, 164–9.

104 In the Keret Epic, Tablet C, Thatmânîtu is the youngest daughter of Keret, who heals her father from illness (there is no 'Sha'taqat', which is merely a causative perfect *š'tqt*). The name means transparently, 'She Who Belongs to the Ogdoad (*taṯmânû*)'; the form is like Accad. *tû'amu*, 'twin', and *takšû*, 'plural birth'; the initial transposition is of common type. This Ogdoad must already have been connected with Thoth, the Egyptian patron of physicians, whose chief appellation in the second millennium was *nb Ḫmnw*, 'Lord of the Ogdoad' (i.e., lord of Hermopolis Magna, later *Ṣhmûne*). Philo Byblius says that Asklepios, i.e., Eshmûn, was the youngest of the eight sons of Sydyk (I, 10, 38; cf. I, 10, 25) by

While there is not the slightest indication in our texts that this figure has any direct relation to Eshmûn, there does seem to be an indirect connexion through the latter's early association with the ogdoad.[105] The fact remains that in the Late Bronze Age there are many references in Hittite, Ugaritic and later in Assyrian tablets to a god whose name appears between c. 1400 and 700 B.C. as *Šulmanuḫa, Šulmanuḫi, Samnuḫa*, and in fuller form, *Šamanminuḫi*, etc.[106] The form of the name is Hurrian, and it obviously goes back to **Šulmān-minuḫi*, 'Shulmân of (the Ninevite temple) Emenue', which is said to have been built by Manishtusu of Accad in the twenty-third century B.C.[107] Furthermore, the consort of Eshmûn at Sidon is said by Damascius to have been Astronoe.[108] When I first suggested that the name *Ešmûn* was a form of *Šulmân* (Can. *Šalmôn*) shortened by dissimilation, I hesitantly observed that this goddess might be the famous Ishtar of Nineveh, who is called 'Astar-Ḫūru in the Egyptian texts of the New Kingdom. It was already known at that time that the cult of Ishtar of Nineveh was widespread, and was particularly popular in Mitanni. But it was not until the publication of the Boğazköy tablets that a prayer came to light in which the goddess in question is begged to come to the land of the Hittites from her different cult-centres

---

one of the birth-goddesses (= Kôsharôt), from which a semantic connexion between the name of the god and the minor goddess may be inferred. We are presumably influenced by a secondary popular etymology in the case of Eshmûn. We must, however, bear in mind that an eighth son or daughter was apparently believed to be exceptionally lucky or well-endowed.

105 This is one of the unexpected partial returns to earlier, prearchaeological, views, derived from classical sources and vigorously rejected by sober critical scholars like W. W. Baudissin (*Adonis und Esmun*, p. 209, n. 6).

106 See AfO VII (1931), 105 f.

107 AAA XIX (1931), 59 ff.

108 On Astronoe in Roman Tyre see H. Seyrig, *Syria*, XL (1963), 21 ff. Astronoe was now associated with Heracles (Melcarth), having presumably been fused with the earlier Asherah.

all over south-western Asia, from the Aegean to the Tigris and from northern Asia Minor to Phoenicia.[109] The loci of these cult-centres are particularly interesting. One is located in Caria and must obviously be identified with Carian Aphrodisias, where the goddess Aphrodite was worshipped—especially since the original name of the place is said, in Greek sources, to be Ninoe, which is hard to separate from Ninuwa, 'Nineveh'. Another cult-centre is even more unexpected. In 1930 I had not yet studied this text so I was puzzled by finding, as I thought, Hurrian deities of ultimately Accadian origin worshipped at Sidon in the Late Bronze Age. The Hittite prayer specifically mentions Sidon as a cult-centre of the goddess Ishtar of Nineveh, so that it is no longer at all adventurous to identify Astronoe with Ishtar of Nineveh, or her young lover Eshmun with Shulmân of Nineveh, who had presumably been worshipped since the twenty-third century B.C. in the temple Emenue. There are, of course, a number of unexpected further identifications. Shulman was identified in Syria with Resheph, and was evidently considered an underworld deity. The Shulamite of Canticles goes back almost certainly to *Šulmānîtu*, name of the goddess of love and war, as well as a figure with underworld associations.[110] As mentioned above, we cannot analyse Canaanite mythology in terms of Aristotelian logic. Eshmûn, the Iron-Age god of Sidon, was also a dying god, with Astronoe playing the rôle of his mistress. Eshmûn also reflects the healing qualities which we should expect from his precursor, Shulmân, literally 'He who (brings) welfare'. The serpents of Eshmûn belong to the chthonic figure named *Rašap-Šulmân*.[111]

[109] See KBo II, 9, i:4, in the middle of a list of Syrian cities, including Ugarit (where her name actually appears in the pantheon; cf. above) and Alalaḫ (Tell Açana). The text was treated by F. Sommer in ZA XXXIII (1921), 85 ff.

[110] See HSSt (Driver volume), 5 ff.

[111] See W. Spiegelberg, ZA XIII (1898), 120.

E. MISCELLANEOUS BELIEFS, SANCTUARIES, AND PRACTICES

The reader of this chapter may have been disconcerted at finding so much detailed interpretation of the names and functions of gods and goddesses, without systematic reconstruction of Canaanite epics, cults, or religious practice. The reason is simple; it is better to limit ourselves at this stage to what is known rather than to launch a frail boat of conjecture upon the treacherous seas of mythological plots and religious observance. Much useful work has been done along this line by such scholars as H. L. Ginsberg, T. H. Gaster, C. H. Gordon, and John Gray. During the past twenty years I have continued my own efforts to interpret difficult passages in the epics without publishing most of my results. Many of the supposed points of reference around which plots have been constructed have proved either to be completely misunderstood or even to be totally non-existent. No one can map little-known areas of research without reliable parameters. For instance, it can be shown conclusively that the so-called goddess Sha'taqat is a figment of the imagination; the supposed name is a finite verb and the figure referred to is the minor goddess of healing, Thatmânîtu.[112] Instead of trying to reconstruct elaborate maps I have preferred to select a few of the more striking motifs for treatment in appropriate places.

Much the same uncertainties present themselves to every investigator of the still scanty data for North-west Semitic sacred buildings. We have surprisingly few clear-cut temple plans and even fewer types of cult objects whose use can be described with any confidence. In dealing with Israelite borrowings from Canaanite religion in Chapter IV, I shall have occasion to refer to the more

[112] See above, n. 104.

important types of temple structure, such as are found in the Middle-Bronze temple of Byblos and the Late-Bronze temple of Hazor, or in the *migdal* temples of Ugarit, Beth-shan and Shechem.

Our knowledge of religious practice will probably be considerably enlarged when the mass of still unpublished ritual texts from Ugarit has become available and when all then-known material has been systematically analysed and compared with similar data in various parts of Mesopotamia and Asia Minor. Such problems as divination and human sacrifice will also be discussed elsewhere in this volume.

The picture which we have drawn exhibits a startling combination of primitiveness and over-sophistication. We are as yet in no position to say that the North-western Semites were more 'depraved' (from a Yahwist point of view) than the Egyptians, Mesopotamians and Hittites, but it is certainly true that human sacrifice lasted much longer among the Canaanites and their congeners than in either Egypt or Mesopotamia. The same situation seems to hold for sexual abuses in the service of religion, for both Egypt and—on the whole—Mesopotamia seem to have raised standards in this area at a much earlier date than was true in Canaan. We shall return to this subject below in various connexions.

IV

The Struggle between Yahweh and the Gods of Canaan

A. THE MOSAIC MOVEMENT

In our survey of Hebrew literary and historical origins (above, Chapters I and II), we have been faced with an apparent paradox, which has disturbed many scholars. Though the Patriarchs were unmistakably immigrants from Mesopotamia, with historical traditions as well as religious lore and customary law derived from the north-east, the Hebrew language and poetic style were quite certainly Canaanite in origin. The seeming difficulty is materially reduced when we bear in mind that the Meso-potamian precursors of the Hebrews were themselves largely of West-Semitic ('Amorite') extraction. Yet it remains a problem for which a solution must be sought.

The solution is probably to be found, paradoxically enough, in the very fact that the immediate followers of Moses belonged mainly to Hebrew groups which had settled long before at the Egyptian end of the old caravan routes between Palestine and Egypt. Elsewhere I will survey the new data which have become available in recent years for the period between the settlement of Jacob and his followers in early Hyksos times[1] through

[1] My detailed study of the Hyksos period in Egypt has been delayed by repeated (and hitherto only partially satisfactory) efforts to decipher the short inscriptions in enigmatic (but not meaningless) hieroglyphic script on Hyksos scarabs. Five names of rulers can be placed in order before the irruption of the non-Semitic Fifteenth Dynasty under Salitis (c. 1650 B.C.): *Šš'* (biblical *Šešay*, though not necessarily founder of the pre-Israelite clan of Hebron

the bitter years of state slavery which followed the triumph of Amosis over the Hyksos in the third quarter of the sixteenth century B.C.[2] This period probably lasted about two and a half centuries, down into the early thirteenth century B.C. That the Israelites did not leave Egypt *en masse* during these centuries, may easily be explained; flight into the desert meant starvation for many, and single persons who could not stand life in Egypt could quite easily find refuge among their kindred in the hill-country of Palestine, where many of the old Hebrew clans still preserved a quasi-ethnic entity: e.g., Judah, Benjamin, Ephraim, Manasseh, and probably others.[3] Aside from occasional short revolts, Palestine remained within the Egyptian empire during almost the whole of this period.

From biblical tradition, confirmed by the alphabetic inscriptions from Sinai (dating between c. 1525 and 1450 B.C.)[4] and Egyptian sources, we know that the pantheon of the authors of the inscriptions consisted chiefly of a mixture of the old Semitic divinities with Egyptian deities; not a single Canaanite god or goddess can be identified with certainty.[5] Hebrew personal names of the age also show that the old Hebrew gods were still revered;

---

bearing this name), *Ya'qub-'âli* (with the same name as Jacob), *'Anatî-'âli, Bbnm* (cf. *Bablimma,* name of a king mentioned in a Qatna inventory, and perhaps the same person). The leader of the invasion (or perhaps the clan to which the dynasty belonged) was probably named *Yam'î* or *Yam'ay* (cf. the two twentieth-century names *Yam'i-'ilu* and *Yam'i-nu'mu* of the Sethe Execration Texts).

[2] For the date see BiOr XXI (1964), 65 and note, as well as BASOR 176 (1964), 44, n. 23. The recovery of Tanis from the Hyksos took place after the eleventh year of Amosis (C. F. Nims, *Thebes of the Pharaohs,* New York, 1965), p. 199. On the period of state slavery c. 1525–1450 B.C. see PSID 10–15, etc.

[3] Cf. provisionally BPAE 32.

[4] See PSID, which contains the results of my decipherment since the appearance of BASOR 110 (1948), 6–22, and especially since the summer of 1957.

[5] PSID 13 ff.

the figure of Shaddai, in particular, appears to have been dominant.[6] But, in general, the Hebrews lived in the north-easternmost part of Egypt, in the region called in the Bible variously the 'land of Rameses', i.e., the region around Tanis-Pira'masese (Gen. 47:11), the 'plain of Tanis' (Ps. 78:12, 43, from the tenth century B.C.),[7] and Goshen (a Semitic name referring apparently to a certain kind of soil).[8] It is no accident that such names as *Ba'al-ṣaphôn*, *Migdol*, *Zilû* and *Sukkôt*,[9] all in this region, are North-west Semitic.

In other words, most Hebrews in Egypt lived in the north-eastern corner of the Nile Valley, where they were effectively prevented by the sea to the north and the desert to the east and south-east from maintaining normal contact with other Semitic ethnic groups. Even had this been practicable, the fact that the former Hebrew donkey caravaneers were despised by their neighbours—Egyptians and Canaanites alike—made close relations difficult at best. Under these circumstances, Hebrew tenacity in maintaining ancient traditions becomes easy to understand. Parallels abound.

When R. Kittel, A. Alt and others compared the Hebrews of the pre-Conquest age to the semi-nomadic *'Arab* (as contrasted with *Bedū*) of the Middle East before the beginning of the automotive age, they made it possible to correct the analogy drawn by J. Wellhausen with the pre-Islamic camel-raising *Bādiya*. I took another step

[6] BPAE 13 f.

[7] On the date, established by O. Eissfeldt, see Ch. I.

[8] The initial voiced g was impossible in Egyptian, as we know from extensive phonological evidence, e.g., Semitic g was transcribed as *q* or *k* in Egyptian, and Eg. *g* appears as *q* in Semitic. *Gošen* appears several times as a South-Palestinian place-name, and Heb. *gûš* (Aram. *gûšâ*) is a word for soil of some kind (cf. also Guš-ḥālāb = Gischala in Galilee).

[9] Baal-zephon was at Tahpanhes = Daphne (*Festschrift für Alfred Bertholet* [Tübingen, 1950], 14, n. 4); Zilû = Roman Silē, formerly *Zaru* of Egyptologists (see JEA x [1924], 6–8).

when, about thirty years ago, I began insisting that the Hebrews were 'ass nomads', not camel nomads,[10] but it was not until 1961 that I realized that they had to be 'donkey caravaneers' (see Chapter II, above). This has completely altered our entire picture of their place in the geographical horizon of the second millennium B.C. They may have been despised, but they were far from ignorant. In fact, since they spent most of their time in activities such as driving donkeys from one country to another, in wandering from pasturage to pasturage with their flocks, in cultivating vineyards and selling wine, as hucksters and traders, in raiding their more settled neighbours, and in serving as mercenaries or as state slaves, they were presumably as clever and as tricky as the Arabs, when judged from Turkish and Kurdish points of view. It is particularly difficult to imagine them as ignorant of international military movements at any time.

Furthermore, the Hebrews in Egypt were settled around the new Ramesside capital and along the routes which led from it by land into Palestine, and by water into the Mediterranean. In a poem to Pharaoh composed under Ramesses II, it is called 'The beginning of every foreign land and the end of Egypt, with beautiful terraces and shining halls of lapis lazuli and turquoise, where thy chariots are marshalled, where thy footmen are mustered, where thy navies reach port, bringing thee tribute.'[11] There they were in a position to learn about troop movements and hear rumours of impending attack from the increasingly unpredictable north. We probably have a definite peg on which to tie the chronology of the Exodus, as we shall now see.

In 1923 Wilhelm Spiegelberg published a list of 679

[10] See FSAC (written in 1939), 119–22, where I published the results of previous years of research on the question. See also JAOS LX (1940), 283, note.

[11] Cf. R. A. Caminos, *Late-Egyptian Miscellanies* (London, 1954), p. 101.

sealings from wine jars from the Ramesseum at Thebes.[12] The place-names in them are, as far as they can be identified, nearly all in the North-eastern Delta, where most of the Egyptian vineyards were located at that time.[13] The personal names are in part Egyptian, in part North-west Semitic, and in part gentilic, such as 'The Cypriote', or 'The Syrian'. The sealings are dated as follows:

Year	1	3	Year	5	72	Year	9	11	Year	13	3
	2	13		6	70		10	6		14	0
	3	48		7	244		11	5			
	4	41		8	146		12	3			

From year 15 to year 52 (when the list ends) there are only 14 sealings in all and never more than 2 in a single year; the last 14 years of the 67-year reign of Ramesses II are missing—presumably because the building in question was no longer used for storing wine. The extraordinary oscillations of wine delivery to the Ramesseum at Thebes in the sixth–ninth years illustrate the fluctuations of the war, as we shall see. During the time of greatest danger the capital was moved south to Thebes, along with many government offices and much military preparation.

In the fifth year of his reign Ramesses II was roundly defeated by the Hittites, as disclosed by Hittite records now supplemented by documents found at Ugarit, in the

[12] ZÄS LVIII (1923), 25–36.

[13] See H. Kees, *Ancient Egypt* (Chicago, 1961), pp. 81 f. and 195 f. for the distribution of vineyards in northern Egypt. Note also that *k3mw*, 'vineyard' is a very old Egyptian loan from *karmu* vineyard (Heb. *kérem*) and that the vineyards mentioned in the Ramesseum material were mostly near Rameses (Tanis), with some coming from near Silē (see above, n. 9). Note further that the proportion of vineyards located in the north-eastern Delta in the early years of Ramesses II is much higher than was true of the jar labels from the palace of Amenophis III at Thebes, where the proportion of vineyards in the north-western Delta was much higher (see W. C. Hayes, JNES x [1951], 35 ff., 82 ff., 156 ff., 231 ff.). Evidently the north-eastern Delta was much more intensively developed in the Nineteenth Dynasty.

light of which we can disregard the claim to victory which Ramesses II makes in his own inscriptions—a claim which turns out to be nothing but a boast that he escaped death by breaking out of the encircling Hittite forces with a small bodyguard. This defeat provoked a general revolt, doubtless incited and supported by the Hittites, which apparently began in the sixth or early seventh year.

The revolt extended at least as far south as Ascalon, which had to be taken before the war could be carried north. In the eighth year the Egyptians finally triumphed over Accho and the rebellious cities in Galilee, the Jordan Valley, northern Transjordan and southern Syria.[14] In the ninth year Ramesses celebrated his triumph and the formal submission of the rebels at Rameses by erecting a basalt stele in Beth-shan,[15] and by his tenth year he had fixed the northern boundary of the Egyptian Empire at Nahr el-Kelb north of Beirut. The outbreak of the general revolt is reflected by the sharp increase in the number of sealings in the seventh year. After the reconquest of the rebellious Asiatic cities in the eighth year of the king, there is a sudden drop from 146 in the eighth to 11 sealings in the ninth year. While the simplest explanation of the drop is that there was much less demand for wine jars at the Egyptian headquarters in Thebes[16] after the bitter fighting of the seventh and eighth years had died down, there is another explanation which may help account for its suddenness, and may well be the true one. We have seen in Chapter II that the 'Apiru of the Late

[14] See J. Simons, S.J., *Handbook for the Study of Egyptian Topographical Lists Relating to Western Asia* (Leiden, 1937), pp. 64 ff. and 149.

[15] J. Černý has recently expressed some doubt about the date, but none was raised by any of the Egyptologists who examined the stele after its discovery. By chance I was the first to read the text, and the date seemed certain to me.

[16] Thebes was still the winter capital, and it was so far removed from the danger of immediate Hittite attack by land and sea that it must have been the seat of government at that critical juncture.

Bronze Age became known as vintagers and vintners, both in Egypt and in Palestine. It is highly improbable that the Israelites would risk flight from near the residence of Pharaoh himself at Rameses (whether at Tanis itself or in the vicinity) unless the opportunity seemed unusually advantageous. But if they fled from the country during the height of the rebellion against Egypt, in the eighth year of the king's reign, the sudden drop in the supply of wine to Thebes might be explained by the shortage of vintagers to take care of the vineyards.

These considerations suggest a date c. 1297 for the Exodus, if we follow M. B. Rowton's new date in 1304 for the accession of Ramesses II.[17] My latest date for the Exodus is relatively about the same as my past dates c. 1290 (when I followed the then standard formula, Ramesses II: 1301–1235 B.C.) and c. 1280 (when I followed Rowton's former date 1290–1224). We now have several independent means of dating the critical phase of the conquest of Western Palestine. The most important of these remains the Israel Stele of Merneptah, on which Merneptah celebrates his victory over the Libyans and at the end refers to his triumph over Israel in Palestine. Apparently the latter took place early in his fifth year, or late in the preceding fourth year. Lachish, in the low hill country of southern Palestine, has yielded important evidence.[18] In the burned level marking the destruction of the Late Bronze town, the sherds of a broken bowl were found scattered over a square metre, indicating that the bowl must have been broken at the time of the destruction. Otherwise the sherds would have been strewn over a considerable area, and it is most unlikely that more than a few would have been found. The bowl bears a

[17] See M. Rowton, JNES XIX (1960), 15–22; R. A. Parker, JNES XVI (1957), 39–43; my 'Chronological Note on the Fall of Ugarit' to appear in C. F. A. Schaeffer, *Ugaritica* V (condensed in CAH², I, ch. xxxiii, pp. 31 f.).

[18] BASOR 68 (1937), 23 f., and 74 (1939), 20 ff.

hieratic inscription mentioning the payment of tribute in the fourth year of a king who must be either Merneptah himself or one of his immediate successors, since it is quite possible to distinguish the script of the fourth year of Merneptah from that of the fourth year of his father and predecessor, Ramesses II, over sixty-six years before, but it is not possible to assign a hieratic text to reigns which were separated by only a few years, as one would have to do in order to distinguish between the script of Merneptah and that of his immediate successors. Since no Egyptian inscribed objects from later reigns have turned up in Bronze Age deposits at Lachish, the attribution of the bowl to Merneptah seems virtually certain.

But there is still more decisive new evidence. In the excavations conducted by C. F. A. Schaeffer at Ugarit in 1957, remains of a tablet oven were uncovered in the stratum to which the final destruction of the city belonged.[19] In this oven were found tablets in the process of being baked at the time of the final destruction. Two tablets are particularly important. One is a letter from the 'great king of the Hittites' to the last known king of Ugarit, 'Ammurapi', saying: 'The enemy has come up against me, (namely) the Assyrian.' This reading was not recognized by the first editor, but examination of the photograph published by Schaeffer in 1963[20] and of the copy and transliteration by Ch. Virolleaud,[21] shows that the word for 'Assyrian(s)' is the only possible reading, spelled as elsewhere in Ugaritic, as well as in later Aramaic.[22]

19 Nothing later (before the Persian period) seems to have been found at the site, and the picture presented by the tablets of the oven and other tablets from the latest stratum of the city outside this area is the same.

20 *Ugaritica* IV, 59, fig. 4.

21 R. S. 18.38, published in PRU V, 84 ff.

22 In an unpublished text (UM 244, No. 296a) *'aṯrym* appears with *Mṣrym*, 'Egyptians' as recipients of wine. Aramaic *Âṯûr*, 'Assyria' goes back to the same source. For *'ltn*, 'has come up against

The other important tablet from the oven is a letter from a Ugaritic field commander to the king of Ugarit.[23] The former has been watching the 'enemy' from Lawazanda,[24] overlooking the Euphrates valley from the west. With him had been the king of Siyanna (capital of a small state just south of Ugarit, and also belonging to the Hittite empire). The only possible enemy which threatened Ugarit and Siyanna as well as the Hittite states to the north (which were then ruled by members of the Hittite royal family) was precisely Assyria. There is only one recorded Assyrian invasion with which we can identify it, namely that of Tukulti-Ninurta I in the first full year of his reign (c. 1234–33 B.C.).[25] The inscriptions of the Assyrian king which mention this invasion of the Hittite empire (from which he carried off 8 *šar* of captives according to his own statement), come from the latter part of his reign; there is no reference anywhere to a later invasion of Khatti. After the king's raid into Commagene he invaded the regions north of Mesopotamia which had once belonged to the Mitannian empire. He then conquered Babylonia (c. 1232),[26] after which he was fully occupied in the south for many years.

---

me', see the rich comparative material for non-accusative verbal suffixes in North-west Semitic gathered by M. Bogaert, *Biblica*, XLV (1964), 220–47.

23 R. S. 18.40 (No. 63, PRU v, 90).

24 Written *Lwsnd* and identified with the Hittite name by M. Astour (AJA LXIX [1965], 257). The following name *Syn* (*Sianna*) was not recognized by Virolleaud; I wish to thank M. Schaeffer for kindly lending several photos.

25 See E. Weidner, *Die Inschriften Tukulti-Ninurtas I und seiner Nachfolger* (Graz, 1959), No. 16:27–30 and 17:23–25.

26 Note that Rowton's Assyrian chronology is ten years too high, as indicated by the agreement of both the well-preserved Khorsabad and S.D.A. tablets of the Assyrian King List against the badly preserved Nassouhi tablet on the reign of Ninurta-apil-Ekur, to which they assign 3 years (c. 1182–80) while the latter assigns 13 years to it. There is another strong argument for the same date, hitherto apparently overlooked. The Fourth Dynasty of Babylon

Though the Assyrian invasion did not reach Ugarit, its exact dating makes it possible for us to date the tablets from the oven within a year or two.[27] In tablets found not in the oven but elsewhere in the latest stratum of Ugarit, we have references to the invasion of Cyprus by seafaring peoples, as well as to the sacking of towns on the coast near Ugarit by the same foreigners.[28] Taken together with the latest inscriptions from Boğazköy,[29] these Ugaritic texts make it clear that the menace of the Sea Peoples was increasing steadily towards the end of the reign of 'Ammurapi', the last known king of Ugarit, and that it is no longer possible to separate these events completely from the Libyan and Aegean invasion of the north-western Delta in the fifth year of Merneptah. Since the latter accuses the Hittites (justly or not) of having sent the marauding Sea Peoples, including the Greek Achaeans, against Egypt, we may safely infer that the Egyptians reacted, not only by resisting the attack in Egypt itself, but also by persuading the Assyrians to mount an expedition from the north-east in order to divert

(Isin II) began c. 1160 B.C., and if we follow the regnal years of King List A, supported by other documents, the reign of Kashtiliash III ended c. 1232 B.C. (but not later than c. 1230 B.C.). If we study the inscriptions of Tukulti-Ninurta I, it becomes rather clear that his initial success against the south-eastern dependencies of the Hittite Empire was not followed up because of the war with Babylonia, in the course of which Kashtiliash III was taken prisoner. Babylonia had been in alliance with Khatti since the Assyrian conquest of Mitanni. In other words, if the raid across the Euphrates took place c. 1234/33, and Babylonia was invaded between 1232 and 1230, our data would fall neatly into place.

27 At an extreme estimate, since it is scarcely likely that any of the originals or copies (translated or not) had been inscribed more than a few weeks (or months, in the case of texts translated from Hittite) before the oven was sealed.

28 See the evidence so far available which has been collected by M. Astour (AJA LXIX [1965], 254 ff.).

29 See H. Otten, MDOG XCIV (1963), 13 ff.; H. G. Güterbock, JNES XXVI (1967), 73–81.

the supposed Hittite vassals from Egypt by a direct attack on the Hittite empire. In one of the latest tablets from Ugarit the king of Ugarit tells the king of Cyprus, who has asked for naval aid, that he has no ships to send, since his fleet is in Lycian waters—obviously to guard against an attack of the Sea Peoples on the Hittite coast! Merneptah may have been wrong in blaming the Hittites for the piratic movements of peoples who were in no sense loyal vassals of Khatti, but who were in fact in open rebellion against the Hittites. That the Egyptians reacted to the supposed situation by encouraging the raiders to attack the coast of Hittite Syria is likely enough; this sort of manoeuvre has always been characteristic of the Mediterranean world.

David Neiman suggested to me in 1964[30] that it is difficult to separate the critical phase of the Israelite invasion of western Palestine from the world situation at the time. Having long schooled myself to keep away from such far-reaching hypotheses, I should probably not have noticed it myself. Not only were the Egyptian coast proper and the coasts of Cyprus and Ugarit menaced by marauding Sea Peoples,[31] but there were also attacks of this sort on Palestine.[32] In any case Egypt's preoccupation with the task of warding off the dangerous invaders gave the Israelites an ideal opportunity to attack the Canaanites on their own account. While it is still too early to be sure that events followed exactly this course,

[30] See now his remarks in *Studies and Texts* (Lown Institute, Brandeis University) III (Cambridge [Mass.], 1966), pp. 127 ff.

[31] Believed by the Egyptians to have been sent by the Hittites (as stated in Merneptah's Israel Stele), and presumably believed by the latter to have been encouraged by the Egyptians. Since Egypt and Assyria were almost certainly allies at the time, both beliefs may have been correct. The Amarna and Boğazköy letters have long since proved that far-reaching alliances against common foes were common in the fourteenth–thirteenth centuries B.C.

[32] See CAH², II, ch. xxxiii, 26 f., 31 f.

the evidence dovetails so well that something of the sort must have occurred.

The evidence sampled in Chapter I for the antiquity of the basic oral traditions about the Exodus makes it quite unreasonable to deny its substantial accuracy. It is true that some of the prose narratives of 'JEP' in Ex. 1–14 reflect later traditions which do not seem to have the poetic or legal basis needed to establish an early date on internal literary grounds alone. As I have long maintained, a period of some sixty years probably elapsed between the Exodus from Egypt and the destruction of the Canaanite towns in the Shephelah (Josh. 10). We may roughly divide this period into three phases: (1) the desert wanderings between Egypt and the settlement in Eastern Palestine; (2) the occupation of Eastern Palestine; and (3) a period of consolidation with the native Palestinian Hebrew groups before the full-scale onslaught against the Canaanite city-states. The first two phases may be roughly equated with the traditional 'forty years in the wilderness', while Phases (2) and (3) may have taken considerably longer than one might assume from the canonical form given to the early traditions in the seventh century B.C. Phase (1) was then correspondingly shorter, and may have taken only a few years.

Any reasonable historical reconstruction must recognize that Moses was an outstanding figure according to any standard.[33] It is impossible to imagine the foundation of such a religious confederacy as that of Israel, without a founder; and the founder of Israel is acknowledged by all independent sources, as well as by all recensional

[33] A substantial part of my forthcoming *History of the Religion of Israel* will be devoted to analysis of the traditions about Moses and his work in order to fix his place in history. A direct approach will be made through traditions preserved in verse or validated by poetic reminiscences of archaic type. Then I shall try to place his work with reference to what we know about pre-Mosaic and post-Mosaic law and institutions.

variants, to have been Moses. It has long been known that the family of Moses was quite thoroughly Egyptianized, since a number of its members bear characteristic Egyptian names, such as *Môšé* = *Mōsĕ*, *Pineḥás* = *Penaḥse*,[34] *Ḥopnî* = *Ḥfny* (*Ḥfnn*), *Merarî* = *Mrry*,[35] and *Pašḥûr* = *Pašḥōr*.[36] Other names have been thought to be Egyptian, including Aaron and Miriam, but only the few mentioned above are clearly Egyptian. The Egyptian name *Mōsĕ* became *Môšê* in Hebrew; it is a common Egyptian hypocoristicon (short form), which is the second element in numerous personal names, all beginning with the name of a divinity (e.g. *Ṭḥutmōse*, *Re-ʿmōse*, *ʿAḥmōse*). The name meant originally, '(such and a god) is born'. It may be that the name *Môšê* was originally connected by a popular etymology with a Northwest Semitic word *mṯ* no longer found in Biblical Hebrew, meaning 'master, lord', and used frequently in the Proto-Sinaitic inscriptions in invoking divinities.[37]

Moses was probably born during the middle decades of the fourteenth century B.C., not long after the collapse of

[34] Eg. *pꜣ-nḥsy*, 'The Dark-skinned One'. When short vowel endings were dropped in Hebrew about the thirteenth century B.C., a helping vowel was inserted. The name was exceedingly common in this period.

[35] Eg. *mrr(w)*, '(He) whom (one) loves' was a very common first element in names of the Old and Middle Kingdoms; it appears more rarely in the New Kingdom (ÄPN I, 162:17–27, 421:22; II, 291:23–25). *Mrri* and *Mrrw* were common hypocoristic forms.

[36] Eg. *Psš-Ḥr* according to W. Spiegelberg, ZDMG LIII (1900), 635. Names with this initial element followed by a divine name seem all to be late. An identification with *Pꜣ-šd-Ḥr*, attested by Alan Gardiner for the twelfth century (ÄPN I, 119:17) is better, since the formation was very common in the New Kingdom (ÄPN I, 119:13, 18, 20). Note that Y. Aharoni's excavations at Arad in southern Judah have turned up sherds at the sanctuary, with names of the old priestly *maʿmādôt*, *Pašḥûr* and *Merēmôt*, in script and spelling of the sixth century B.C., so the former may have been much older than generally thought.

[37] PSID, 41 f.

the Aten revolution. We do not know whether there was any direct relationship between the Aten revolution and the Mosaic movement. The two do share certain general features, such as monotheism—both emphasize that their god is the sole creator and lord, 'beside whom there is no other'—though Amarna monotheism centred around a triad, in which the king was also divine. Yet the *aten* was not the sun-god, but was the solar disk, the glorious refulgence of Rē', not Rē' himself. The ethical level of Atenism was much lower, from our post-Israelite and post-Hellenic point of view, than that of Mosaic society. 'Truth' (*mu'a*)[38] was essentially the acceptance of the new standards of the élite in language and art. The charming freedom of manners, shown in court scenes, went hand in hand with total demoralization of the royal family, where incest was glorified as never before or since in Egyptian history. Yahweh, unlike the Aten, does not reflect any force or phenomenon of nature, but is the God who created all and reigns over all. There are, however, other interesting points of contact. For example, both emphasize the official 'teaching' (Eg. *sbăye*, whence Coptic *sbŏ*, and Heb. *tôrāh*).

How new the religion of Moses was, and how much of it was derived from older Hebrew sources, is difficult to say. In the case of every great religious reformer the same problem arises: is he a reformer or an innovator? A great reformer nearly always innovates. He cannot help innovating, since so many things seem wrong with the old society and its inherited beliefs. On the other hand a great reformer seldom, if ever, is a deliberate innovator, but someone concerned to restore the ancient heritage, which he tends to see in the light of his own ideals. We find this dual rôle in all outstanding figures of Judaeo-Christian religious history, and we should therefore ex-

[38] Conventionally transcribed 'maat' since early Egyptological days; on this concept at Amarna see R. Anthes, JAOS, *Supplement* 14 (1952).

pect to find it also in Moses. And indeed there are very ancient elements in the Mosaic tradition. Among them we may count a strong basic tendency towards monotheism (see above), and a hitherto unparalleled emphasis on the Covenant between the supreme God and his worshippers.

The Covenant or Pact between God and Israel is now known, as shown by G. E. Mendenhall,[39] to have followed the pattern of suzerainty treaties in late second-millennium Anatolia and Syria (see Chapter II). In these treaties a suzerain makes a pact with a vassal, the rôle of suzerain being, of course, more important than that of vassal. There is a parallel sequence of subject-matter in these treaties, virtually all of which start with a historical preamble and end with the statement that the text of the treaty is to be deposited in the temple of the chief god of each country. Exactly the same pattern is found in Joshua 24, which thus appears to be the oldest description in the Bible of a covenant between God and His people —instead of being one of the latest, as used to be thought by critical scholars in the absence of material to the contrary. This epoch-making discovery by Mendenhall has been rejected or modified by other scholars, but erroneously. It has been pointed out recently by Herbert B. Huffmon (CBQ XXVII [1965], 100 ff.) and others that critics of Mendenhall's views have overlooked certain facts and have disregarded vital differences between the suzerainty treaties of the second millennium B.C. and the Assyrian and Aramaean treaties from the first millennium B.C. For example, the historical preamble has disappeared completely from the first-millennium treaties. Above, at the end of Chapter II, emphasis was laid on the vital function of pacts or covenants at all stages of early Hebrew life.

[39] See especially his classical treatment, *Law and Covenant in Israel and the Ancient Orient* (The Biblical Colloquium, Pittsburgh, 1955, reprinted from BA XVII [1954], 26–46 and 49–76).

Another important religious principle handed down through Moses was belief in 'the god of the fathers'. The 'god of the fathers' was not the same as the Accadian translation, 'god of the father', of the name of the great patron of ancestral worship, 'El'eb, among the North-western Semites.[40] As pointed out by A. Alt[41] and J. Lewy,[42] this is, rather, akin to what we have later in the Nabataean and other North-Arabic inscriptions of mercantile and caravaneering families, as well as in the Old Assyrian tablets from the Patriarchal age itself. The god(s) of a man's father, the teraphim,[43] could be carried around by a man when he was unable to attend to his cultic obligations in an established sanctuary. Yet the Accadian translation 'god of the father' does show that the concept of *theos patrōos* was familiar in the Late Bronze Age as well as in the Patriarchal period; it therefore serves as another bridge between Abraham and Moses. It was Moses' acceptance of the old faith in the god of the fathers that led him to identify Yahweh with the 'god of the fathers' as well as with Shaddai. Belief in the Covenant and the God of the Fathers are undoubtedly the two most important elements taken by Moses from Patriarchal tradition.

The long debate over the original meaning of the name *Yahwêh* shows no sign of abating, and the most incredible etymologies are still advanced by otherwise serious scholars. The indicative form of the name is clearly demon-

40 See above, Ch. III, § c, and below, § d.

41 *Der Gott der Väter* (BWANT III:12 [1929]), reprinted in KSGVI I, 1–78; cf. JBL LIV (1935), 188.

42 RHR CX (1934), 50 ff.

43 On the teraphim cf. ARI, 114 and 207, n. 63. As a possibility I may now add that *tĕrāfîm* may be a contemptuous deformation of a hypothetical noun (**tarpa'u*?) from the stem *rp'*, from which the name of the Rephaim (the spirits of ancestral heroes in Ugaritic, Phoenician and Hebrew) is derived. Note also the name *Ub-rapi'*, belonging to a very ancient Hebrew tribe (see Ch. II), and containing the name of the archetype ancestral deity Ub.

strated by the ending; otherwise we should expect to have a jussive as in the case of the hypocoristic form *Yahū*, which can be traced back as far as the ninth century B.C., thanks to Assyrian transcriptions. We must remember that in Hebrew and cognate dialects there was a tendency to reduce imperfect verbal elements in personal names to jussive form, precisely because the original form of nearly all such elements in composition was jussive.[44] It is rather obvious that a *qal* interpretation of the name, though possible for 'Amorite'[45] and normal for Arabic verbs *tertiae infirmae*, would have a strange meaning. In those days of emergent empirical reasoning about theological matters,[46] a rendering such as '(He) is' or '(He) will be' makes no sense. On the other hand, a causative explanation was perfectly intelligible and has hosts of parallels; the notion that a causative meaning would be 'too abstract for early Israel' is nonsense, since no semantic category which is represented by special morphemes and innumerable individual cases in any language can be considered too abstract for the genius of that language. We might just as well say that the *ung/ing* ending had too abstract a meaning for the early Germanic peoples. The stem *HWY* itself appears in both Hebrew and Aramaic, the only known Semitic tongues in which it was regularly used. It is true that the *hif'il* of this verb has disappeared from normal use in Classical Hebrew, but Aramaic dialects exhibit both *pa'el* and *af'el* in causative sense, 'cause to be', 'create'. Similar formations are common in other Semitic verbs with the same meaning: e.g.,

44 As pointed out in JBL XLVI (1927), 153–78, M. Noth's treatment in *Die israelitischen Personennamen im Rahmen der gemeinsemitischen Namengebung* (Stuttgart, 1928) leaves the question open most of the time. In general we find utter confusion among biblical scholars today, though the evidence for jussive form and meaning has been increasing steadily.

45 See APNMT, 66–73, and especially pp. 72 f. and 159 f.

46 On this subject see especially HACH, 83 ff. and Albright, *New Horizons in Biblical Research* (London, 1966), pp. 17 ff.

in Phoenician and cognate names we have both *kûn* and the corresponding causative, indicative *yakîn* and jussive *yakĭn*; in Accadian names we have *bašû* as well as *šubšû* ('cause to be, create'); in Egyptian *sḫpr*, 'to cause to come into existence, to create', is also common in personal names.

It has recently been argued that the *qal* would be more natural, and Accadian forms like *Ibašši-ilu* are cited as relevant.[47] But the corresponding Canaanite-Hebrew form would almost certainly be *'Iṯ-Ba'al*, 'Baal (actually) exists'. The Hebrew name *'Iš-ba'al* or *'Eš-ba'al* corresponds to the formula in the Baal epic, '(I know that) the Prince, Lord of the Earth, exists (*'iṯ*)'.

There is another solid reason for objecting to the *qal* interpretation: in Ugaritic and Hebrew (as well as in South Canaanite of the Amarna period) the Barth-Ginsberg law holds, that there was dissimilation from very early times in the vocalization of the intransitive imperfect; the normal form of the intransitive *qal* imperfect (indicative) would be **yihwayu*〉*yihyê* (Hebrew).

The indicative *qal* form *Yahwê* (jussive *Yahu*) is extremely significant, since it must normally be an abbreviation of a longer formula. This idea is not at all adventurous, since it is assumed in the explanation of the name given in Ex. 3:14, where God informs Moses that his full name is *'ehyê 'ašer 'ehyê* and commands him to tell the children of Israel that his name is *'ehyê*. It has long been recognized by many scholars that the vocalization is wrong and that the full name had to be in the first person (when spoken by God) *'ahyê 'ašer 'ahyê*, with *'ahyê* as the short form. The absence of any known reflection of this formula elsewhere in the Hebrew Bible suggests that it is a secondary theological adaptation of an original formula in the third person, 'It Is He Who

[47] W. von Soden, 'Jahwe "Er ist, Er erweist sich"', *Die Welt des Orients* III (1965), 177–87.

Creates What Comes into Existence', like Eg. *sḫpr.f pw wnn.ty.fy* and *qmꜣ wnn.t.*[48] I pointed out a good many years ago that *Yahweh* appears as the first element of other names of obvious liturgical origin such as *Yahwê Ṣebā'ôt*; D. N. Freedman has followed with other suggestions,[49] to which I shall add elsewhere. That the appellation is pre-Mosaic seems to be shown by the following considerations: (1) the 'Amorite' personal name *Yahwī-il*, spelled *Yaḫwi-il* and *Yawi-il*, is quite common in Old Babylonian transcriptions (the double writing is due to the fact that there is no *h* in Accadian); (2) the element appears as a place-name written *Y(a)hw(e?)* in a fourteenth–thirteenth-century Egyptian list of south Palestinian place-names; (3) the appellation *Yahwê* is used as an alternative designation for *'Elôhîm*, 'totality of the gods, the supreme god', as far back as the Song of Miriam and other poems from the thirteenth and twelfth centuries B.C.[50] This use in poetic parallelism, either in A or B position, lies entirely within normal Canaanite practice and suggests that it was introduced into Israel at a very early date. The preservation of the name as the indicative verbal element in ancient liturgical formulas is so archaic and was so little understood in later times that it must go back to extremely early times. For the use of old cultic formulas as divine appellations there are a great many examples in Canaanite, Egyptian, Sumerian,

[48] For the first reference to these Egyptian parallels see JBL XLIII (1924), 370–8; cf. also JBL XLIV (1925), 158–62. I may also repeat what I have said above, that many Sumerian, Egyptian and Canaanite divine names and appellations are abbreviations of liturgical formulas.

[49] See my review of Wambacq, JBL LXVII (1948), 377–381, and D. N. Freedman, JBL LXXIX (1960), 151–6, as well as F. M. Cross, Jr., HTR LV (1962), 250 ff.

[50] On the early use of *Yahweh* and *'Elôhîm* in parallelism, one taking position A, the other position B, according to the 'school' to which the poet belonged, see CBQ XXV (1963), 1–4 and 9–11, and above, Ch. I, § D.

Accadian, etc. If my interpretation is correct, a number of cases appear already in the Proto-Sinaitic inscriptions.[51]

With these remarks we take leave of this subject for the present; it will be considerably expanded elsewhere.[52] The evidence is now so clear and extensive that it is hard to see how it can be refuted.

B. THE ANTIQUITY OF MOSAIC LAW

Turning to the case-laws of Exodus, we have already seen (Chapter II) that they are much more ancient than their present context suggests, and that they must have been —at least in large part—brought from Mesopotamia by the ancestors of the Hebrews and kept alive in Egypt as well as Palestine. Among them is, however, some material of apodictic and generalizing character which points to Mosaic or post-Mosaic reworking or editing.

This apodictic material appears as insertions scattered in blocks through Ex. 21–3, especially at 21:12–17, 22:17 (Heb.)–23:3, and 23:6 ff. It is scarcely ever stated in the conditional form of case-laws but always as declarations, either in the form of prohibitions or more rarely as positive commands. Their content is religious, moral and humane; the brilliant analysis by Albrecht Alt[53] clarified the difference between the originally non-Hebrew customary law in case form and the apodictic law found in the Book of the Covenant and elsewhere in the Books of Moses. Their general character reminds one of the Egyptian Negative Confession (Book of the Dead, Ch. 125),[54] which goes back at least to the sixteenth cen-

[51] PSID, 13 f., etc.

[52] See my forthcoming *History of the Religion of Israel.*

[53] *Die Ursprünge des israelitischen Rechts*, originally published in the *Verhandlungen* of the Leipzig Academy, LXXXVI:1 (1934) and now reprinted in KSGVI I, 278–332.

[54] See J. A. Wilson in ANET, 34 ff., and for the latest treatment see T. G. Allen, *The Egyptian Book of the Dead . . .* (Chicago, 1960), pp. 196 ff.

tury B.C. and was very popular during the centuries immediately preceding and following the time of Moses. The Egyptian statements are couched as protestations of innocence, e.g.: 'I have not committed murder, I have not ordered murder to be committed, I have not treated anyone unjustly, I have not reduced the food offerings in the temples, I have not debased the bread of the gods, . . . I have not had homosexual relations, I have not defiled myself, I have neither increased nor diminished measures (of capacity), I have not tampered with the balance', etc. The Negative Confession shows a remarkable lack of systematic order or selectivity with regard to different types of sin which will cause a man to be rejected by the judges of the Nether World. A striking difference is the relative lack of specific cultic regulations among the apodictic rules in the Book of the Covenant. At the same time the Hebrew texts lay much greater stress than the Egyptian on humane treatment of men and animals. The Decalogue consists of a similar intermixture of prohibitions and positive commands, but its content was remarkably well selected from a much larger body of similar material in the apodictic law. We have no way of telling whether the Decalogue is younger than the apodictic law as such, or not; the differing recensions found in Ex. 20 and Deut. 5 show that different forms of it had diverged early, while, on the other hand, use of words like *melā'kāh* in the sense of 'labour' or 'business' shows that the text was put into Classical Hebrew form at a date subsequent to the time of Moses.[55] But the use of relatively late words does not mean that the Decalogue as such is necessarily later than Moses, since the wording of such a popular list of moral norms for behaviour might easily be changed quite often in the course of its history

[55] On the meaning of Ugar. *ml'akt* at that time (a meaning which it still has occasionally in Hebrew verse), see BASOR 150 (1958), 38, n. 14.

and there has obviously been some expansion of items.[56] Elsewhere I shall present extrinsic arguments for an original date of the Decalogue no later than the thirteenth century B.C.[57] The generalized pattern of the norms of the Decalogue is very striking and places it in a different category from the Negative Confession or corresponding Babylonian lists of sins and taboos, also from the latter part of the second millennium B.C.[58] Most remarkable is the generalized statement of the *lex talionis* in Ex. 21:23–25. A. Alt pointed out in 1934 that the formula in question appears in very similar terms in Punic inscriptions of about the third century A.D. from North Africa. In the Latin text we have *anima pro anima, sanguine pro sanguine, vita pro vita*, which is so like the Hebrew formula in Exodus (together with its variants in Lev. 24:20 and Deut. 19:21) as to be unmistakably derived from the same ultimate source.[59] On the other hand, the two formulas are not sufficiently alike to make direct borrowing likely, even if it were not excluded by the totally different context in each case: the Punic formula involves substitution of animal for human sacrifice, whereas the Hebrew adumbrates the principle of equal justice for all. We may, therefore, be reasonably sure that this formulation of the *lex talionis* goes back to not later than the seventh century B.C., after which there was little fresh influence from Phoenicia on Carthage.

In the Hebrew formula, we have what may be the earliest enunciation of a generalized legal principle known anywhere in the world. Though it has not yet

[56] One hopes that no student has been misled by the fanciful additions to the text of the Decalogue made by Shapira, the antiquities' dealer of Jerusalem. A recent attempt to whitewash him and to prove that the leather strips of 'Deuteronomy' were authentic, has been made by J. M. Allegro, *The Shapira Affair*; cf. my review in the *Baltimore Sun*, 31 March 1965.

[57] See my forthcoming *History of the Religion of Israel.*

[58] Cf. FSAC², 228 ff., 268 f.

[59] ZATW, N.F. XI (1934), pp. 303 ff., KSGVI I, 341 ff.

attained the level of a generalized abstract proposition, it reaches its purpose by listing several related concrete propositions to illustrate the scope of the generalized principle. Since the Old Testament shows little trace of protological thinking after the thirteenth–twelfth centuries B.C. but is throughout a monument of empirical logic,[60] we need not have any hesitation about tracing this legal generalization back to the beginnings of the Mosaic revolution—either to Moses himself or to a 'school' of interpreters who endeavoured to harmonize the ancient case law with the body of apodictic law which had been developing since the time of Moses. The latest probable date for the collection of their material is the tenth century B.C., as will be argued below.

Since it is not our purpose here to discuss the entire Mosaic *corpus* of apodictic law, we shall limit ourselves to a necessarily brief discussion of certain features of the dietary and sanitary codes attributed to Moses.[61]

A detailed analysis of the dietary and hygienic rules of the Pentateuch is still premature, though I have attempted it in a still unpublished manuscript. We have much material for the laws of purity in the ancient Near East in the collections of ritual taboos which were prepared in Egypt and especially in Babylonia during the second millennium B.C. It is noteworthy that the Hebrew rules are much more highly developed than the corresponding ancient Near Eastern lists of taboos. For this we may adduce a number of reasons. In the first place, there is a strong flavour of sympathetic magic—sometimes even of professional magic—about the taboos in such cuneiform collections as Shurpu and Maqlû. If we knew more about corresponding Egyptian forms of ritual, we should doubtless find much the same situation in Egypt where, to quote Adolf Erman, some aspects of Egyptian culture tended to resemble newly hatched chicks which

[60] See above, n. 46, for recent discussions.

[61] See n. 57, above.

carry bits of eggshell about on their backs for days after they emerge from the shell. It must also be recognized that there had probably been much more revision and interpretation of the content of the Hebrew laws of purity, with addition of later interpretation and commentary, than would be true of case-law or simple apodictic declarations. This is probably because the case-law as preserved in the Pentateuch is at best extremely fragmentary, containing essentially only laws about homicide, slavery, and torts,[62] and because the early apodictic law is even more fragmentary and less systematic. The relatively systematic presentation of the rules of purity strongly suggests a later date for them than for the less complete tradition of civil and moral law. The codification of the laws of purity may well come down to the seventh century B.C. in their present form (chiefly in 'P' and 'D').[63] On the other hand, we shall see that no part of the Hebrew Bible is more clearly empirico-logical in its background than the rules of purity; the body of rules in question carries us directly back to the lessons learned from common experience.

After a long period in which anthropologists were accustomed to explain all such regulations as going back to totemism or animism, there is now a striking reaction. It is being increasingly recognized that men have always learned from experience and observation, especially in the ancient Near East, where sedentary culture began long before its origin in most other parts of the world. Everywhere man has a natural capacity, not only for observing closely, but also for remembering what he has observed. Such memories are carried down by collective activity. In other words, the elders teach what they have heard from the elders of their generation, supplemented

[62] For a striking Greek parallel to this partial preservation of case laws dealing especially with homicide, see BPAE, 99, n. 46.

[63] See now the judicious analysis by W. L. Moran, S.J., in CBQ XXVIII, 271–7.

by their own experience, to younger people who, in turn, transmit it to the next generation, in such a way that the experience of one person is checked by that of others and that of one chronological group by the experience of the following. I have repeatedly pointed out that the Hebrew Bible is the greatest existing monument of empirical logic and that this logic is more exact than formal logic in some important respects. After all, it is based on the cumulative experience of men, and not on postulates or presuppositions which may or may not be correct, as is inevitably true of most postulational reasoning outside of mathematics and the exact sciences.

Just as the Chinese had long known the curative properties of *mahuang* before it was exported to the West and finally replaced by its active alkaloid, ephedrine, so the ancient Egyptians discovered the curative function of many medicinal plants and preparations, which they duly transmitted to the Greeks, who in turn passed on their pharmacopoeia to mediaeval Europe.

It is equally natural that men should have learned through the experience of many centuries to distinguish between poisonous and non-poisonous serpents, mushrooms, etc. For example, they early learned the danger involved in eating pork. Since trichinosis has been endemic in all Near Eastern lands from antiquity, and since there are several other dangerous maladies which come from eating insufficiently cooked pork, some connexion must have been recognized at an early date, at least in areas where the habits of domesticated pigs had become unusually filthy. Since they knew nothing specific about the causes of illness contracted by eating pork, they did not realize that adequate cooking would dispose of the dangers. The common explanation for the biblical legislation concerning pork—that it was not eaten because it was sacred among pagan peoples—is sheer nonsense. The pig was sacred in certain places and periods, but large and small cattle were even more generally sacred, so that it is quite irrational to single out the economically and religiously much less important pig, and to explain its prohibition in Israel by its alleged religious significance. If there were any doubt about the empirical explanation, it should be removed by the fact that both the hare and the hyrax (*šāfān*) were also prohibited. This can be explained only by the fact that both animals are carriers of tularemia, which comes from infected cuts received in the process of skinning and dismembering the animals. While it is true that the hyrax belongs to an entirely different mammalian family from the hare, it is also true that their habits of life have converged almost completely, and it is now well known that the hyrax, like the hare, carries this disease.

The most remarkable distinction of this kind in the regulations distinguishing clean from unclean animals in Lev. 11 and Deut. 14 is that made between fish with fins and scales and fish without fins and scales. It is only in the water of extremely muddy and slow-flowing rivers such as the Nile that the distinction is important for health.[64] Fish with scales and fins are normally free-swimming, whereas fish without scales and fins, such as eels, are usually mud-burrowers and therefore hosts to a great many more parasites than free-swimming fish. (Of course there are periods in the life cycles of some aquatic animals when they are free-swimming, and periods when they are not, but in general this distinction holds true.) Animal parasites and native inhabitants often establish a symbiosis, but foreign visitors to the Nile valley have not established immunity, so that parasites can be quite lethal, for the number of diseases carried by aquatic animals in the Nile valley is prodigious. For foreigners, then, the distinction is extremely significant. The most reason-

[64] It is true that the rabbis remarked on this very fact with reference to the Sea of Galilee, but there is absolutely no comparison today between this lake and the Nile as a refuge for pathogenic organisms and the aquatic animals which carry them.

able explanation of its origin seems to be that this distinction was discovered by early Semitic settlers in Egypt, and passed on by them to the Hebrews during the centuries in which they lived in the Nile valley. It is thus a vivid example of the antiquity of some of this legislation which is often thought to be very late. In salt water the distinction is not generally valid, and it could not have been noticed in the clean salt waters of the Mediterranean, or in the Dead Sea, where there are no fish at all. It might conceivably have arisen in the Jordan Valley and the Sea of Galilee, but there is nothing to show that fisheries played a significant economic rôle there in Israelite times. An ultimate Babylonian origin is possible but not very likely, since we have no trace of it in our extensive Babylonian rituals of purity such as the Shurpu and Maqlû codes.

Another case is that of the camel. The camel, as far as we know at present, was not generally domesticated even in Arabia until the end of the Bronze Age. By the late twelfth century it was being used to mount large-scale raids, as well as presumably for trade. The camel was certainly known through this entire period and had been since Pleistocene times, at least. Since camels are notoriously stupid, it is highly probable that herds of them were kept in half-wild state in order to provide milk, flesh, hair and skins for the nomads. Camel flesh, as far as known to medical science, is harmless though extremely tough. But the Egyptians were much less hospitable to the camel than the Semites. In fact there is no evidence for domesticated camels in Egypt until the Persian period—and this evidence comes from texts copied in Roman times. The Arabian camel was not introduced into North Africa west of Egypt until still later. It is therefore probable that the prohibition against camel flesh was also Egyptian in origin.

The most striking feature of the dietary laws in the

Pentateuch is that for the first known time in history we have generalized classification of complex zoological phenomena according to observed criteria. In this connexion it is scarcely relevant to point out that the classification of clean and unclean animals according to parting the hoof and 'chewing the cud' is not quite accurate, since hares, for example, do not actually chew their cud but merely move their lips. Nor is it significant that these rules can scarcely have been drawn up on the basis of any knowledge of the aetiology underlying the prohibition of certain mammals, fish, and other animals. It is rather a kind of mnemonic device to make abstention from certain kinds of flesh easier for the young or unsophisticated person. And yet we find no classification as logical as this in any of the elaborate cuneiform lists of fauna or of ritual taboos.

In the case of hygienic regulations, it is perfectly obvious that their ultimate basis rests on the observed facts of contagion and infection. It could not possibly escape the sharp eyes and active mind of the proto-physician that certain diseases were communicated from person to person or from contaminated locations or areas to persons. In this case the background is reasonably clear. Both in ancient Near Eastern medicine and post-biblical Jewish folklore the rôle played by demons in transmitting disease was well known. (In practice there is little difference between belief in demons and in pathogenic organisms as a basis for transmitting infection!) In the Mosaic tradition the rôle of demons had been almost always cancelled by the process of demythologizing which set in with Moses. But the facts of experience remained and were presupposed in the hygienic laws. Thanks to the dietary and hygienic regulations of Mosaic law, held firmly together and developed along empirico-logical lines by post-Mosaic commentators down to the seventh century B.C., subsequent history has been marked by a tremendous advantage in this respect held by Jews over all other comparable ethnic and religious groups. It is only in our own times that advances in medicine have made it possible to replace rule-of-thumb regulations of former times by medical and hygienic practices which obtain similar results by scientific methods.

One of the most remarkable features of Mosaic legislation—always using the term in its widest sense, of laws approved or introduced by Moses and developed in later Israel—is its humanity to man. It is the most humanitarian of all known bodies of laws before recent times. The laws about slavery, which envisage the liberation of Hebrew slaves after seven years, are a good example. But there are also laws protecting the poor: interest (always high in the ancient East) was prohibited, and again there was a moratorium on payments after a term of years. Furthermore, it was not permitted to take a man's clothing in payment for a debt. Even strangers, who normally had very little protection in antiquity, except when they were citizens of a strong neighbouring state which might step in and protect them by force of arms, are exceptionally well cared for by Mosaic law. Not only do we find numerous special provisions for the humane treatment of human beings, but even the well-being of animals receives attention; as for example in the command, 'Thou shalt not muzzle the ox that treads out the grain' (Deut. 25:4). The original practice may well have been connected with pagan cult, as so often, but the apodictic law has been depaganized.

In 1950 I pointed out that the laws of Exodus could scarcely be later than the ninth century B.C., because they contain no hint of the royal appointment of judges which was introduced under king Jehoshaphat, according to II Chron. 19.[65] We can be reasonably sure that the

[65] See my study, 'The Judicial Reform of Jehoshaphat' in the *Alexander Marx Jubilee Volume* (New York, 1950), pp. 61–82.

tradition has an historical basis for three reasons: (1) The compiler of Chronicles was very much interested in legal matters and should therefore be particularly reliable in treating them. This reason would be even stronger if I am correct in maintaining that the first edition, at least, of this work is due to Ezra, who was himself a jurist.[66] (2) The reform is said to have involved setting up a mixed tribunal of royally appointed judges of both priestly and non-priestly origin, which can be closely paralleled in fourteenth- and thirteenth-century Egypt. (3) Our respect for the accuracy of both the written and the oral tradition recorded by the Chronicler has been notably enhanced in recent years.[67]

The legislative material of Exodus was not intended to be a digest of current or proposed legislation, but as just what it purports to be—an account of the legislation of Moses, drawn up and edited in its present form in the seventh and sixth centuries B.C., but not including anything then known to date after the Mosaic age. When one combines the material presented in this chapter with what was given in Chapter II, one realizes that it is no longer rational to deny the antiquity of the Pentateuchal laws in general, and that there is no reason why we should date the case laws later than the Patriarchal Age. The older legislation was presumably accepted by Moses and adapted where necessary to the situation of Israel in his day. The apodictic law also reflects pre-Mosaic sources, but has been so thoroughly reworked in the spirit of the Mosaic movement that its originality cannot be denied.

66 For this obviously correct view see the demonstration by H. H. Schaeder, *Esra der Schreiber* (Tübingen, 1930).

67 On the historical value of the Chronicler's work see Jacob M. Myers, *Chronicles*, in two volumes (Anchor Bible, 1965), especially the Introduction to Vol. I.

C. EARLY PAGAN VESTIGES IN HEBREW LITERATURE: ARCHAIC DEMYTHOLOGIZING

There is much confusion in dealing with pagan survivals in the Hebrew Bible. If we had the necessary evidence we might be able to distinguish clearly among: (1) pagan elements in Hebrew religion as Moses found it, (2) elements borrowed by the Israelites at an early date from the Canaanites among whom they lived, (3) elements of early date which continued in use among the Israelites and are accidentally found only in later literature, and (4) later borrowings from Phoenicia. In this section we shall deal with the first three groups of material, without attempting to isolate them. At the same time that these pagan elements were handed down through Mosaic channels or appeared subsequently, there tended to be a process of excising or transforming obviously pagan ideas. This process we have called 'archaic demythologizing'. We owe the term 'Entmythologisierung' to Rudolf Bultmann, but it is scarcely necessary to point out that we are using it in a quite non-Bultmannian sense, since we are not employing any form of existential philosophy in order to reach our conclusions.[68]

The reader may wonder why we have not dealt with material survivals of cultic structures or with the pagan elements in Hebrew ritual, but the fact is that nearly all pertinent evidence is extremely fragmentary and elusive because of our lack of knowledge of substantive data. It is therefore safer to begin with what we actually do have, Hebrew literary survivals, such as names of divinities with some information about their functions, etc.

The process of demythologizing pagan myths undoubtedly took a long time, beginning in the thirteenth century

[68] For my attitude towards existential philosophy and its use in biblical interpretation see HACH, 272–84.

and not ending until the seventh or even the sixth century B.C. Since no religion can exist without the use of concrete language and symbolism to express the ineffable, it is, of course, impossible to eliminate all 'myth' in the post-Platonic sense without destroying the best part of our religious heritage. When I use the term 'demythologizing' I am using it in the sense of eliminating specifically polytheistic elements in the narratives of Genesis as well as poetic survivals or pagan borrowings in Old Testament literature. A very good illustration comes from the first chapter of Genesis. We do not know the age of this chapter, and can say only that it had a complex history which certainly went back to remote times, and can probably be followed in still preserved structural elements partly to the Late Bronze Age and partly to about the tenth century B.C., reaching its extant form in the seventh century B.C.[69] In other words, it belongs with the 'Priestly Code' in general as well as with the 'later Elohist', which is so closely related in many ways to 'P'. Here, as first pointed out by the late G. A. Barton, appears the ancient myth of the destruction of the dragon of chaos which we find alluded to so frequently in the Prophets, especially Amos[70] and Isaiah. In verse 2 we read: 'And the earth was empty and chaotic, and there was darkness over the primordial fresh-water ocean' (Heb. *tehôm*). Then we are told that 'the spirit of God was soaring over the waters'. There is obviously some kind of break between these two passages. Now, whereas in Canaanite just as in Babylonian mythology, the dragon or dragons of chaos preceded the regnant divinities, in Gen. 1 the monsters are created by God himself. We read in verse 21 that

[69] See my discussion in *Mélanges bibliques . . . André Robert* (Paris, 1957), pp. 22–6; J. B. Bauer, 'Das Heptaëmeron' in *Biblische Zeitschrift*, 1957, Heft 2 (and the independent study by S. E. Loewenstamm, IEJ xv [1965], 121–33).

[70] One such reference in Amos 7:4 has been clarified by Delbert Hillers; see CBQ xxvi (1964), 221–5.

'God created the sea-monsters' (Heb. *tannînîm*), using the plural of a word which in Canaanite was employed in the singular for the dragon of chaos which was destroyed by a god at Creation. It follows that there was originally a statement in verse 2 mentioning specifically and succinctly the triumph of God over the great Deep (*Tehôm* = Acc. *Ti'āmat*), which was later deleted. In any case it is obvious that the pagan archetype was thoroughly demythologized at some stage in the history of Gen. 1. There are many other cases of demythologizing in the cosmogonic narratives of Genesis as well as in the Patriarchal stories. In later Israel the tendency to eliminate polytheistic references was spasmodic, depending presumably upon periodic reform movements and efforts to eliminate remaining traces of paganism. It may confidently be stated that there is no true mythology anywhere in the Hebrew Bible. What we have consists of vestiges—what may be called the 'débris' of a past religious culture.

There are, however, a great many minor vestiges from Canaanite religion among the Hebrews. The names of many pagan gods and goddesses continued to be used in Hebrew for religious or nonreligious purposes, just as in English. For instance, when we speak of eating breakfast cereal we certainly do not mean to imply worship of the goddess Ceres. The word has simply been borrowed and applied to products previously believed to be under the special protection of the goddess of that name. Similarly we celebrate Easter, which bears the name of the Anglo-Saxon goddess Eostre, without intending to venerate her at all. If anyone insists that these etymologies prove the mythological character of our beliefs, we should have every right to laugh him out of court, and yet such reasoning is still common among historians of religion. In the Bible the goddess Ashtaroth appears in the term *'aštĕrôt (haṣ-)ṣôn*, meaning 'sheep-breeding' (several times in Deut.). Since Astarte was best known as the patroness of sexual reproduction, this is a very natural development, quite acceptable in Israel, as the Israelites had little feeling for the religious connotations of the expression. The three words *dāgān*, *tîrōš*, and *yiṣhār*, referring to grain, wine, and oil, respectively, often appear together. *Dāgān*, 'grain', comes from the name of the god Dagan (which became *Dagôn* in Phoenician), on whom see above. Similarly, it is now virtually certain that *tîrōš*, 'wine', Ugar. *trṯ*, 'wine', is derived from the Canaanite divine name *Tiršu*, which appears at Hazor and Ugarit; the name has nothing to do with unfermented wine, as was formerly thought on the basis of imaginative etymologies.[71] In view of these parallels, *yiṣhār* which takes the place of the ordinary word for oil, *šemen*, is almost certainly the name of an old god of olive oil, though so far this name has not been identified among the references to pagan divinities in Palestine and Syria. The name itself is obviously the normal imperfect of the verb *ṣhr* (**ẓhr*), 'to be bright'.

A pair of names in Hab. 3:5 has often been mentioned since it was first discovered that Resheph was the name of a Canaanite god. Here Resheph and Deber appear as angels.

Before Him Pestilence marched.
And Plague went forth at His feet.

On Resheph see above, Chapter II; Deber has not yet been identified as a divine name in Ugaritic literature, but it is quite likely that it was, since divinities of this type tend to appear in pairs in Canaanite mythology.

It was seen long ago that the plant-beds of Na'man (*niṭ'ê na'mānîm*) in Is. 17:10 mean 'plant-beds of Adonis', who may be referred to under this name in the Ugaritic

[71] The word is probably non-Semitic; the extant form may reflect the name of the god after it had reached the status of a proper noun with helping vowel *ă*. The name would then become *Tîrōš* in Phoenician and North Israelite.

texts. In any event, there can be no doubt that the designation *Na'mân—Nu'mân—Na'môn*, 'the Charming One', was employed for Adonis by the Phoenicians.[72] The so-called Adonis gardens enjoyed a long life in the ancient Mediterranean world and ultimately became popular Easter customs of the Greek churches, where they still exist today in some places. Eshmun, Sidonian god of healing (see above, Chapter III), and also, like Adonis, a dying and reviving god, clearly appears in Is. 59:10 as well as in the first Isaiah scroll of Qumrân in the form *'ešmûnîm* (with *plene* spelling of the middle vowel). The context makes it perfectly clear that *'ešmûnîm* is the opposite of *mētîm*, 'dead, death', just as the preceding *ṣŏhŏrayim*, 'noon', is the opposite of *nešef*, 'dusk'. *'Ešmûnîm* is here an abstract plural meaning 'health'. In Chapter III we have already referred to *kôšārôt*, 'the process of birth', originally the goddesses of birth (Ps. 68:7). We have also shown that *kîšōr* (Prov. 31:19) is derived from original *Kôšar*, the Canaanite name of the god of skill.

In a number of poetic passages Canaanite deities appear, going back ultimately to pagan compositions. For instance, in Is. 14:12 Hêlêl[73] is called 'son of *Šaḥar*', the Canaanite name of the god of dawn, to whom a liturgical text is devoted at Ugarit.[74] In Cant. 7:1 f. the Shulammite appears in a context which almost certainly refers back to the war goddess named *Šulmânîtu* (on whom see Chapter III).[75] In Ps. 68:24 f. I have proposed to divide the first four letters, which read an impossible *le-ma'an*, into *LM 'N* and to insert a fifth letter *T*, which would

[72] HACH, 172 f.

[73] Certainly an appellation of 'Athtar; the LXX would not be likely to be ignorant of its meaning when they translated ἑωσφόρος. Its etymology is obscure.

[74] The composition celebrating the birth of the 'beautiful and gracious' gods Šaḥar and Šalim, Dawn and Dusk, respectively.

[75] See also my remarks in *Hebrew and Semitic Studies . . . Godfrey Rolles Driver* (Oxford, 1963), pp. 5–6.

involve a haplography of the fifth letter of the verse (*T*). The text would then read:

Why, O Anath, dost thou wash Thy feet in blood,
The tongues of thy dogs In the blood of the foes?[76]

As emphasized above in Chapter I, Ps. 68 is an anthology of opening lines and strophes of ancient poems, and it would not be at all surprising to find such echoes of pagan material in it. Note that in none of these cases is there any reason to suppose that the Hebrew writers were deliberately employing pagan expressions. Some of the names of pagan divinities have simply become secular Hebrew words with no pagan meaning; mythological expressions are used as poetic symbolism without indicating the slightest reverence for the original pagan deities, just as in many Christian poets of the fifteenth–seventeenth centuries A.D.

We have dealt at some length with this material (which we have in no way exhausted), in order to make it easier to deal with two classes of ancient divine names and appellations where there is still much disagreement. We have, as authentic Hebrew appellations of Yahweh/Elohim, the names *El*, *Ṣûr*, *'Al* or *'Elî*, *'Elyôn* and *Šadday*, which are all particularly common in very early texts and reappear archaistically in late books. It has been urged that the Patriarchal religion had a kind of 'El-monotheism' which recognized El as the Supreme Being and disregarded most other divinities. This point of view is quite possible, but I must confess to serious doubts about its validity. The name *Ṣûr* (on which see Chapter I) means literally 'mountain'; 'cliff' or 'rock' are very inadequate renderings. But since 'mountain' was often a synonym for 'god' in Syria and Anatolia, it is not surprising to find that *Ṣûr* is simply a synonym of *El* in early Hebrew lit-

[76] See HUCA XXIV, Part I, 28–9.

erature. *Šadday*,[77] 'He of the Mountains', though a more obviously secondary appellation, belongs semantically with *Ṣûr*. *'Al* or *'Elî* means, of course, 'the Exalted One' and has been recognized in recent years in a number of Hebrew religious poems as well as an element in personal names.[78] *'Elyôn* is a variant of it, going back to high antiquity.[79] We must emphasize, however, that there is not the slightest reason to suppose that any of these names were used for members of an Israelite pantheon of divinities. Just as in Canaanite religious literature, we often have synonymous divine names and appellations used in parallelism. No inferences as to the dominance of polytheism can be drawn from them.

We have reserved for the end of this treatment of depotentized or transformed divinities a group which is intimately related, both linguistically and semantically, to *'El*. The feminine of *'El*, Canaanite *'Elat*, 'goddess', which is also applied to Asherah as *the* goddess, El's consort, is found in the Hebrew Bible, so far as we know, only as the ordinary word for 'terebinth'. The terebinth (*Pistacia palaestina*) is one of the finest shade trees in Palestine, with a broad oval crown and with small fruit which may be roasted and eaten as nuts. Ben Sira describes the terebinth as follows (24:16):

> Like a terebinth I have extended my branches,
> And my branches are branches of glory and grace.

As in other parts of the eastern Mediterranean outside of forested mountains, a fine shade tree such as a terebinth

[77] See JBL LIV (1935), 180–93 (with many subsequent additions, such as the name *Sadê'ammî* in Egypt c. 1300 B.C., and the parallel noun formation *Rabbâyu*, of a tribe of bowmen in the Mari letters); Manfred Weippert, ZDMG CXI (1961), 42–62; F. M. Cross, Jr., HTR LV (1962), 244–50 (on Shaddai as God of the Fathers see pp. 226–32).

[78] See especially M. Dahood, ThSt XIV (1953), 452–7.

[79] For recent treatments of *'Elyôn* see J. A. Fitzmyer, S.J., JAOS LXXXI (1961), 193.

was highly regarded and early became deified, just as was true of the sycomore fig (Heb. *šiqmāh*) which was deified in Egyptian as *nūhe* (*Nht*). The oak tree was probably also deified, as in other Mediterranean lands (see below); it is certain that Heb. *'allôn* means 'oak' and probable that the word *'ēlôn* should be vocalized *'allôn* in some cases. It is, in any case, hard to separate *'ēlôn* from Aram. *'îlânâ*, 'tree', which replaced '*q*)' ', the older Aram. equivalent of '*ēṣ*. (When a word is reduced so completely to a mere hiccup, its utility is at an end, according to well-established principles of dialect geography, so a new, longer word replaces it, in this case a common word for 'oak'.) There is much confusion here, owing to the variety of different species of *Quercus* as well as of the Arabic *ballûṭ*, which have been given varying scientific names by different taxonomists. In antiquity there were undoubtedly many more of the high oak species in the hill country of Palestine and Syria than remain today, when the *ballûṭ* is generally a dwarf oak. The familiar word *ballûṭ* is therefore an unsafe guide to the type of oak which was meant. That the oak was also sacred is clear. Greek *dryas* (from *drys*, 'oak') and *hamadryas* both refer to minor divinities ('nymphs') whose life is bound up with that of the oak tree to which they were attached. It is quite possible that the Ugaritic *'elnym* which stands in parallelism with *'elm*, 'gods', refers to minor divinities of the same type. The etymology of the word is, in any event, quite clear; it must be derived from a double adjectival formation pronounced *'elânîyîma* (accus.). On the other hand we cannot be sure that these particular minor divinities were attached to oak trees as such. It is to be noted that *'ēlôn* tends to have the specific meaning 'sacred tree' and is sometimes used with reference to a dead tree or even to a post replacing an original tree, as for example in Jud. 9:6, interpreted in the light of the LXX and of Samuel Iwry's discovery of the true meaning of the word *nimṣā'* in Hebrew.[80] The plural *'ēlônîm* (found only in the construct) probably has the same formation as Phoen. *'elônîm*, plural of *'el*, just as *'Elôhîm* = *'ēlîm* is plural of *'Ēl*. *'Elônîm*, 'gods', would then go back to *'elônîyîm*, contracted as normally in Phoenician and Hebrew to *'elônîm*. In this case *'ēlôn*, 'sacred tree' (e.g., I Sam. 10:3, Gen. 35:8, Josh. 19:33, Gen. 14:13, etc.) might be a back-formation from the plural *'elônîm*.

The name *'Ašērāh* is a special case.[81] Originally, as pointed out above, it was a shortened form of the phrase *'Aṯíratu yammi*, 'She Who Treads on the (dragon) Sea', or the like. Later it became an ordinary term for a grove of trees which was popularly considered as sacred. This we know from the LXX, which translates it by *alsos*, as well as from the context of the word in various Hebrew passages. Such groves of high trees were rare in ancient Palestine, and by the 1920's they had become very much rarer; old groves on hill-tops were then still attached to saints' shrines (*welis*).

Since H. Wheeler Robinson's famous paper of 1944,[82] many additional references bearing on the divine council in Israel have been brought together from the Hebrew Bible.[83] At the same time much new information bearing on the subject has been collected from Sumerian, Accadian and Ugaritic sources. In I Kings 22:19 ff. we have a vision of the heavenly court in which the angels make suggestions. In Isa. 40:1 ff. several scholars have shown that the agents of Yahweh are the angels of the heavenly council. In Psalms 82 and 89 we have references to the

80 *Textus* v (1966), 34–43. See provisionally my remarks in BASOR 169 (1963), 28 f., n. 32.

81 On this question see the survey by W. L. Reed, *The Asherah in the Old Testament* (Yale thesis, published at Fort Worth, Texas, 1949).

82 JTS XLV (1944), 151–7.

83 See F. M. Cross, Jr., JNES XII (1953), 274–7, and R. E. Brown, CBQ XX (1958), 417–21.

divine assembly in which Canaanite terminology is transparent. On the other hand, we have an interesting case of demythologizing in Gen. 1:26, where God speaks in the plural, 'Let us make man in our image and likeness', with a striking Ugaritic parallel. The term *sôd* at that time meant undoubtedly 'assembly, council', just as *mswd* did in South Arabia. In Job the angels appear as members of the council of God, but they do not take an active part, only standing to receive orders. In other words there was a tendency, which becomes accentuated with the progress of time, to change the divine assembly from an actual council to a forum where God's orders are transmitted to his messengers (angels), who then go out to execute them. In view of the great antiquity of the conception of the Sumerian ukkin, Accadian *puḫru(m)*,[84] and the fact that the same word is used in Ugaritic for the divine assembly, it is probably quite unnecessary to assume a Canaanite origin for the concept in question. On the other hand, there can be no reasonable doubt that Canaanite ideas did influence specific details of the concept of the divine assembly in early Israel. In Deut. 32:8 we read:

> When the Most High distributed lots,
> When he separated the children of men,
> He set the borders of the peoples,
> Like the number of sons of God.[85]

The sons of God are the angels, as elsewhere in Hebrew, and not the gods as in Ugaritic. The number of the *banū 'Aṯirat* is given in the Baal epic as seventy, in accord with the statement in the Haggada that 'seventy angels were appointed by God to rule the seventy nations'—these seventy nations corresponding to the roughly seventy peoples of Genesis 10. In a minor detail like this it is clear

[84] See Thorkild Jacobsen, JNES II (1943), 159–72 and ZA LII (N. F. XVIII, 1957), 91–140. Cf. my remarks in HACH, 183 ff.

[85] See VT IX (1959), 343 f.

that Israelite thought was indeed influenced by Canaanite mythological patterns. It is probable that similar patterns would appear in many other areas of religious thought where basic Hebrew conceptions were derived chiefly from Mesopotamia, but were later modified in detail by Canaanite terminology. It is noteworthy that such Canaanite patterns were depotentized and demythologized rapidly, so that by the end of Old Testament times official Yahwist religion had been demythologized to a rather extreme degree. In fact, too little place was sometimes left for anthropomorphic expression of abstract religious concepts.

D. SOME ASPECTS OF EARLY ISRAELITE CULT

In the area of specific divine names or appellations and their functional evolution among Canaanites and Israelites, we are on much more solid ground than when we attempt to combine the archaeological remains of the Hebrew and Canaanite cults with literary material. This may seem strange, since the concrete, excavated remains and the specific descriptions of Tabernacle and Temple, Ark of the Covenant and Altar of Burnt Offering, etc., seem to provide us with a mass of objective data on which to base sound inferences. In dealing with the rich sacrificial ritual of Leviticus, we appear to be situated even more favourably for comparative research. Actually this is not true at all. We have few clear temple and sanctuary sites of the Canaanite Bronze Age and almost none of the Phoenician Iron Age. The Tabernacle was mostly of cloth, leather, and wood, and the original Ark of the Covenant was mostly wood, so all traces of both, as well as of possible parallels, have perished. We have no satisfactory analogies between the Pentateuchal descriptions and Canaanite sources. Only in the description of the temple of Solomon do we have parallels, and even there they are often more puzzling than clarifying, as in the case of the pillars of Jachin and Boaz. We have almost no description of ritual in the entire Ugaritic literature. What we have consists chiefly of lists of gods and offerings, as well as later sacrificial tariffs, none of which can be found in the Pentateuch. In short, our points of contact are so vague that we must still turn to ancient and modern Beduin parallels to find plausible analogies from non-Israelite cultures. How unsatisfactory this kind of analogy may be, we have had occasion to see above. Presumably there were close parallels between portable sanctuary and cult objects of Israel as described in Exodus, and similar sanctuaries and objects in the cult of the ancestral Hebrews as well as of nomadic and semi-nomadic Semitic peoples of the Bronze Age. Since practically every trace of the latter has disappeared, this must remain an assumption—though in itself highly plausible. In short, where we ought to have parallels, they do not exist, and if it were not for the general picture which has emerged from consideration of divine names and functions as well as for a number of sometimes unexpected points of contact in material cult, we should find ourselves in a relative vacuum.

Quite aside from the witness of biblical tradition to the existence of shrines, sacred objects, divination, etc., in early Israel, we now have direct archaeological evidence to explain some otherwise enigmatic details. The first wave of Israelite invaders in the late thirteenth century B.C. was certainly hostile to image worship, as we can illustrate by finds at Tell Beit Mirsim in the south and Hazor in the north. In the 1930 campaign at the former site, we found a shallow pit containing bones of sacrificial bovides, including the skull of a young ox, and also two cult objects: a large libation bowl of soft chalk limestone with a lioness and two cubs in relief (30 cm. across) and a lion in somewhat harder limestone (over

50 cm. long).[86] These objects had been thrown into the pit and were standing on their sides in it, among the débris. The temple from which they must have come lay just outside our excavated area. These remains all came from the last Canaanite destruction level. In Hazor, Yigael Yadin discovered that the image of a standing bull which had, we may suppose, originally supported an image of the storm god, had been deliberately broken before the destruction of the temple in which it stood.[87] This was also found in the destruction level marking the end of the Canaanite occupation of Hazor about the third quarter of the thirteenth century B.C.

The excavation of Shechem, begun by a German expedition directed successively by E. Sellin and G. Welter, and successfully resumed in recent years by G. Ernest Wright, has shown that in the acropolis area there was a special enclosure which was fortified for at least part of the time. This enclosure lasted from about 1700 B.C. or a little earlier, to the Israelite period.[88] Here we have, almost certainly, the sacred precinct of Shechem, called *āl ili*, 'city of god', in the Amarna Letters.[89] According to biblical tradition Shechem was sacred to the Hebrews from the time of Abraham to its destruction by Abimelech. It was believed to have become Hebrew in the days of Jacob. This seems to be confirmed by the correspondence of Lab'ayu, ruler of central Palestine in the Amarna Age, with his Egyptian suzerain.[90] In the correspondence of another Palestinian prince, 'Abdu-Kheba of Jerusalem, with Shuwardata, prince of the adjacent territory to the south, we are told that Shechem had be-

[86] AASOR XVII (1938), 65 ff. (§§ 75–7).

[87] For details we must await the publication of the text volume of *Hazor* III–IV. See provisionally BA XXII: 1, pp. 4 ff.

[88] See G. E. Wright, *Shechem* (New York, 1964), pp. 80 ff., 123 ff.

[89] See my remarks, CAH², II, ch. XX (1966), p. 19 f.

[90] See *ibid.* for details.

come Hebrew, thanks to the activities of Lab'ayu and his sons.[91] In any event this sanctuary was completely destroyed in the late twelfth century B.C. And just as was true of the sanctuary at Shiloh, discredited after its abandonment by Yahweh and its destruction by the Philistines, so was the fate of the old sanctuary at Shechem. The temple which existed on Mt. Gerizim in late Persian and Hellenistic times was in quite a different location, and it is not likely that any connexion was ever admitted by the Samaritans.

There were undoubtedly many local sanctuaries in Israel during the time of the Judges, most of which probably went back to earlier tradition, as in the case of Shechem, Bethel, Beersheba (?), etc. There were also local sanctuaries whose nature must remain in doubt even after they have been cleared by excavation. For example, the sanctuary of Hazor found in Stratum XI from about the eleventh century B.C., has been described by Y. Yadin as 'an idolatrous Israelite cult place'.[92] In it were found two incense stands, similar in shape to eleventh-century incense stands from Megiddo, a jar full of votive bronzes, including a figurine of a seated war-god, etc.[93] Since Hazor was at this time so close to the indefinite border between Israel and Canaan, it would be quite unrealistic to expect a consistent Yahwist tradition there.

The latest excavation of the Israeli Department of Antiquities at Laish (Dan) in the spring of 1966, under the direction of Avram Biran, has yielded clear evidence of a somewhat earlier destruction of the town followed by a reoccupation.[94] This confirms the account in Judges of the destruction of Laish (later Dan) by the Israelites as well as the subsequent occupation by the latter. The

[91] *Loc. cit.*, p. 20.

[92] BA XXII:1 (1959), 12 f.

[93] *Ibid.*, Fig. 10 (the axe-head has been stuck to it by the oxidizing process).

[94] See, e.g., *News from Israel*, No. 56 (7 July 1966), p. 3.

Israelites are said to have erected an idolatrous object (*pesel*) of some sort and to have made Jonathan, son of Gershom, son of Moses[95] its priest (Judg. 18:30 f.). The close association of a descendant of Moses with idolatry cannot be taken at face value, since the accounts of the origins of the cult at Bethel and Dan were both edited by the same Deuteronomic historian in the late seventh century B.C. It is stated explicitly in the text that Jonathan's descendants remained priests of Dan until the Assyrian captivity. Unfortunately, the terms *pesel* and *'ēfôd* are very obscure (see below); this sanctuary was, however, definitely Israelite and not pagan, though obviously paganizing in tendency.

In connexion with the erection of a 'golden calf' at Dan (I Kings 12:28 ff.) as well as at Bethel, we must remember what was said about Exodus 32 in Chapter I. As shown there, with examples from prose and verse, the content of this chapter is in large part archaic; it refers specifically to an attempted return by the Israelites of Moses' time to the ancient practice of representing the chief divinity in the form of a storm-god standing on a young bull. This practice had doubtless been shared by pre-Mosaic Hebrews with the pagans among whom they lived, and its restoration by Jeroboam is simply a return to early Hebrew tradition. It may well have been found by the Danites at Laish, though we do not know whether or not the figure of the god standing on the young bull was supposed to be visible or invisible. The latter was true later. In view of the archaism of Exodus 32 and Jeroboam's obvious intention, over 350 years later, to restore pre-Solomonic faith and practice rather than to create a new paganism, it is much safer to assume that the Israelites did not erect a visible image at either Bethel or Dan.

95 MT has an impossible 'Manasseh', but Greek MSS going back to Lucianic (now called by F. M. Cross, Jr., 'Old Palestinian') tradition read 'Moses'. Of course, Gershom was one of Moses' sons, not a Manassite clan.

It has long since been pointed out that in glyptic art there is a clear development from a young bull with a storm-god on his back, carrying a sheaf of lightning bolts, through a bull with only the sheaf of thunderbolts on his back, to a young bull without anything on his back. The first two of these types are documented from cylinder seals of the Bronze Age,[96] and the third is found on an Israelite seal dating no later than the early ninth century B.C., as is clearly shown by the extraordinarily archaic *mem* and *aleph*.[97]

There are a good many illustrations of reaction against paganizing tendencies in early Yahwism. For example, we read in Deut. 32:17, from the eleventh century B.C.,

> They sacrificed to demons,[98] not divine,
> Who are too deaf to approach,[99]
> Gods whom they knew not,
> And whom their fathers did not know.

In the official Deuteronomic history from the late seventh

[96] See Th. Obbink (ZATW XLVII (1929), 264–74) and my observations in FSAC² (1957), 298–300; my detailed study has, unfortunately, not been published as promised. For some of these early seals see W. H. Ward, *Seal Cylinders of Western Asia* (Washington, 1910), pp. 171 ff. For a seal with only the thunderbolt standing on the bull see p. 174, Fig. 468.

[97] See H. Gressmann, *Altorientalische Bilder zum Alten Testament* (Berlin, 1927), pl. ccxxvi, No. 582, and p. 165. The seal reads, 'Belonging to Shemaiah son of Uriah' (not Azariah), and dates no later than the early ninth century B.C., as shown by the very archaic *mem* and *aleph*, with which the other characters agree. It is probably the earliest known inscribed Israelite seal; it has been overlooked partly because it was published over a century ago (1862).

[98] Whether we read *šēdîm* or *śĕʿîrîm*, or both in parallelism (in which case something has dropped out of the text), is quite irrelevant for our purpose here.

[99] Reading the consonantal text and vocalizing *ḥērĕšîm miqrob* ⟨*ʾalēhem*⟩, comparing Hab. 1:13 for the syntax and inserting a third word as haplography before *ʾelōhîm*. On the verse see VT IX (1959), 341 f.

century B.C. this theme is resumed, especially in the book of Judges, indicating that according to official tradition the Israelites backslid at every opportunity and during every period of relative peace and prosperity. There is no reason to doubt that this point of view was essentially correct, though details may have been exaggerated.

The unrealistic approach of the late Yehezkel Kaufmann,[100] who held that there was no backsliding in Israel except possibly during the period of Ahab and Jezebel in the ninth century B.C., is, in my opinion, quite untenable. The religion of Yahweh was far ahead of the popular level in its abstract approach to theology, and at the same time far too intolerant of objectionable pagan practices to be an easy faith to follow. Since the entire subsequent Judaeo-Christian tradition is full of reform movements, both in theology and in moral practice, it is incredible that the Israelites should have formed an exception. After all, they were surrounded by pagans and were constantly engaged in trade with them. Besides, virtually all art, music and 'science' were then saturated with pagan elements.

In Judg. 6:25 ff. we have a most instructive account of a phase of the struggle with paganism about the middle of the twelfth century B.C. Gideon, whose original name was Jerubbaal,[101] was a strong supporter of Yahwism. In

[100] See the excellent English condensation of Kaufmann's great work, *Toledot ha-'emunah ha-yisre'elit* (in eight volumes, 1937–56), by Moshe Greenberg: *The Religion of Israel* (Chicago, 1960), especially pp. 18–19, 134–47. It is a theme to which the author returns again and again.

[101] The name 'Gideon' (*Gid'ôn*) is obviously a *kunyah* (kenning) of *Yarîb-Ba'al* ('Jerubbaal'), so I suggest that it was applied to the hero after he had gained a reputation as an image-destroyer (Greek *eikonoklastēs*). Since quite different verbs are used of his destruction of a Baal altar and Asherah at Ophrah (Judg. 6:25 ff.), though *gd'* is used specifically of destroying idols in Deut. 7:5; 12:3, etc., this explanation is reasonable. (In this case the popular elimination of oral tradition as an historical source by assuming an aetiological explanation for nearly everything is incredible.)

pursuit of his mission he destroyed an altar of Baal in his native town of Ophrah and cut down the sacred *'ashērāh*, thereby incurring the wrath of his fellow citizens. Note that his father bore the Yahwist name of Joash, and yet Gideon is said to have borne a name formed with 'Baal'. Just what this oscillation in the use of theophorous personal names meant, we do not know, but its very existence indicates that there was still much uncertainty as to whether 'Baal' could be used as an appellation of Yahweh in the sense of 'lord'. To complicate our problem, Gideon later set up a golden ephod in Ophrah. Similarly we are told in the prelude to the Danite story (Judg. 17:5), which probably dates from a slightly earlier period, that a Levite named Micah or Micaiah[102] set up a silver ephod somewhere in mount Ephraim, where he had a 'house of God' (*bêt 'elôhîm*). The last expression is obscure enough in Hebrew, but it is supported by both Greek recensions of Judges. Besides the ephod we hear of a *pesel* and of *tĕrāfîm*. We also hear that Micah made one of his sons priest of his shrine. While we are obviously not yet able to solve the problems which arise in connexion with this tradition, which may not have been put into writing until the late seventh century B.C., we must treat it with the utmost care, since tradition was often exceedingly tenacious. In this case it is even less likely to have been invented, since there is nothing to prove a specifically anti-Ephraimite bias.

The problem of the ephod has been attacked from different directions, but no previous efforts seem to have been successful. Fortunately, we now have Old Assyrian and Ugaritic material for the interpretation of the word. In the nineteenth century B.C. the word appears in the Cappadocian tablets as *epādum*, pl. *epādātum* (CAD IV, 183a), which almost certainly means something like

[102] Since he is a Levite the longer form is probably authentic. His original name may have been 'Michael' (*Mî-kā-'El*), the normal hypocoristic of which is 'Micah'.

'plaid robe'. The singular of this word, pronounced *'epd*, that is, *'epâdu*, appears at least twice in now available Ugaritic materials. In text 17.125 from the palace of Ugarit[103] we read in an inventory (line 3), 'a woman's robe of hy[r]ax skin, an ephod'—in Ugaritic *md. ṯ⌜p⌝n. 'epd*. The word *md* is used specifically in Ugaritic for a woman's garment. The second word is almost certainly *ṯpn* = Heb. *šapan*, Arab. *ṯafan*, 'hyrax'.[104] Hyrax skin was covered with a fur not unlike rabbit fur, so that a garment of it should be quite acceptable for winter wear. The *'epâdu* was a specific kind of robe, presumably a wrap-around plaid something like a *sari* but not so wide, i.e., a strip which was wrapped around the body and fastened at the shoulder, leaving one arm free. In the Baal epic we have another reference to the ephod. The context probably refers to the impending slaying of Leviathan by the goddess Anath.[105] The text reads as follows:

When thou dost smite Lôtân, the primordial serpent,
  When thou dost destroy the winding serpent,
    Shalyaṭ of the seven heads,
The heavens will wither,
  And will sag like the fastening(?) of thy ephod.

There are numerous parallels in the Hebrew Bible to the concept that the heavens will waste away: cf. particularly Ps. 102:26 f.; cf. also Is. 51:6; Job 26:11. In Heb. 1:10 ff. there is an interesting variation in the first passage based on the LXX: 'and like a mantle shalt thou roll them up'. Though the Hebrew text is probably right, there can be little doubt that the Greek comparison was suggested by the winding of a plaid robe, which became a simile for the revolving vault of heaven. In representations of Babylonian divinities from the ninth to seventh centuries B.C.

[103] PRU II, 182, No. 152:3.

[104] Also as a proper name *Ṯpn* (= Shaphan), PSID, 45.

[105] See BASOR 83 (1941), 39–42 and 84, 14–17. While other translations have been proposed, none of them makes good sense.

they are clad in outer robes studded with stars.[106] In much later times we have a description by the poet Nonnus (fourth to fifth century A.D.)[107] of the star-studded garment (*astrochitōn*) of the Tyrian Heracles (Phoen. Melcarth).

In 1936 the eminent classical archaeologist, Hermann Thiersch, devoted an important volume to a comparison of the form and function (but not the name) of the Greek *ependytēs* and the ephod.[108] In this volume he dealt particularly with a Greek outer garment which was often completely covered with gold and silver and other rich decoration; in Greek iconography it is represented as a robe fastened tightly around the upper middle and lower part of the body, often resembling a mummy-case. The best-known example of this garb is the outer garment of the goddess Artemis of Ephesus.[109] There is another extremely interesting example of a famous goddess of Oriental origin who wears an elaborate *ependytēs*—the Aphrodite of Aphrodisias in Caria (originally called *Ninoē*).[110] As we have seen in Chapter III, this is the Hurrian goddess Ishtar of Nineveh who was worshipped in Caria in the Late Bronze Age, as we know from Hittite sources. The best-known male deity shown wearing the

[106] How deep-rooted this Babylonian symbolism was, may be seen from the fact that a common word for the firmament in which the stars were set was *burūmu*, literally, 'what is embroidered'. The stem *barāmu* and its derivative *birmu* are used regularly of embroidered garments (cf. CAD II, 103, 257 f., and 344 f.). On the general idea of the starry firmament as the garment of God, see R. Eisler, *Weltenmantel und Himmelszelt* (1908) and A. Jeremias, *Das Alte Testament im Lichte des alten Orients*[3] (1916), p. 581 (on Psalm 104:10).

[107] *Dionysiaca*, 40:408. The same word is used of 'star-clad night' in much older, Orphic, poetry.

[108] *Ependytes und Ephod: Gottesbild und Priesterkleid im alten Vorderasien* (Stuttgart, 1936).

[109] *Op. cit.*, pp. 54–8.

[110] *Ibid.*, pp. 59–72, and pls. viii–xii. On this goddess (originally the Hurrian Ishtar of Nineveh) see also above, Ch. III.

ependytēs is the Syrian storm-god of Baalbek, called *Jupiter Heliopolitanus* in Roman times.[111]

As worn by the high priest, the ephod with its *ḥošen* (gem-set breastplate) was quite distinct in function from the ephod as a separate cult object. This question has been so well discussed by Thiersch[112] that it is not necessary to go into detail here. As a cult object the ephod was probably taken over from pagan sources in Palestine, either as a direct adaptation of an older Canaanite object, or as a legacy from early Hebrew times. The God of Israel, being invisible, was represented only by His heavenly glory—a monotheistic offshoot of the *astrochitōn* concept. Such a rich costume covered with gold or silver and studded with stars and other cosmic symbols could be interpreted as an idol by Yahwists adhering to the strict Mosaic tradition, or treated simply as the visible symbol of the invisible deity in the official Yahwist cult of the day. I need scarcely point out that in cult images of all periods, both among pagans and Christians, there has been a strong tendency to turn the garb of a sacred statue into the most significant item of its ensemble. From this to the veneration of the outer garment, richly decorated with cosmic symbols, as a substitute for the image of the divinity, was a natural step. We may, therefore, provisionally consider the ephod of the time of the Judges as on a par with the golden bullocks of Bethel and Dan, which were visible but whose function was to support the invisible presence of Yahweh, as we have seen above.

In 1956 I presented a paper at the Strasbourg Congress of Old Testament Scholars on 'The High Place in Ancient Palestine'.[113] This paper was strongly influenced in its presentation by the work of L. R. Farnell, *Greek Hero Cults and Ideas of Immortality* (1941) and Martin P. Nilsson, *Greek Popular Religion* (1940). As the result

[111] *Loc. cit.*, pp. 73 ff. and pls. xii–xix.
[112] *Ibid.*, 120 ff.
[113] VT, *Supplement* IV (1957), 242–58.

of archaeological excavations and explorations in Palestine and neighbouring areas, it had become clear that the *bâmôt*[114] must have been connected in some way with the stone cairns which are found in Palestine, Sinai and Arabia both in cultic areas and on the summits of hills and ridges. The *bâmôt* were in different ways strikingly parallel to Greek hero-shrines, which were primarily devoted to the veneration of ancestors. It has since become clear from Ugaritic evidence, which agrees closely with biblical and Mesopotamian data, that the cult of ancestors was much more widespread in antiquity than I had supposed a decade ago. Important contributions to my understanding were also made by R. de Vaux and Yigael Yadin.[115] This is not the place to go into detail, since the subject was adequately treated in the original publication and new material will be added in the proper place. The main point in which we are interested here is that there was a flourishing cult of 'heroes' in second-millennium Palestine, which perpetuated both ancestral Hebrew and Canaanite practices.

Since 1963 we have learned something about the cult of deceased kings both at Ugarit and among the Amorite rulers of Babylon and Asshur. We have already seen in Chapter III how important were beliefs in *'El'eb*, the mysterious deity who seems to have been the patron of all respectable ghosts, and who apparently embodied their collective cult in his own person. In this connexion

[114] The etymological observations, *ibid.*, pp. 255 f., still hold as made, though many more phonetic parallels can now be given. CAD II (1965), 76, is quite wrong in rendering *bāmātu* as 'plain', or as 'plains in the mountains(!)'; it should be rendered 'ridge(s)'.

[115] Yadin has since called attention to II Sam. 1:19, where the Greek text requires a reading *haṣṣîb* instead of MT *haṣ-ṣĕbî*. I suggest that the two following words *bâmôt* and *ḥălāl* be transposed; the text would then mean

Set up, O Israel, Burial cairns over thy slain.

This at least makes complete sense.

we also saw that the word *'ōb* appears more frequently in the Hebrew Bible than had been supposed, and that *'el 'eb* seems to appear at least once in the same sense (attested also by a Palestinian seal). The practice of necromancy, which is somewhat obscurely attested in Hittite and Mesopotamian cuneiform sources, appears in the famous narrative of the 'witch of Endor' who called up the *'ōb* of Samuel from the grave, as well as in the frequent denunciations of the practice of calling up the ghosts of the dead (*'ōbôt*) in Pentateuchal legislation and elsewhere in the Hebrew Bible.

The word *bâmāh* not only denoted a memorial stone cairn but also was often transferred to the standing stone, or *maṣṣēbāh*, which stood on or in the cairn. For instance, on the Mesha Stone the stele is called 'this *bmt*'. And in the Greek Bible throughout the Pentateuch *bâmāh* is regularly translated *stēlē*. The *bêt bâmôt* would thus be a house of (burial) stelae, like the *temple des obélisques* of Byblos from the latter part of the Egyptian Middle Kingdom, or the thirteenth-century funerary shrine at Hazor which originally contained at least 27 funerary stelae.[116] Even more striking in some ways is the open-air sanctuary containing a whole row of massive standing stones of earlier date at Gezer. To what extent the cult of the Canaanite divinity Asherah was associated with the *bâmôt* we do not know, but the constant association of *'ashērîm* in the sense of 'groves' with *bâmôt* in the Bible makes it virtually certain that this was the case.[117] In any event the cult of the *bâmôt* was a paganizing survival and so had to be rejected by official Yahwism, just as was true of the ephod and various other cult objects. Below, in Chapter V, § A, we shall deal briefly

[116] See Y. Yadin, *Hazor* I (1958), pp. 83–90; II (1960), pp. 97 f. I was wrong (*op. cit.*, p. 252) in quoting the number '45'; only 27 stelae were found in and around the shrine.

[117] See my remarks *op. cit.*, pp. 254 f. For additional details see W. L. Reed, *The Asherah in the Old Testament* (1949).

with an attempt to reform the *bâmôt* cult in the time of Samuel.

In this chapter we have endeavoured to draw sharp distinctions, wherever possible, between the Patriarchal Hebrew heritage, the unique contribution of Moses and the movement which he founded, and the influence of contemporary Canaanite culture on the Israelites who were exposed to it. The latter is an exceptionally complex problem, since the early Hebrews were influenced by their Canaanite neighbours, there were beliefs and practices common to both, and there were later borrowings and adaptations from Canaanite culture during the period of the Judges as well as of the subsequent Monarchy. The picture is, accordingly, by no means simple. Yet we can state definitely that it does not support the extreme position of the late Yehezkel Kaufmann, who maintained in his great 'History of the Faith of Israel'[118] that Mosaic monotheism was a phenomenon entirely peculiar to Israel. According to him, Moses founded Israel, and Israel created monotheism; or, to put it another way, Moses was himself a member of the people which he brought into existence, and because he was an Israelite he was able to create monotheism. Mosaic monotheism was, he thought, a creation of Israelite religious genius, as the intellectual achievements of Greece in the sixth–fourth centuries B.C. were a product of Hellenic secular genius. Neither phenomenon can be explained by ordinary evolutionary processes. According to Kaufmann, the Israelites were completely unable even to understand the nature of polytheism, since it was totally foreign to their entire higher culture. Kaufmann's point of view certainly has an element of truth. Without monotheism, Israel, as we know it, could not have existed. It was indeed Moses who was the principal architect of Israelite monotheism.

118 See the condensed English translation quoted in n. 100, especially pp. 60 ff., 212 ff. and Index, *passim*.

The pious Israelite probably knew little about many pagan beliefs. But, on the other hand, there was so much exchange of cultural influences between Israel and its neighbours on all sides of its tiny territory, and there were so many irruptions of paganism into Israel, that the ignorance presupposed by Kaufmann's view is simply incredible. We shall see that there was profound influence from Phoenicia on the literature of later Israel. This Phoenician contribution was pagan in background, but Israelite authors were able to utilize it without permitting it seriously to distort their monotheistic approach. In much the same way Christian authors of the second–fifth centuries A.D. utilized the literary and philosophical heritage of pagan Greece without allowing it, in general, to paganize their religious outlook.[119]

[119] For the best treatment of this subject yet produced, see Harry Austryn Wolfson, *The Philosophy of the Church Fathers*, vol. I: *Faith, Trinity, Incarnation* (Cambridge, Mass., 1964).

V

The Religious Cultures of Israel and Phoenicia in Periodic Tension

After our descriptions of the background and character of each of the two contrasting religions, one would expect violent conflicts to break out when the two directly confronted one another. Before the tenth century Canaan had influenced Israel strongly, but there is no evidence for a similar impact of Israel on Canaan. In the time of Solomon the Israelites seem to have given something to the Phoenicians as well as to have received much from them. But what they received is certainly far better known to us today, in both earlier and later times.

A. THE PROPHETIC MOVEMENT IN ISRAEL

In some ways the ethical monotheism of early Yahwist faith was not so directly opposed to the crude polytheism of Phoenicia as the prophets of the Hebrew Bible were to Phoenician hierophants. Without the great rebirth of conscience which the entire subsequent world owes to the spiritual revival of the Mosaic movement led by Samuel, the religion founded by Moses could not have flowered into normative Judaism and Christianity.

Many years ago H. Torczyner (Tur Sinai) pointed out that *nābî'*, 'prophet', must be derived from the word which appears in Accadian as *nabā'um*, 'to call (especially of a man by a god)'.[1] More recently the same verb has turned up repeatedly in 'Amorite' proper names at

[1] FSAC², 303, which was independent of H. Torczyner's previous suggestion. See also SBPM, 5 ff.

Mari, with the same use as in Accadian personal names.[2] The *nābî'* was, accordingly, one who was called by God for a special purpose, or who believed that he had received such a call. He was, then, a charismatic religious figure without hereditary right or political appointment, but authorized by his vocation to speak or act for Yahweh. Before the time of Samuel, the term is seldom used. In Gen. 20:7 God says of Abraham, 'he has a call from me', not 'he is a prophet' as vocalized in the Hebrew text.[3] Moses is explicitly contrasted with the *nābî'* class in Num. 12:6–8;[4] and in Ex. 7:1 f. he is to appear before Pharaoh as 'God', while Aaron is to go to Pharaoh as his representative (*nābî'*). In the period of the Judges the later 'prophet' (*nābî'*) was still called 'man of God'—a term that, in the early monarchy, appears simply as a synonym of *nābî'*.

In Chapter I we have discussed a passage quoted in Hosea 12:13 ff., the archaic form of which fixes its origin no later than about the eleventh century B.C.; here we have a clear reference to Moses as a *nābî'* like Samuel:

'Through a prophet did Yahweh bring Israel up from Egypt.'

Even more striking is Jer. 15:1, where Moses and Samuel are mentioned together as possible defenders of Israel at the heavenly assizes: 'And Yahweh said to me, "Even if Moses and Samuel stood before me, I should not favour this people."'[5] Jeremiah evidently considered Samuel as founder of the prophetic movement in Israel, just as Moses was Israel's great teacher and lawgiver.

The description of Samuel's activities after the destruction of Shiloh is extremely interesting. He replaced the

[2] APNMT, 236.
[3] Vocalize probably: *kî nĕbî'î hû'*.
[4] See above, Ch. I, § E.
[5] SBPM, 9.

lost central sanctuary at Shiloh with *meqômôt*, 'places' (I Sam. 7:16), at Bethel, Gilgal and Mizpah. The use of this word as a generic term for local shrines foreshadows a general later use in Hebrew, regardless of whether the cult was Jewish or pagan (cf. Deut. 12:2 f.). Later still it was to be used in Samaritan of the 'tabernacle' on Gerizim.[6] In Aramaic the equivalent *'athrâ* in *'athrâ qaddîšâ*, 'holy place', had a similar semantic development. In any event, the shift which led Samuel and his ecstatic followers to give up the official 'Tabernacle' and its cultic equipment in favour of the ancient Hebrew-Canaanite *bâmôt* is hard to explain unless the idea of fixed holy places had been replacing that of the movable Mosaic shrine for some time.[7]

The religious behaviour associated with these shrines was that of 'revival' groups. In a recent book entitled *Battle for the Mind*,[8] the eminent neuro-psychiatrist, Dr. William Sargant, examines the effects of religious revivals in the history of the Christian church, especially among Quakers, Methodists, and Baptists. Similar phenomena appear also among Muslims and Jews. When tremendous emotional stress is accompanied by continuous dancing and instrumental music, a subject will often go into a trance and become a typical ecstatic. Dr. Sargant is aware of the great power of such methods in stirring up the emotions, which can result not only in brainwashing, but also in true religious conversion, which establishes a reserve for later spiritual life. The two have much in common when seen through the eyes of a perceptive psychologist and neurologist. However, Dr. Sargant's comparisons are not intended to disparage revival experiences—quite the reverse. He emphasizes that religious revivals produce both valuable results and gross

[6] Here I depend largely on still unpublished work of Abram Spiro.

[7] See above, Ch. IV, § D.

[8] *Battle for the Mind* (London, 1958, 1961).

perversions. In human affairs every important mass phenomenon can be used for evil as well as for good, as has always been recognized by careful observers. While it is quite natural for members of an established religious organization to be afraid of such a movement, frequently with good reason, it is also probable that their own organization could not have been established originally without an emotionally supercharged beginning. Although Dr. Sargant does not mention Samuel, the biblical account of Samuel's activities contains elements more characteristic of the situation he describes than Pentecost, or than most revivals among early Quakers, Baptists, and Methodists.[9]

As the founder of a great new movement of unparalleled spiritual significance, Samuel left his stamp indelibly impressed on the pages of religious history. At no other time and in no other place, so far as we know, has there been an institution quite comparable to Israelite prophetism. Though often dishonoured by 'false prophets', it revived again and again. Represented at its best by one great figure after another, it persisted through the five centuries of Israel's life as a nation, and did not die out until after the Restoration. In this light Samuel appears as second only to Moses in his impact on the religious history of Israel.[10]

Samuel was born a Nazirite, vowed to the life of a *nāzîr* by his mother before his birth—apparently a common practice in Israel.[11] He grew up at the tabernacle or temple in Shiloh; he must have been deeply impressed

[9] SBPM, 7 ff.; AHAEBT, 64 f.

[10] On Samuel in general see AHAEBT, 42–65. Both 'JE' and 'D' reflect prophetic editing in the tenth–seventh centuries; the late Edward Robertson even over-emphasized the relation between Samuel and Deuteronomy; see his papers in BJRL and his book *The Old Testament Problem*: *A Re-investigation* (Manchester, 1950).

[11] Evidence from LXX, DSS, Ben Sira and Mishnah. See AHAEBT, 47 f.

by the reported corruption of the priests who officiated there and especially by the ensuing disaster. After the Philistines had won a great victory over Israel near Aphek, they destroyed the temple at Shiloh and slaughtered its priests, as presupposed by Jer. 7:12 ff.; 26:6 ff., favoured by archaeological excavations at Seilûn, and stated explictly in Psalm 78:60, 64.[12]

Israel was now under the heel of the hated Philistine, with the priests scattered and no generally accepted cult of Yahweh left. This new situation made it possible for a mass ecstatic movement to develop with extraordinary rapidity. That this movement was new at the time may be inferred from the numerous references in I Samuel to bands of prophets who, dancing and singing to the accompaniment of musical instruments, worked themselves up into a frenzy, and then fell into trances (see above). References to ecstatic votaries appear in the Mari texts and thereafter in Mesopotamian records, and their generic designation, *maḫḫû*, was also used of madmen, without any clear distinction. Similarly, a Hebrew denominative verb, derived from *nābî'*, is employed in the sense 'to behave like a madman, to rave'. In the Wen-Amun report (c. 1060 B.C.) there is a remarkable reference to an ecstatic who delivers an oracle to Zakar-Baal, king of Byblos.[13] Since this was probably within a decade or two of the fall of Shiloh, we may perhaps suppose that there was some indirect connexion.[14] The movement in Israel may have formed part of a general surge of this phenomenon through south-west Asia, as has not infre-

12 On the date of Psalm 78 see O. Eissfeldt in *Das Lied Moses* . . . (above, Ch. I, notes 41 and 58).

13 For the meaning of the reference see A. Scharff, ZÄS, 1938, 147. The determinative reappears in the Onomasticon of Amenemope, resting on more ancient tradition, together with names of musicians and dancers, with *kumru* = *komer*, 'eunuch priest' (FSAC[2], 234 f., n. 34).

14 See below, § E, on the ecstatic prophets in Phoenicia.

quently been surmised in the past. It may be that it began in Anatolia, where such phenomena were particularly well attested in antiquity. However this may be, in Israel it achieved positive significance, since Samuel, fired with zeal for the reformation of the cult of Yahweh and for the expulsion of the Philistines, was present to give it direction.

We have no indication in our extant tradition that Samuel took any interest after the fall of Shiloh either in the central sanctuary or in the Ark of the Covenant.[15] At first this may seem strange, but a little reflection shows a clear pattern. In the first place, we have often seen how the destruction of a sanctuary led to its abandonment, and even to the complete secularization of its site. This is particularly evident in the case of the sanctuaries at Shechem (see above) and Shiloh. In the latter case Israel was so overwhelmed at the thoroughness of Yahweh's punishment of an allegedly wicked priesthood, that the people looked for spiritual leadership outside the priesthood. In the ecstatic prophets they found a natural substitute for the disgraced priests. In any event the latter had by this time become an established hierarchy, with formalized cultic practices which had developed far beyond the simple liturgy of the original tabernacle. New religious leaders generally organize very simply at first, avoiding the formation of a complex hierarchy—which would remind them of the reasons for their original revolt. Illustrations abound all through the Judaeo-Christian religious tradition.[16] The emergence of the Essenes in the second century B.C. was accompanied by *de facto* sectarian replacement of priests by laymen. Priests were still highly respected in the sect if they were descendants of Zadok, but in the ordinary affairs of the community they were replaced by elders and especially by overseers,

[15] See SBPM, 16 ff. and AHAEBT, 56 ff.
[16] See SBPM, 19 ff. and AHAEBT, 63 ff.

who were to become the prototypes of Christian bishops.[17] Among the Pharisees religious teachers took the place of priests in the practical life of the sect. The *rabbânîm*, or rabbis, were not ordained priests, but laymen who showed unusual knowledge of the law and an unusual talent for interpreting it; they were eventually ordained in their turn.

In Christianity the apostolic church kept only the twelve laymen of the Essenes' governing body of twelve laymen and three priests.[18] However, since it is always necessary to have leaders, Christians began to follow the example of the Jewish sectarians from whose ranks many of them had come, and at an extremely early date—scarcely later than the middle of the first century A.D.—set up *episkopoi*, 'overseers', who became bishops. In the later Christian church the same thing happened over and over again. In the sixth century A.D., for example, the Benedictine order was formed in order to compensate for the over-formalized hierarchic organization of the secular clergy. In the thirteenth and fourteenth centuries the mendicant friars emerged—again in protest against corruption and inefficiency among both secular clergy and religious orders. Just as in later Israel the long-continued tension between priests and prophets led to a remarkably well-balanced structure, so in the Roman church the elaborate system of checks and balances between the secular clergy and the religious organizations has maintained stable equilibrium for several centuries.

In the Reformation there was an even more vigorous change of this kind. Lutherans and Calvinists replaced ordained priests by 'shepherds' of both priestly and lay origin. These pastors soon became the ordained equivalents of the Roman priests. In the eighteenth century John Wesley, though an Anglican all his life, introduced a

[17] See especially the discussion by C. S. Mann in Johannes Munck, *Acts* (Anchor Bible, 1967), Appendix 4.

[18] See C. S. Mann, *loc. cit.*

new system of lay preachers which was directly responsible for Methodism's break with the Church of England. This break was followed by the establishment of a new hierarchic organization in American Methodism. The same phenomenon reappears in some of the youngest Protestant sects. Turning back to the Jews, we note that the Hasidic movement of the eighteenth century replaced orthodox rabbis by saints and miracle workers, who themselves were called rabbis (*rebs*) by their followers. This process is characteristic of any religious movement which, like Judaeo-Christianity, has a built-in tendency to correct its own weaknesses and reorganize its structure in order to keep spiritual devotion and moral action in the forefront of life.

The 'renewal' feature of Israelite prophetism can be documented from the works of the canonical prophets, especially Amos, Micah, Isaiah and Jeremiah. After the prophetic movement died out in the late sixth or fifth century B.C., it was replaced in part by the spread of apocalyptic thinking, which despaired of a solution on earth, and awaited a general catastrophe, national or cosmic, to be followed by a new world under the direct rule of God. This movement also had its roots in the pagan world, as the author has tried to show in still unpublished studies.

There were other exceedingly important aspects of the prophetic movement in pre-exilic times. Continuing the Israelite tradition that the prophets were originally called *rô'îm*, 'diviners' (I Sam. 9:9), as well as the tradition in Chronicles that the synonym *ḥôzîm* was applied to archetype poet-musicians,[19] the prophets of Israel were expected to predict the future and to compose their oracles in good lyric verse. Such emphasis was laid on these points that their message was validated in part by

[19] Cf. below, § E, on Phoenician analogies among the hierophants.

the accuracy of their predictions, and the literary quality of the canonical prophetic oracles is nearly all high.

Though it is very doubtful whether there were true 'cult prophets' in Israel,[20] there were certainly prophets who were also priests, like Jeremiah, or 'singers' (poet-musicians), like Habakkuk. Even Samuel appears as member of the hereditary guild of singers, according to tradition preserved by the Chronicler.[21] The members of prophetic guilds were also custodians of the literary heritage of Israel's faith, especially of the 'JE' and Deuteronomic traditions.[22] To what extent they overlapped the class of scribes is very difficult to estimate on the basis of our available sources. It is becoming increasingly clear that some prophets attained high prestige as advisers to the king, who greatly appreciated favourable oracles. The rôles of Isaiah and Jeremiah, though very different, illustrate this point. The oracles of Amos are even more instructive, since they show that even the poorest citizen might feel duty-bound to speak out as a prophet on delicate points of international significance.[23]

Two recent studies by Delbert Hillers[24] and Isaac Rabinowitz,[25] respectively, throw light on the rôle of the prophet in international relations. Hillers has demonstrated that the sanctions ('curses') invoked by the prophets are substantially identical with the sanctions in

[20] For the classic treatment of this theme see I. Engnell's article 'Profeter' in *Svenskt Bibliskt Uppslagsverk* II (1952), 729 ff.

[21] Cf. SBPM, 26, and on these guilds see ARI^2, 125 ff., 209 ff., 227 f., 230, n. 70, as well as below.

[22] Cf. above, n. 10.

[23] It is still uncertain whether *lô'* in Amos 7:14 is negative or asseverative (as in Amos 1:3, 6, 9, 11, 13; 2:1, 4, 6). Zech. 13:5 is considerably later, but is also rather ambiguous, in spite of the negative attitude taken towards prophets.

[24] *Treaty Curses and the Old Testament Prophets*, Rome, 1964.

[25] 'Towards a Valid Theory of Biblical Hebrew Literature' (*The Classical Tradition . . . in Honor of Harry Caplan*, Ithaca, 1966, pp. 315–28).

contemporary treaties from Syria and Assyria, thus making it virtually certain that these prophets were familiar with diplomacy. Rabinowitz has pointed out that the 'word' of Yahweh as transmitted to foreign lands and rulers by the prophets was believed to embody power far more effective than any ordinary diplomatic exchange could possibly be.

Under § C below I shall discuss the relation between the hierophants of Phoenicia and the prophets and wise men of Israel. In spite of basic differences this relation was closer externally than I, for one, have ever suspected in the past. But superficial resemblances in origin, terminology and function only emphasize the fundamental contrast between the spiritual monotheism of Israel and the physiocentric[26] polytheism of Canaan.

B. PHOENICIA AND PHOENICIAN HIGHER CULTURE

In Chapter III we dealt with the religion of Canaan in the Bronze Age, that is, roughly before the twelfth century B.C. Our evidence came from contemporary texts and excavations, particularly at Ugarit, north of Phoenicia proper. We occasionally drew on later sources, where they corroborated evidence from the Bronze Age. In this chapter our sources are much scantier, for two reasons. Owing to the displacement of clay tablets and cuneiform script by papyrus and sheepskin, on which alphabetic script was written in ink, the available written material is very much reduced by the action of time. Furthermore, strange to say, there has been almost no excavation in Iron Age levels of any Phoenician town or site. Evidence comes chiefly from biblical and classical sources. There are many scattered stone inscriptions, chiefly from North Africa, and there is much Egyptian and Assyrian material for comparison. We are greatly

[26] For this term see HACH, 265.

helped by numerous points of agreement between Bronze Age data from Ugarit and information provided by late Greek writers, which bracket the Iron Age.

In the early Iron Age the political and cultural situation in Phoenicia changed radically.[27] After the thirteenth century B.C. the Canaanites were restricted to Phoenicia proper and its hinterland, with some extension southward along the coast of Palestine and into the low plains of Galilee. Otherwise the area once dominated by Canaanite culture in Syria was in the hands of the Aramaeans, while Israel and the Sea Peoples occupied Palestine. Under Philistine hegemony, the Sea Peoples established control of the eastern Mediterranean, with their cultural foci in Cyprus and the coast of Palestine. From before 1060 B.C.[28] until the middle of David's reign (c. 975 B.C.) the Phoenicians were at the mercy of the Sea Peoples, and were thus unable to expand their sea trade. The power of the Philistines was then destroyed by an alliance between the Tyrian kings Abibaal and his son Hiram (c. 969–936 B.C.), on the one hand, and David on the other.[29] During the middle decades of

[27] See *Historia Mundi* II (1953), 362 ff.; BANE, 340 ff.; CAH^2, II, ch. XXXIII (1966).

[28] For this date of Wen-amûn add 130 years to the accession of Shishak c. 935 B.C. and deduct five years. The latter date is based on the Tyrian chronology as transmitted by Menander of Ephesus through Josephus; see my papers in BASOR 100 (1945), p. 20; 130 (1953), pp. 4 ff.; 141 (1956), pp. 26 f.

[29] This is clear from II Sam. 5:11 and I Kings 5:15, expanded in Chronicles and Phoenician records cited by Josephus, *Apion* I, 108 ff. Note that, as pointed out by M. Rowton, BASOR 119 (1950), pp. 20 ff., the Tyrian date for the building of Solomon's Temple agrees exactly with mine. As proved by W. L. Moran, citing the observations of J. A. Montgomery, *Kings* (ICC, 1951), 132 ff., in CBQ XXV (1963), 77 ff., the word *'ôhēb*, used of Hiram's relation to David, refers specifically to political ties of alliance. The usual cavalier disregard of clear biblical evidence is not 'critical' but just the opposite. See also H. Huffmon, BASOR 181 (1966), 31 ff.

the tenth century B.C., the foundations of a great maritime empire were laid.

There was no great competing Mediterranean power at the time, so the new Tyro-Sidonian empire rapidly established trading stations in different parts of the Mediterranean in order to barter for the mineral wealth of Cyprus, Sardinia and north-western Spain. Before the end of the tenth century there were Phoenician ports in Cyprus (Citium) and Sardinia (Tarshish),[30] as well as probably at Gades (Cadiz) in Spain and Utica in North Africa. Direct evidence is lacking for such intermediate stations as Malta and Motya. The biblical tradition about Hiram's fleets of ore-carrying vessels (*'ŏnîyôt Taršîš*) in the time of Solomon is completely in accord with our present evidence, though every new piece of concrete evidence will be welcome. When we remember how rapidly the Spaniards spread over the New World between 1492 and 1542, by which time Chile had become a province, the coast of California had been explored, and the Philippines had been discovered by Magellan and were already being colonized, there is no difficulty in accepting a comparable speed of expansion on the part of the Phoenician mariners and traders. After all, their ships were built of the splendid forest trees of Lebanon, hewn

[30] Since Sardinia was, next to Cyprus, the principal source of copper ore in the Mediterranean, it is really unimportant whether *Taršîš* was originally a Phoenician word for 'refinery' or a non-Semitic place-name in Sardinia. In either case the connexion with Tharros, where quite early Phoenician remains (e.g., D. B. Harden, *The Phoenicians* [1962], pp. 30 f., etc.) have been found, would stand. It must be remembered that Greek *rr* often stands for earlier *rs*, as in Attic Τυρρηνοί = Doric Τυρσανοι (the Tursha = Etruscans). [The new 5-line Phoenician inscription 'Hispania 14' from Seville (M. Solá Solé, *Rivista degli Studi Orientali* XLI [1966], 97–108), probably from the early eighth century B.C., favours an early date for Phoenician colonization in both Spain and Sardinia. On the ninth-century Nora stone see most recently BASOR 180, 42.]

and shaped with iron tools for the first time in history. They did not need the magnetic compass of the Spaniards, since they sailed in the dry season, when the sky was seldom overcast for long. In addition, the then recent development of the art of building watertight cisterns made it possible to provide island strongholds such as Tyre and Arvad, Malta and Motya, with plenty of fresh water. (In the Amarna Age Tyre was still dependent on the mainland for water.)

The wealth of the Tyro-Sidonian empire became fabulous, and the arts and crafts flourished as never before. Our concrete evidence is still restricted chiefly to ivories and work in gold, silver, and bronze, since the even more important work in woods of Lebanon, dyed and embroidered textiles, and leather has disappeared—until some chance find in a desert cache like the caves of Murabba'at, brings samples to light. Israel was one of the chief indirect beneficiaries of the rapidly expanding wealth of Phoenicia, since virtually the entire western boundary of North Israel was shared with the Tyro-Sidonian state in most periods of the Monarchy. From Tyre south the Israelite border can seldom have averaged over ten miles from the Phoenician coast. Israel provided agricultural products and manpower; it also controlled the shortest caravan routes between Arabia and Phoenicia. Even when Phoenicia was dominated by Assyria and Babylonia its commerce remained enormous; cf. Ezek. 27–28.

Probably the most characteristic feature of Phoenician civilization in the first millennium B.C. was its dependence on Egyptian motifs and prototypes. During the Pyramid Age (Dyn. IV–VI) and the Middle Kingdom (Dyn. XII) Byblos had been the most important foreign colony of Egypt. Before the end of the nineteenth century B.C. it became an autonomous vassal state, which retained its Egyptian culture down at least into the early

Hyksos period, after c. 1700 B.C.[31] Rib-Adda, prince of Byblos about 1370 B.C., assures Pharaoh that his city is as Egyptian as Memphis.[32] A few years later the official scribe of Abimilku of Tyre wrote a whole series of letters to Akhenaten in the customary Babylonian cuneiform, but the numerous mistakes, use of Egyptian words and translations of Egyptian verse into Accadian prove that he was himself an Egyptian.[33]

Phoenicia's awareness of its debt to Egypt is well illustrated by the Wen-Amun report, dating from shortly before the middle of the eleventh century B.C. In this report an Egyptian envoy named Wen-Amun tells the story of his adventurous mission to Byblos on behalf of Ḥrḥor, high priest of Thebes. With the necessary authorization from Smendes, first king of the Tanite Dynasty in the north-eastern Delta, the envoy sailed up the coast of Palestine and Phoenicia in order to procure timber for the construction of a new barque for the god Amun at Thebes. In the past this account was generally regarded as a romance, but J. Černý has demonstrated conclusively that it was actually an official report. The author, whatever his success as a diplomat, was certainly a man of letters, and he was also an accurate observer, apparently writing down just what he saw and heard.[34] (This does not, of course, mean that he reported incidents that might reflect on his judgment or honesty!)

Wen-Amun puts the following words into the mouth of Zakar-baal: 'See, Amun created thunder in heaven when he gave Baal his kingdom. For when Baal founded

[31] BASOR 179 (1965), 38 ff.

[32] EA 84, lines 37 f.; 139, lines 8 f.

[33] JEA XXIII (1937), 190–203.

[34] On the Wen-Amun report as an official document see J. Černý, *Revue d'Égyptologie*, VI (1949), 41, n. 8, and *Paper and Books in Ancient Egypt* (London, 1947), p. 22. On its historical value see my remarks, *Studies Presented to David Moore Robinson* (St. Louis, 1951), 203–31, and B. Mazar, *The Israel Academy of Sciences and Humanities, Proceedings*, I:7 (1964), pp. 3 ff.

all lands, he founded them after first founding the land of Egypt, whence thou comest; for craftsmanship issued from it to reach the region where I am, and instruction issued from it to reach the region where I am.'[35] Zakar-baal was not necessarily trying to flatter the Egyptian envoy; he was simply stating what most Phoenicians probably regarded as the plain truth. Similarly, in Gen. 10, which has long been recognized as an adaptation of a Phoenician model of some sort,[36] Canaan appears as one of the sons of Ham, that is, as a younger brother of Egypt.

In the Ugaritic epics, dating in their extant form before c. 1365, but composed much earlier, there is little evidence for direct Egyptian influence on any phase of Canaanite mythology. The only clear case is the identification of Koshar (*Kôthar*) with Ptaḥ of Memphis, which recurs in the Sidonian cosmogony of Mochus, as we shall see. The latter appears to be a mixture of elements from Phoenician and Egyptian sources. That the account of it which was transmitted by Damascius, a Neo-Platonist of the fifth century A.D., is substantially correct, seems clear, once we have discarded his post-Platonic theosophy.[37] There are several undeniably Egyptian elements in the accounts of the Sidonian cosmogony attributed by Damascius to Eudemus (fourth century B.C.) and Mochus. The latter seems to be more reliable; Eudemus' informer may have been inadequately informed himself. First in the scheme of Mochus came (in Greek translation)

[35] See JAOS LXXI (1951), 261. The previously enigmatic *mlk.f* is simply 'his kingdom', Can. *mulk*, not *milk* (from *mălĭk*), 'king'. The syntax has been revised after F. Hintze, *Untersuchungen*, II (1952), p. 261.

[36] It is obvious from the place-names of Ezek. 27, which certainly rests on Phoenician sources, that most of the names in Gen. 10 were also derived through Phoenicia.

[37] It was this secondary theosophical dress, borrowed from Middle Platonic and Stoic sources, which led earlier scholars to consider the data in question as worthless.

Aithēr and *Aēr* (= *Aēr* and *Aura* according to Eudemus). From them was born the Phoenician *Ūlōmos*, who begot the Phoenician *Chūsōr* by masturbation, like Atum and other Egyptian creator-gods. *Chūsōr* created the cosmic egg, which he then split into heaven and earth in his name as the 'Opener' (*Anoigeus* = Ptaḥ; see below). Here we have elements of the creation myths of Memphis (Ptaḥ) and Heliopolis (Atum). (As is well known, there was some confusion in later times between the cosmogonies of these two neighbouring cult centres, as well as with the cosmogony of Hermopolis Magna.) Among such elements are: Ptaḥ as creator, the cosmic egg,[38] and masturbation as the chief method of divine procreation.

The date of Mochus would be quite obscure if he were not obviously a native Phoenician writer.[39] The relative archaism of the cosmogony of Mochus is obvious when it is compared to the highly sophisticated cosmogony of Taauth, handed down to us by Sanchuniathon in the sixth century B.C. (see below).

Thanks to Eusebius of Caesarea, who wrote his *Praeparatio Evangelica* in the early fourth century A.D., we possess a substantial transcript of the mythological part of the 'Phoenician History' of Philo Byblius. According to Eusebius, Philo (who wrote in Greek c. A.D. 100) quoted faithfully from Sanchuniathon, who had written in Phoenician, drawing in his turn on such older sources as the 'Cosmogony of Taauth'. Moreover, the meticulous accuracy with which Eusebius reproduced his sources, wherever we can check his quotations, was demonstrated

[38] See Siegfried Morenz, 'Ägypten und die altorphische Kosmogonie', in *Aus Antike und Orient* (*Festschrift Wilhelm Schubart*, Leipzig, 1950), pp. 64–111. Note Eduard Meyer's recovery of two references to the cosmic egg in the Mochus tradition (GA II:2[2] [1931], p. 180, n. 2).

[39] The name is not *Moschus* (e.g., in WM), but a hypocoristic Μωχος = Punic *MKY* or Hebrew *Mākî* (or a parallel **MK'*).

conclusively by the late Karl Mras.[40] Since the decipherment of the Ugaritic texts there has been a steady flow of material (still continuing) to confirm the statements of Philo Byblius about Phoenician mythology. That Phoenician was still written (and read) is certain from coins of the third century A.D. inscribed in Phoenician.[41]

It is no longer possible to suppose that the work of Philo Byblius is full of secondary Greek euhemeristic speculations. We know now that simple euhemerism was common in the ancient Orient.[42] Furthermore, the Phoenician milieu in which Sanchuniathon lived was favourable to demythologizing—though scarcely in a monotheistic sense.[43] Although Sanchuniathon makes little effort to distinguish between the pantheons and myths of different cities, it must be observed that by the sixth century B.C.—to say nothing of Philo in the late first century A.D.—it was probably no longer possible to distinguish the sources of particular myths or divine figures. A gradual transfusion of practices and beliefs, resulting from extensive trade and movement of population between Phoenician cities, must have rendered any such analysis extremely difficult, if not impossible.

[40] See especially his lecture on 'Die Stellung der *Praeparatio Evangelica* des Eusebius im antiken Schrifttum' (Vienna Academy: *Anzeiger, Phil.-hist. Klasse,* 1956:17, 209–17).

[41] IEJ IV (1954), 8 (reign of Gordian, A.D. 238–244).

[42] Note especially the Sumerian King Lists and fragments of chronicles (see especially Jacobsen, *The Sumerian King List* [Chicago, 1939]), where names of gods and human beings are interspersed. Still more important for us is the Turin Papyrus, copied in the thirteenth century B.C. and beginning with a long list of gods (Rē', Geb, Osiris, Seth, Horus, Thoth, etc.). All regnal years preserved are abnormally long, just as in the case of early Sumerian rulers.

[43] For this see especially the discussions in my forthcoming volume 'Experience on the Road to Reason: Phoenicia, Israel and Ionia'. The demonstration will also be given in more concise form in my study 'Neglected Factors in the Greek Intellectual Revolution', to appear in PAPS.

While we cannot date Mochus with any confidence, Sanchuniathon was a refugee from Tyre who settled in Berytus about the second quarter of the sixth century B.C.[44] In my opinion the cosmogony of Mochus is older and may easily go back to the seventh or eighth century B.C., if not earlier.

But the cosmogonies of Sanchuniathon and Mochus were much earlier than the time of these writers. In Sanchuniathon there are a number of very archaic forms, such as *Taauth* for *Ṭăḥáwtĕ* (later *Thōth*), and *Thūrō* (*Thourō*) for *Tĕwūrĕ* (later *Thoēris*).[45] Both these names have kept their New Kingdom pronunciation in Phoenician; accordingly they cannot have been taken over from Egyptian after the thirteenth century B.C. Moreover, the designation of Kôshar (late Phoenician *Kûšōr*) by Damascius as the 'Opener' (*Anoigeus*) means that the name *Ptaḥ* had been explained as *pattāḥ*, with the same sense. Again we have to reckon with the change of *pattāḥ* to *pattōḥ* between c. 1200 and 1000 B.C.—this time in Phoenician. This phonological point is quite independent of the fact that a specific connexion is made in the Baal and Aqhat Epics between Kôshar and Memphis, Ptaḥ's home. It is by no means impossible that the identification of Kôshar with Ptaḥ goes back to the Pyramid Age (see Chapter III).

The Tyrian cosmogony of Sanchuniathon was based on a very ancient Hermopolite myth of the beginning, centring around Thoth, the patron divinity of Hermopolis Magna in early Middle Egypt. That Taauth was indeed

[44] For details see above, n. 43; the evidence is much stronger than I should have expected twenty-five years ago, when I did not venture to date Sanchuniathon more closely than between 700 and 500 B.C. (e.g., FSAC [1940 ed.], 243, 334 [= 1957 ed., 230, 317 f.]), though I then preferred the seventh century.

[45] E.g. *Tȝ-wr.t*, lit., 'The Great One'. Before the twelfth century B.C. long (accented) *ē* in an open syllable was regularly *ū*; see VESO, 16–18, and for the corresponding masculine *Pȝ-wr*, Amarna *Pawuru, Pauru*, etc., see JNES v (1946), 19.

Thoth was well known to all these writers, including Eusebius. (For his rôle as a Phoenician hierophant and a Hebrew sage, see below.) Taauth is called by Sanchuniathon 'the wisest man that ever was under the sun'. The expression 'under the sun'—one of the most characteristic Phoenician traits in this account—is, of course, characteristic of the strongly Phoenicianizing book of Ecclesiastes (see below), and also appears in Sidonian inscriptions from the fifth century B.C., as well as occasionally in the dramas of Euripides, also from the fifth century B.C. The use of this expression sheds light only on the date of Sanchuniathon, not on that of the Taauth cosmogony, which was certainly older.[46]

C. PHOENICIAN AND ISRAELITE RELIGION IN CONTACT

Turning from late compilations back to primary sources, we have a most valuable Iron Age pantheon of Tyre preserved in the treaty concluded between Esarhaddon of Assyria and Baal of Tyre in the early seventh century B.C.[47] In the last section of the preserved part of the treaty is a list of the deities called upon to sanction details of the treaty, first those of Assyria, followed by an enigmatic line of divinities with Aramaic names,[48] then

[46] Cf. Uvo Hölscher, *Hermes* LXXXI (1953), 394. Hölscher is clearly right about the Semitic character of the verse underlying the condensed translation of the original poem into Greek prose, but there is no trace of second-millennium repetitive style. I should date the original poem between the tenth and eighth centuries B.C. —i.e., before the time of Gen. 1–2:3a.

[47] See R. Borger, *Die Inschriften Asarhaddons Königs von Assyrien* (AfO, Beiheft 9, Graz, 1956), 107–9 and pls. iii–iv.

[48] See Col. IV:6 with Borger's discussion in VT VII (1957), 102 ff. The paired names ^{d}*Bait*(*i*)-*ILĀNI*^{pl} and ^{d}*Anat*(*i*)-*ba*[*it*(*i*)-*IL*]-*ĀNI*^{pl} are, therefore, reasonably certain, and reflect Aramaic names **Bait-'elâhayyâ* and *'*Anat-bait-'elâhayyâ*, 'House-of-the-Gods' and 'Anath-of-the-House-of-the-Gods'. Some 250 years later these Ara-

the Phoenician deities of Tyre. First come three Baals: ^{d}*Ba-al-sa-me-me*, ^{d}*Ba-al-ma-la-ge-e*, and ^{d}*Ba-al-ṣa-pu-na*, followed by Melcarth (*Milqartu*) of Tyre, Eshmun (*Iasumunu*) of Sidon, and 'Ashtart (*Astartu*).[49] These three are called upon in the curse formula to punish any violator of the treaty by sending storms against the ships, tearing up mooring-posts, causing the ships to be swamped by mighty seas. It is particularly interesting to find the god Baal-shamêm here as a Tyrian deity, since, while the cult of the Lord of Heaven is so far unattested in Bronze Age Canaan proper, it becomes very important in Iron Age Phoenicia. That it had been known farther north in Syria is shown by a number of references to ^{d}*IM-ša-me-e* = Can. *Ba'al-šamêm* in fourteenth-century treaties between the Hittites and Ugarit.[50] The oldest reference to it in Phoenicia proper is in a Byblian inscription dating from the tenth century B.C.[51] The name *Baal-malagê* has certainly been misread. But there is a simple solution at hand. We have only to read the sign *ad* for the middle *la* (which is almost identical in form), and we have *Baal-madgê*, meaning something like 'Lord of Fishing (Fishery)'.[52] It

---

maic gods appear at Elephantine as 'Bethel' and 'Anath-bethel'. See for my latest published views (which require modification today) ARI (1956 ed.), 173 f.; 222, n. 132; 230, n. 74.

[49] Note that Assyrian *s* and *š* (in normal Accadian spelling) were pronounced *š* and *s* respectively, as we know from a host of transcriptions in both directions.

[50] Cf. several passages in PRU IV including Nos. 17, 227, line 51 (p. 43); 17, 340, line 17 (p. 51), to which Dr. Hillers has called my attention. In the Amarna Tablets, ^{d}*IM* stands for Baal as well as for Adad.

[51] In the Yeḥîmilk inscription; see JAOS LXVII (1947), 157 and n. 34.

[52] This may be the meaning of Ugar. *mdgt* in Aqhat I:147. The line was plausibly read *yqbrnn . bmdgt . bknrt* by G. A. Barton, JBL LX, 217; I suggest rendering 'They (?) buried him (?) in the fishing place at Kinnereth' = Tell el-'Oreimeh on the Sea of Galilee,

would be equivalent to *dûgāh*, if this word has been correctly preserved in the MT of Amos 4:9. This divinity may be the fisherman of the sea-goddess Asherah (*dgy 'Aṯrt*), mentioned twice in the Baal Epic. Melqart and Eshmun are to lay the country waste and take away food, clothing and oil. Astarte, the goddess of war, is invoked to destroy the weapons of the Tyrians in the event of their rebelling against Assyria.

The figure of Ba'al-shamêm (Aram. *Be'el-šamên*) has never been adequately explained, so far as I know, though a valuable paper was devoted to the subject by Otto Eissfeldt in 1939.[53] The original identity of the divinity might have been recognized long ago, if the Aramaic inscription published by J. A. Montgomery in 1907[54] and studied by M. Lidzbarski somewhat later[55] had been taken seriously. The inscription was found in Cilicia and dates from about the fifth century B.C.; it invokes the sanctions of Be'el-shamên 'the great', and of the Aramaic moon-god Sahar and sun-god Shamash upon the violator of a boundary. In other words, Ba'al-shamêm was neither the moon nor the sun, but a god who was above both. This god was presumably the same as the South-Arabic Dhū-samāwi, 'Lord of Heaven', properly 'Athtar, god of Venus-in-the-Morning, and thus equivalent to the North-Arabic *Atar-samayin* of the seventh century B.C.[56] i.e., Aram. *'Attar-šamayin*, 'Morning Star of Heaven'. The reason why the name is so rare in the Bronze Age is simply that the appellation only began to displace the original name towards the end of the Bronze Age, centuries after the appellation *Ba'al* had displaced

---

with M.B. and L.B. remains, including a basalt stele fragment from the fifteenth century B.C. (cf. JEA XIV [1928], 36 ff.).

[53] 'Ba'alšamēm und Jahwe', OEKS II, 171–98.

[54] JAOS XXVIII (1907), 164 ff.

[55] *Ephemeris*, III, 64.

[56] In inscriptions of Esarhaddon and Asshurbanapal. Note again that the Assyrian pronunciation of the sibilant was reversed.

Hadad (Adad). The cult of Ba'al-shamêm was probably in the act of sweeping over Phoenicia in the tenth century B.C., as acutely observed by B. Mazar.[57] Besides the reference in the inscription of Yeḥimilk of Byblos, cited above, where Ba'al-shamêm is placed at the head of the pantheon, even before Ba'al-gebal himself, there are very important statements by Dius and Menander, quoted by Josephus.[58] The latter, who got his material from good Tyrian sources, states that Hiram, son of Abibal, 'dedicated the pillar of gold in the (temple) of Zeus'; the inscription was presumably visible for several centuries. Dius also mentions the building of 'the temple (*hieron*) of the Olympian Zeus'[59] explicitly. Menander further mentions Hiram's construction of sanctuaries (*naoi*) for Heracles (Melcarth) and Astarte. Evidently the cult of Ba'al-shamêm occupied a favoured place in Phoenicia at the time of Solomon!

There is an extraordinary tradition preserved by Sanchuniathon about the beginnings of the cult of Ba'al-shamêm (*Praep. Evang.*, I, 10, 7). It is said of the offspring of the primordial human pair, Genos and Genea, that they 'populated Phoenicia, and when droughts came, they raised their hands skyward towards the sun. The latter, he [Sanchuniathon] says, they considered as the only god, lord of heaven,[60] whom they call Beelsamēn, that is "Lord of Heaven" in Phoenician, and Zeus in Greek.' It is possible that this curious story goes back to an identification of the head of the Tyrian pantheon with the Egyptian sun-god (Aten) in the Amarna period,

57 *Israel Academy of Sciences and Humanities*, I, No. 7, pp. 19 f.

58 *Apion*, I, 113, 118 f.

59 On Ba'al-shamêm = Zeus Olympios in the early second century B.C. see, e.g., Elias Bickermann, *Der Gott der Makkabäer* (Berlin, 1937), pp. 90 ff., and O. Eissfeldt, *op. cit.* (n. 53), pp. 191 f.

60 The Greek text has clearly: '. . . θεὸν . . . μόνον οὐρανοῦ . . .', without variant readings.

when Tyre became the personal property of Meritaten (*Mayāti*).[61] This might account for the otherwise undocumented identification of the god with the sun.

However this may be, Mazar has made a plausible case (on other grounds), for recognizing some direct connexion between the cult of Ba'al-shamêm and Hiram's association with Solomon in planning, building, and equipping the Temple in Jerusalem. According to the data transmitted by Josephus, the temple was built (i.e., founded) in the twelfth year of Hiram, which overlapped the fourth year of Solomon, c. 958 B.C.[62]

G. Ernest Wright and I have written at length about the extent to which the Temple of Solomon reflects Phoenician culture, in architecture, art, and cultic furnishings.[63] We now know much more about the evolution of the plan itself, thanks to the work of Y. Yadin at Hazor (Late Bronze)[64] and to the finds of M. Dunand at Byblos (early Middle Bronze).[65] The former shows the same tripartite division along an axis running lengthwise; the passage from each section to the next is longer and narrower than in the Temple of Solomon. The much earlier structure at Byblos shows three sections at angles to one another, with still longer passages between them. It was thus impossible to see through the building along the axis. It is likely that the longitudinal axis was introduced into the tripartite scheme under Egyptian influence, perhaps in the latter part of the Middle Bronze. The familiar model of Solomon's temple and of the sanctuary of Ta'yinat in North Syria is probably no earlier than the end of the second millennium.

61 EA, No. 155, *passim*. On this letter see above, n. 33.

62 See M. Rowton, BASOR 119, 20 ff.

63 ARI², 142–55; WBA, 129–45.

64 IEJ IX (1959), 81 ff.; *Hazor*, III–IV (Jerusalem, 1961), pls. ci–cxxix.

65 *Fouilles de Byblos*, II, *Textes*, Part 2 (Paris, 1958), especially Fig. 767 on pp. 640–1; see also BASOR 155 (1959), p. 32.

There is a striking reflection of Phoenician imagery in the short poetic dedication preserved in the Hebrew text of I Kings 8:12 f. and the corresponding Greek text in the same chapter, verse 53a, which contains a line lost or deleted in MT. With due caution we may render (3+3:3+3):

Yahweh hath created[66] the sun in heaven—
  Doth He desire[67] to tent in the storm clouds?[68]
Truly I have built Him a majestic house,
  A dais on which to be enthroned for ever!

Here Yahweh is placed above both Ba'al-shamêm, Lord of the Morning Star, whose chief glory is the sun, and Ba'al-ṣaphôn, the older Hadad, Lord of the Storm. One must, however, note that there seems to have been an actual quasi-monotheistic current among some Phoenicians and most Aramaeans, which attributed a place to Ba'al-shamêm far above all other divinities of their pantheons. For instance, Zakir, king of Hamath in the early eighth century, in setting up a stele to his north-Mesopotamian god Iluwer, ascribes all successes of his life to Be'el-shamayin. It is more than likely that the Israelites of the tenth century B.C. played a considerable rôle in encouraging this quasi-monotheistic movement, though they can scarcely be credited with the Egyptianizing identification of the god in question with the sun, as we have just seen.

A curious episode in the Baal Epic, where 'Athtar tries

66 For the best treatment of this text see J. A. Montgomery, *Kings* (ICC), pp. 189 ff. My own rendering is new. For Greek ἐγνώρισεν lit. 'he made known', render probably 'he created' (cf. Acc. *šuma nabû*, 'to call by name' = 'create'). The often proposed *hēkîn* would also mean 'he created' in Phoenician.

67 Read perhaps *ḥamád* = *baḥár*, 'to choose', instead of *'amár* (MT, LXX).

68 Heb. *'rpl* cannot mean 'black darkness' (LXX γνόφος) but 'storm cloud(s)', *'rp* in Ugaritic. Actually the strange εκνοφου of GB should probably be read ἐκ νέφου, 'from a cloud'.

to usurp the throne of Baal while he is in the underworld, suggests that there had actually been intense rivalry between the Canaanite followers of Hadad Ba'al-ṣaphôn and the adherents of 'Athtar at an early date, well before the middle of the second millennium. The defeat of 'Athtar is vividly described in a Canaanite mythological dirge quoted in the seventh or sixth century B.C. (Is. 14:12 ff.):

How hast thou fallen from heaven,
  Helel, son of Shaḥar (Dawn)!
Thou didst say in thy heart,
  'I will ascend to heaven,
Above the circumpolar stars (*kôkăbê 'El*)[69]
  I will raise my throne
And I will dwell on the Mount of Council
  In the back of the north (*ṣāphôn*);
I will mount on the back of a cloud,
  I will be like unto 'Elyôn (= Baal).'

There must have been intense hostility between the priests and votaries of Melcarth, lord of Tyre, and the followers of Ba'al-shamêm. About the middle of the ninth century B.C. the cult of Melcarth had not only taken Israel and Judah by storm, but had also been accepted by Ben-hadad of Syria.[70] A few years later Israel and Judah had risen against the foreign intruders and we hear no more of Melcarth among the Aramaeans. On the contrary, Be'el-shamên had regained his prestige, as we know from the Zakir inscription (see above). Melcarth had become the chief god of Carthage, Tyre's chief colony, and c. 450 B.C. Herodotus (II. 44) places the gold monument which Menander and Dius locate in the temple of Olympian Zeus (= Ba'al-shamêm), in one of the

[69] This phrase (also found in the Phoenician inscription from Pyrgi, c. 500 B.C.) refers to the far northern stars which never set (Eg. *iḫmw sk*); it symbolizes eternity.

[70] BMB III, 65–76; BASOR 84 (1941), 7–12; G. Levi della Vida, BASOR 90 (1943), 30–2.

two temples of Heracles; Zeus is not mentioned at all. Of course Tyre had been destroyed by the Chaldaeans c. 572 B.C.,[71] but the loss of influence on the part of Baʿal-shamêm remains noteworthy.

The official foundation of the Tyrian colony at Carthage in 814 B.C., according to the oldest and most solidly established Phoenician tradition, brought with it the introduction of a slightly modified pantheon. The chief deities of Carthage ('New Town' = *Qart-ḥadašt*) were Baʿal-ḥammôn, Melcarth, and Tennît ('Tanit'). We have already discussed the names and have touched briefly on the functions of the divinities in question. Following Greek identifications (at least in the first two cases), the Romans identified them with their own Saturn (Greek *Kronos*), Hercules (*Heraklēs*), and Juno (especially in her rôle of *virgo caelestis*).

One of the most significant aspects of Punic religion consists in its archaic appearance and secondary specialization. The name of the chief god, *Baʿal-ḥammôn*, 'Lord of the Brazier',[72] first appears in Syria together with *Baʿal-ṣmd*, 'Lord of the Mace',[73] and *Rakkâb-el* in the inscription of Kilamuwa of Sham'al (Zincirli), c. 825 B.C. The sequence of gods corresponds, as pointed out by B. Landsberger,[74] with the three gods listed in two inscriptions of the eighth century from the same city: Hadad, El, and Rakkâb-el. That the 'Lord of the Mace' is a form of Hadad is obvious, and the identification of Baʿal-ḥammôn with El follows naturally. This combina-

[71] For this date see the convincing paper by O. Eissfeldt (OEKS II, 1 ff.).

[72] This underlying meaning was established in ARI[1] (1942), 215 f., and was first applied to Ba'al-ḥammân by J. Février, JA CCXLVIII (1960), 179, but his association of the name with the sun will not do—Saturn was certainly not Helios nor Apollo.

[73] Since Baal smites Yam with a *ṣmd* in the epic, and since he is often depicted with a mace, this rendering is much more probable than the usual 'team (of horses)'.

[74] *Sam'al* (Ankara, 1948), pp. 45 ff.

tion provides a clue to the nature of the chief god of Carthage. Sanchuniathon furnishes the complementary evidence by describing: (1) how Elos (=Kronos), in order to stop a destructive plague, sacrificed his only (*monogenēs*) son to his father Heaven (*Ūranos*), introducing the practice of circumcision to commemorate the occurrence; (2) how Elos, during a great war, sacrificed his only son by 'the nymph Anobret', after dressing him in royal attire and preparing a special altar.

We are not told by Philo Byblius how the sacrifice was performed, but in Carthage Ba'al-ḥammôn (=El) was honoured down to the third century A.D. by having children sacrificed as burnt offerings—presumably to recall the debt which the Phoenicians owed to him for his own sacrifices to save their forefathers. That El should be the patron of human sacrifice may seem strange, in view of the fact that he appears in early sources as the 'Merciful One' (*d̲û-pe'di, d̲û-ṯôbi*, etc.),[75] but it is only another of the many paradoxes exhibited by polytheism everywhere.

Greek and Roman authors have provided us with a wealth of information about the practice of human sacrifice in Phoenicia and North Africa.[76] Thus Quintus Curtius (first century A.D.), the chronicler of Alexander's campaigns, says that when the inhabitants of Tyre were threatened by Alexander's siege of the city, they decided to resort to a practice which had been in disuse for centuries, namely, revival of the institution of human sacrifice in order to appease the anger of the gods. From his statement we might infer that it had been abandoned for 'many centuries' (*multis saeculis*), but we may safely limit ourselves to several centuries (see below). In any event, it was still being practised in Phoenicia when the early Punic colonies in the western Mediterranean were founded (tenth to eighth centuries B.C.). Among classical

[75] See F. M. Cross, Jr., HTR LV (1962), and Heb. *'El ḥannûn we-reḥûm*, 'God, merciful and gracious'.

[76] See the bibliography given by W. Röllig in WM, 300.

authors who have transmitted details about the burning of children as sacrifices to Kronos (Saturnus) are especially Diodorus Siculus (first century B.C., on events of the late fourth century B.C.) and Tertullian (late second century A.D.). Diodorus followed Timaeus, a Sicilian who was contemporary with the events in question, whereas Tertullian was himself an African of pagan parentage, whose background in law gave him valuable information about the efforts of successive Roman emperors to stamp out the practice of human sacrifice.

In spite of the documentation available in pagan and Christian sources about human sacrifice in Phoenicia and Carthage, the rationalistic critics of the nineteenth and early twentieth centuries refused to believe that the reports had any basis, especially since archaeological work seemed not to furnish any support.

In 1921 the situation changed with the discovery at Carthage of a pointed stele from about the third century B.C. dedicated to Tennît (as shown by the symbols), with the representation of a priest holding a human infant in the usual position for offering a lamb.[77] This isolated find was followed in 1930 by the discovery at Ngaus in eastern Algeria of five stelae inscribed in Latin, dating from the second or third century A.D.[78] From these texts there emerged interesting variations of a dedicatory formula 'To the holy lord Saturn (Ba'al-ḥammôn), a great sacrifice of night-time (*sacrum magnum nocturnum*), *molchomor*, breath for breath, blood for blood, life for life'. It was quickly pointed out that the Punic expression corresponded exactly to an already published *MLK 'MR*, the second part of which was known to mean 'lamb' in Punic (as in Ugaritic and Aramaic).

The finds at Ngaus made it possible to explain previously excavated stelae from el-Ḥofra (Roman Cirta, near

[77] For an excellent photograph see Jacques Allibert, *Archéologia* I:1 (1964), 82.

[78] MOPH, 1 ff.

Constantine in eastern Algeria). Among the 1875 finds were pre-Christian Punic inscriptions, some of which replaced *MLK 'MR* by *MLK 'DM*, occasionally followed by the words *BŠR(M) BTM*.[79] Evidently there had been an increasing tendency to substitute a lamb for a child, a fact which would explain the substitutionary formula 'life for life', etc.

In 1935 Otto Eissfeldt published a monograph[80] in which he brought the evidence together, combining it with the data for biblical 'Moloch'. He showed convincingly that *mōlek* was a sacrificial term and not the name of a Canaanite divinity. Punic *molk* and Heb. *mōlek* (vocalized correctly by MT) are in fact the same word, and both refer to a sacrifice which was, for Phoenicians and Hebrews alike, the most awe-inspiring of all possible sacred acts—whether it was considered as holy or as an abomination. Reception of Eissfeldt's drastic reinterpretation of the meaning of 'Moloch' was mixed; most accepted it, with slight modifications here and there.[81] There are probably few competent scholars who now believe that a god Moloch is intended in any biblical passage referring to human sacrifice.

Meanwhile, exploration has continued, with increasing success.

[79] There has been much discussion of the meaning of this expression. Since G. Levi della Vida's demonstration that *btm* was rendered in Latin (first century A.D.) *de sua pecunia* (Accademia dei Lincei, *Rendiconti*, Ser. VIII, Vol. IV, fasc. 7–10 [1949], pp. 400–5), the meaning 'paid with his own funds' has been widely accepted (e.g., by H. Cazelles, *Dictionnaire de la Bible: Supplément* v [1957], 1341—but contrast J. Février, JA CCXLVIII [1960], 172). I should, however, prefer to equate it with Heb. *be-tōm*, and render 'completely'. In the Lepcis inscription it would mean '(paid) in full'. Our formula then means '(whose) body (cf. Prov. 14:30) (is) intact'.

[80] MOPH. Cf. my enthusiastic review in JPOS XV (1935), 344, as well as my more nuanced statement in ARI[1] (1942), 162 ff.

[81] The only real difficulty came with the discovery of a place-name *Ilummuluk* or *Ilumalik* at Mari; see below.

In 1950, seventy-five years after the first important discovery of stelae with Punic inscriptions at Cirta (el-Ḥofra), came the sensational find of no fewer than 700 stelae (or fragments), over 300 of which were inscribed. This lot, which covers at least seven centuries, was admirably published in 1955; a number of these Punic texts mention *MLK 'DM* as well as *MLK 'MR*, thus notably increasing our documentation.[82]

About 1920, stelae of the same types began to be found by natives in Carthage itself, in the area which became known as the 'Precinct of Tanit', now generally called the 'Tophet'. In 1925 excavations were carried out by a Franco-American expedition headed by Francis W. Kelsey, with Donald Harden among its members.[83] Since then other excavations have been undertaken at this rich and still only partly excavated site, notably by Pierre Cintas. Here we have a stratified site, consisting of three main strata, the lowest of which seems to date from the ninth–seventh centuries B.C.[84] This period has yielded many urn-burials of children (mostly very young infants)[85] and sacrificial animals, all of which had been cremated, but no stelae; the stelae begin only in the second period, in the seventh century B.C. No other Punic 'tophet' is so early, though the finds at el-Ḥofra cover a longer period. Other 'tophets' have been located at Sousse (Hadrumetum), and elsewhere in Punic Africa; the former is particularly important, since it also yielded a cremation pit like one described by Diodorus (see

[82] See André Berthier and René Charlier, *Le sanctuaire punique d'el-Hofra à Constantine*, Paris, 1952–55.

[83] Cf. L. Poinssot and R. Lantier, RHR XLIV (1923), 32–68; F. W. Kelsey, *Excavations at Carthage, 1925: A Preliminary Report*, New York 1926; Donald Harden, *The Phoenicians* (London, 1962), 95 ff.

[84] Cf. Harden, *op. cit.*, p. 100.

[85] See R. de Vaux, *Studies in Old Testament Sacrifice* (Cardiff, 1964), pp. 82 f., reporting on the examination of skeletal remains by Dr. J. Richard.

above).[86] In the pit all contents had been reduced by the heat to a mass of burnt and calcined matter. In the Phoenician settlements in Sardinia and Sicily, a number of examples of sanctuaries of the 'tophet' category have now been excavated, especially at Nora, Tharros (Tarshish?), Sulcis and Monte Sirai in Sardinia, and at Motya in Sicily.[87] Some of the Sardinian urns go back to Greek geometric patterns—no later than the eighth century B.C. and probably earlier. The stelae are closely related to North-African prototypes. None of the island stelae appears to be earlier than the sixth century B.C., and most are several centuries later.

The relatively late date at which the practice of setting up commemorative stelae in connexion with 'tophet' sacrifices was introduced, makes it improbable that they were derived from Phoenicia proper. There is not the slightest reason to connect them directly with the stelae set up at Gezer, Hazor and Byblos to commemorate ancestors.[88] On the other hand, there is a certain resemblance in function to sacrificial stelae from the temple of Dagon at Ugarit, which bear inscriptions recording mortuary offerings.[89] That sanctuaries of the 'tophet' class have not yet been found in Syria-Palestine may easily be accounted for. Like Tophet in Jerusalem, they must preferably have been located near the bottom of valleys on the south or east of the towns to which they belonged. By now most of them must be covered deep with débris, blown or washed over them.

86 Cf. J. Février, JA CCXLVIII (1960), 174 ff.

87 On Nora, Tharros, Sulcis in Sardinia see the survey by Gennaro Pesce, *Sardegna punica* (Cagliari, 1960, pp. 41 ff.). For recent work at Monte Sirai and Motya see *Monte Sirai* I and II (Rome, 1964, 1965) and *Mozia* I (Rome, 1964).

88 On the latter see *Supplements to VT*, IV (Leiden, 1957), 252 f., and my discussion above, Ch. IV, § D.

89 R. Dussaud, *Syria* XVI (1935), 177–80, and my discussion, ARI[1], 203, n. 30, together with David Neiman's paper, JBL LXVII (1948), 55–60, which I heartily endorse.

There is also a substantial amount of written evidence for the existence of human sacrifice among the Moabites and Aramaeans during the tenth–seventh centuries B.C. The biblical evidence with respect to Moab is found in II Kings 3:26 f. and Amos 2:1. In the former passage Mesha, king of Moab, is said to have sacrificed his first-born son, heir to the throne, on the city wall before the horrified besiegers. In his own long inscription, Mesha reports that he had slaughtered the entire population (7,000) of Nebo, whom he had devoted to ritual destruction (*ḥerem*) for 'Ashtar-Chemosh. Since Chemosh, as lord of Moab and its king, is mentioned ten times elsewhere in the inscription, we may safely assume that he was identified with the morning star, the lord of heaven (see above). J. Gray is, therefore, justified in bringing in St. Nilus' account of his adventures in Sinai, where his younger son had a narrow escape from being sacrificed to the god of the morning star by the nomad Arabs who had migrated into this region from eastern Arabia.[90] It is true that the reliability of Nilus has been impugned by various scholars, including J. Henninger.[91] However, no anachronisms have been shown to exist in the work of Nilus, ostensibly composed in the early fifth century A.D., and most recently Philip Mayerson has demonstrated the accuracy of Nilus' topographical information.[92] That such

[90] See LC², 170 f., and for a criticism of his use of Nilus see A. Caquot, *Syria* XXXV (1958), 50, n. 7.

[91] In his important monograph 'Ist der sogenannte Nilus-Bericht eine brauchbare religionsgeschichtliche Quelle?' (*Anthropos*, L [1955], 81–148). While I sometimes disagree with Henninger's views, we are all under tremendous obligation to him for his wealth of learning which he has brought to bear on ancient Arabia.

[92] See his paper, 'The Desert of Southern Palestine According to Byzantine Sources' (PAPS CVII [1963], 160–72). He has shown that the narrative of Nilus agrees closely with the archaeological and documentary data recovered by the Colt Expedition. If we remember that Nilus had been an accomplished Byzantine courtier, we shall not be worried by the suggestion of critics that he imitated then popular romances in writing his story. True adventures in the

a broadly educated man as Nilus wrote in a sophisticated style showing the influence of the pagan Greek novelists is no argument against the veracity of his account. Civilized travellers in desert regions often have unusual adventures, as I can attest from extended personal contact with adventure-prone archaeological explorers. There is, besides, ample documentation in Aramaic and Arabic sources for human sacrifices made to the evening star (Aram. *Kawkabtâ*, Arab. *al-'Uzzā*).[93]

Returning to human sacrifice in Moab, H. Tur Sinai (Torczyner) has offered a convincing revocalization of the consonantal text of Amos 2:1,[94] which should be pointed to mean (with a further correction of my own):

'Thus Yahweh has spoken,

"Because of three offences of Moab,
Because of four, I shall surely requite him!
Because he burns the bones . . .
. . . of a human sacrifice to a demon."'

The usual Massoretic pointing, which means 'because he burned the bones of the king of Edom into lime', yields a very strange sense. How can one burn bones without calcining them? By simply changing the pointing to read *mōlek 'ādām laš-šēd* instead of *mélek 'Edōm laś-śîd*, one obtains a perfectly satisfactory text, closely parallel to Psalm 106:37.[95]

Human sacrifice to the god Adad is attested among the Aramaeans of Gozan at the source of the Khābûr in northern Mesopotamia (late tenth century), in Late-

Arabian desert have often sounded quite incredible, as I know from my own earlier life.

[93] See J. Henninger, 'Menschenopfer bei den Arabern' (*Anthropos* LIII [1958], 721–805); on sacrifice to the evening star see p. 742.

[94] LS 1 (1948), 64 ff. Tur-Sinai did not change the last word; see n. 95 for an exact parallel.

[95] 'And they sacrificed their sons and their daughters to demons (*laš-šēdîm*).'

Assyrian economic texts under Aramaean influence, and in the North-Syrian cult of Sepharvaim (Dead Sea Scroll Isaiah *SPRYYM*, elsewhere *Sibraim* = Assyr. *Šabarain*),[96] where children were sacrificed (II Kings 17:31) to the god Adrammelech (= Assyr. Adad-milki, attested in Aramaean personal names from late cuneiform tablets.[97]

What evidence do we have for 'moloch' sacrifices at Ugarit? There is surprisingly little—and even that is controversial. Schaeffer, following Virolleaud's first interpretation of the liturgical text 19.15, discovered in 1955 and published ten years later, has insisted that the text has nothing to do with human sacrifice,[98] but Virolleaud has meanwhile become more cautious in the light of Février's article.[99] Unfortunately, the text is incomplete; the first two lines run:

> (1) Wine which is measured by the hand of [ ]
> (2) in the *mulk* sacrifice (*dbḥ* . *mlk*).

A horizontal line separates line 2 from 3. In line 3 we have only 'sacrifice of the north' (*dbḥ ṣpn*); in 7, 10 and 11, 'the palace' (*bt*.*mlk*); in 14, 'sacrifice of Baal' (*dbḥ*.*b'l*). The divinities Astarte and Resheph are also mentioned, both in enigmatic context.

That *mulk*〉*mōlek* meant originally 'kingdom, royalty' is certain; it often appears in the Bible in this sense, and it is also found in Ugaritic, South Canaanite, and early Aramaic.[100] Such cases of abstract nouns assuming a concrete meaning, like *Qdš*, 'Holiness' (appellation of Asherah), or Aramaic *qudšâ* as title of God, are very common; a case in point is *Molk-'aštart* (not *Milk-'aštart*),

96 On the transcription see n. 49.

97 A. Ungnad in *Die Inschriften von Tell Halaf* (AfO, *Beiheft* 6, Berlin, 1940), p. 58.

98 *Ugaritica* IV (Paris, 1962), 77–83.

99 PRU V (1965), 8.

100 H. L. Ginsberg, BASOR 87 (1942), 35, n. 20; Albright, JBL LXIII (1944), 218, n. 70; many others more recently.

literally 'Royalty of Astarte'.[101] There was a town in eighteenth-century Mari named *Ilumuluk* or *Ilumalik*,[102] literally 'God-Royalty' or 'God-King'; for the form cf. *Iluwêr* and *'El'eb*. It is reasonable to suppose that the name originally referred to the god of the king or the royal god, and that **d̲abḥu mulki* came to mean 'royal sacrifice', i.e., the noblest possible sacred act. Eventually *mulk/molk* developed the sense 'princely sacrifice' by itself, after which the transition was easy to 'vow of exceptional sanctity', and finally 'solemn promise' (Syriac *mulkânâ*).

In view of the denunciation of such sacrifices in all recorded stages of Mosaic law, it is in the highest degree unlikely that 'moloch' ceremonies were tolerated in Israel before the eighth century B.C., though there were doubtless occasional occurrences of them among pagan or paganizing elements of the population. Otherwise we should find some specific reference to them outside of 'P' in Leviticus, Jer. 32:35, and II Kings 23:10. As I have elsewhere maintained, the re-introduction of the practice into Israel presumably came with the growth of pagan Aramaean influence from the time of Ahaz on.[103]

The story of Abraham's plan to sacrifice Isaac had probably been handed down from the Patriarchal Age. We now know that there was a striking change in Babylonian burial practices between the Third Dynasty of Ur (lowest date c. 2060–1950) and the death of the Amorite king 'Ammiṣaduqa (c. 1562 B.C.). In the former a number of

[101] On this divinity see especially A. Caquot, *Semitica* xv (1965), 29–33, who has shown that it is masculine. I strongly suspect that the figure in question is androgynous like Phanebal of Ascalon (see Ch. III).

[102] See ARM xv (1954), 127: spelled *I-lu-um-mu-lu-uk(KI)*, *AN-mu-lu-uk(KI)*, with gentilic *AN-mu-lu-ka-ya(KI)*, *I-lu-ma-li-ka-ya(KI)*.

[103] ARI², 161 ff.

persons were put to death and buried with the king,[104] just as in the Royal Tombs of Ur (c. twenty-fifth century B.C.) and the tombs of the First Dynasty in Egypt (c. twenty-ninth century B.C.). In the case of 'Ammiṣaduqa the only death seems to have been that of an officer who fell into the burial pit.[105] This shift in practice took place during the Patriarchal Age, *latiore sensu.*

I still maintain (cf. above) that the official Phoenician cult which was brought into Israel in the time of Jezebel, and which even obtained a foothold in Judah under the queen-mother Athaliah, was that of Melcarth, which certainly enjoyed a revival of popularity in Tyre as well as in neighbouring Aram about this time. Like Nergal, whose name meant 'Lord of the Great City', Melcarth, 'Lord of the City' (the Nether World) was at home both in the Upper and the Lower World; his identification with Heracles illustrates the basically chthonic nature of the latter's cult. It was Heracles who conquered the three-headed monster Cerberus, and therefore became the defender of all who were threatened by the dread powers of the Nether World. Like Nergal, who was worshipped at Tyre in Graeco-Roman times, Heracles was *par excellence* the conqueror of dreaded monsters; this was certainly an attribute of Melcarth. Human sacrifice is nowhere mentioned as an issue in the conflict between Elijah and the followers of Baal and Asherah. This fact also militates against identifying the Baal in question with

104 This was true of the tombs of both Shulgi and Amarzuen, in each of which there were two chambers, one intended for the king and the other containing the bodies of persons buried with the king (Woolley, *Excavations at Ur* [London, 1954], p. 157). Evidence from Sumerian literary texts confirms the situation; see S. N. Kramer, BASOR 94 (1944), 2–12 (legend of Gilgamesh), but this text describes burial of a whole retinue, as in the Royal Tombs of c. 2500 B.C. There is still some difference of opinion; cf. the discussions by C. J. Gadd and S. N. Kramer in *Iraq* XXII (1960), 51–68.

105 See Addendum.

Baʿal-shamêm, originally the god of the morning star, as we have seen. It is not impossible that the decline of the practice of human sacrifice at Tyre was partly connected with the increasing popularity of Melcarth and Eshmun, gods who healed instead of destroying. However this may be, it is very hard not to give Israel credit for having helped by its example to encourage the opponents of human sacrifice in Phoenicia.

D. PHOENICIAN HIEROPHANTS AND THEIR METAMORPHOSES

A striking contrast between Phoenicia and Israel is the great popularity in the former of specifically named hierophants, inventors, and sages in general, whereas in Israel native hierophants in this sense were virtually unknown, and emphasis was laid on 'men of God' or 'men called (by God)', as we have seen in § A. The absence of native hierophants in Israel is all the clearer because of numerous appearances of Canaanite and Phoenician hierophants to fill the place of native figures missing in extant Israelite literature. Outstanding among Phoenician–Canaanite hierophants is Taauth, who was called by Sanchuniathon 'the wisest man who ever lived under the sun'. This wisest man, Taauth (the best spelling preserved in the MSS), is always identified in the text of Eusebius with the Egyptian god Thoth, the older form of whose name down to about 1200 B.C. was *Ṭaḥawte* (still earlier *Ḏḥwty*, i.e. *Djaḥáwtey*).[106] Since the later form with *ô* instead of *aw* displaced the archaic form in Egypt before c. 1100 B.C. at the latest, it is clear that the

[106] Note that *Ṭḥt* is the normal early equivalent of the name in Semitic but that assimilation of the first to the second of two such 'litterae incompatibiles' ultimately yielded *Tḥt* as the later Aramaic form of the month-name *Thōth*, especially when the first two consonants fell together as a strong aspirate (= *t* not *ṭ*), Greek *thēta*, in transcription.

figure of the ibis-headed moon-god of wisdom had been taken over by the Canaanites not later than this time and perhaps at a considerably earlier date.

The most important literary text attributed to Taauth is the Cosmogony of Taauth, which was based on the native cosmogony of the chief city of Thoth, Hermopolis Magna in Middle Egypt. I shall demonstrate elsewhere[107] that there is no clear evidence for any of the syncretistic forms of this cosmogony which appear in later Egypt. There is indeed a tendency to replace the Egyptian gods by natural phenomena, but this process of rationalization has virtually nothing in common with the metaphysical reinterpretation of the Sidonian cosmogony of Mochus by Damascius (see above). To what extent the rationalistic thought of Sanchuniathon has actually changed details of the Taauth cosmogony must remain uncertain.

Thoth was also credited by the Egyptians with the invention of script, just as Taauth was among the Phoenicians. Taauth as inventor is bracketed in Job with an enigmatic figure which has hitherto remained completely without reasonable explanation. In Job 38:36 we have the following couplet:

> Who put wisdom in *Ṭḥwt*?
> Or who gave understanding to *Škwy*?[108]

A number of years ago, after beginning systematic work on the Phoenician material in the Bible, I saw that the enigmatic *ṭḥwt* must refer to Taauth as the hierophant of Sanchuniathon. It is true that the Hebrew *Ṭḥwt* has often

[107] In my forthcoming *Experience on the Road to Reason: Phoenicia, Israel and Ionia.*

[108] On earlier exegesis of this long enigmatic verse see Marvin Pope, *Job* (Anchor Bible, 1965), pp. 255 f. We may add that the Greek translators in the second century B.C. had no better idea of the meaning—they rendered:

> Who has given wisdom to skilled weaving women,
> Or understanding to (!) a skilled embroiderer?

been connected with the Egyptian god Thoth, prototype of Taauth. Others have rendered the word as 'ibis', Thoth's sacred bird (!). The parallel name, vocalized *Śekwî*, has a very curious history, as we shall see presently.[109] (Note that the distinction between *ś* and *š* is in the pointed, not the consonantal, text.) Since the discovery of the Hebrew and Ugaritic word *ṯkt*, 'bark' (Hebrew plural *šekîyôt*),[110] it has become clear to me that if the basic consonants are right, *Škwy* ought to mean 'mariner, navigator', like Ugaritic *dgy*, 'fisherman', from *dg*, 'fish'. That the name has been correctly transmitted has now been demonstrated by the discovery of a carved seal in script of the fourth century B.C., at Tell Makmish, a Phoenician seaport on the coast of northern Palestine. The seal reads: 'Belonging to Ḥanan, son of *Škwy*'.[111] On the basis of a rabbinic prayer, 'Blessed be Thou, O Lord our God, king of the world, who didst give to *Śkwy* the intelligence to discern between day and night', the word was explained by mediaeval Jewish commentators as meaning 'cock, barnyard fowl'. Though this explanation sounds ridiculous, it gives us an important clue. Why was the cock considered as the creature which was able to tell day from night? Naturally because the cock crows before the first break of dawn. But this made the barnyard fowl a natural alarm clock for fishermen on the Sea of Galilee, who set out in their boats well before the first break of dawn in order to assure a good catch. Fish in the Sea of Galilee go deeper into the water after dawn and are no longer

109 There is no such Coptic name as *Sūchī* = the planet Mercury, as supposed by G. Hoffmann (letter of 5 Sept. 1962, from H. J. Polotsky). Actually the word was invented by modern European students of Coptic, who copied one another's misunderstandings, going back to the element—σουχις (from older *Sbk*, name of the crocodile-god) in late personal names.

110 See my remarks (partly suggested by H. L. Ginsberg) in the Bertholet *Festschrift* (Tübingen, 1950), pp. 4 f., note.

111 I wish to thank Dr. N. Avigad for showing me a photograph of the seal, which he was then about to publish.

easy to catch.[112] Half humorously, the Galilaeans living around the lake seem to have given the title 'Sailor' to the cock.

Close relationship between Taauth and *Škwy* is confirmed by Sanchuniathon's statement that Taauth was the son of Misōr (Phoen. *Mîšôr*), while his brother Sydyk (Phoen. *Ṣedeq*) begot sons who are said to have invented the ship. That these myths are early is shown by the fact that the same pair *Mšr* and *Ṣdq* has recently been found in Ugaritic texts.[113] Taauth himself is said to have invented the script and to have planned in detail for the symbolism and iconography of the gods; he was finally placed by Kronos (El) over the land of Egypt. Taauth was, moreover, not only an inventor himself but the direct or collateral ancestor of a large family of divine or quasi-divine inventors.

The figure of Taauth appears again in the Bible, in the sense of 'esoteric lore', or the like. In Psalm 51:8 (51:6 in English), we may probably render:

> Truly Thou takest ⟨no⟩ pleasure in esoteric lore[114]
> But hidden wisdom[115] Thou shalt teach me.

The best illustration comes through Porphyry, whom Eusebius (I. 10, 43) quotes as follows:

> Taauth, whom the Egyptians call Thoth, who excelled in wisdom among the Phoenicians, was the first to organise re-

[112] Cf. Franz Dunkel, C.M., *Biblica* v (1924), 380; G. Dalman, *Arbeit und Sitte in Palästina*, VI (1939), 356.

[113] These are, of course, Heb. *mîšôr-mêšārîm* and *ṣedeq*; cf. *ṣedeq ū-mêšārîm*, etc.

[114] Reading *'ĕmét⟨lô'⟩ḥafaṣtā bĕ-ṭaḥût* instead of *hēn 'emét ḥafaṣtā ba-ṭûḥôt: hēn* is vertical dittography from v. 7; *lô'* is required by the context. Another possibility is that we have here the *bĕ* of comparison, first pointed out by M. Dahood: 'Thou dost prefer truth to esoteric lore.' This was my first rendering of the passage and Father Dahood tells me that he has also employed this syntax in his forthcoming *Psalms*, II (Anchor Bible).

[115] The word *sātûm* is ambiguous; see p. 248.

ligious worship, (removing it) from the ignorance of the common people to systematic practice. After long ages he was followed by the god Sūrmūbēlos and ⟨the goddess⟩[116] Thūrō, whose name is equivalent to *Chūsarthis*; and they clarified the theology of Taauth, which had been concealed and obscured by allegories.[117]

As shown on pp. 137 f. the two deities are Ḥaurôn, pronounced *Ḥûrûn* in later Phoenician, and his consort, who appears on the first Phoenician incantation from Arslan Tash as the protectress of women in child-birth. Thūrō is older Egyptian *Tewūre* (Greek Thoéris), and Chūsarthis is older *Kôšart*, goddess of child-birth, the singular of the *Kôšārôt* of Psalm 68:7, Phoenician *Kûšart*. We may safely suppose that Ḥaurôn and Kôshart were singled out of the crowd of divine and semi-divine personalities because of the abundance of incantations credited to them. For the Psalmist the name *Ṭaḥût* had become a word embodying the esoteric wisdom of the hierophant. To the author of Job, who was directly acquainted with Phoenician literature, *Ṭaḥût* was just what Sanchuniathon called him in the sixth century B.C., 'the wisest man who ever was under the sun'.

In this connexion, another Phoenician hierophant may be mentioned: Daniel or Dan'el, father of Aqhat, hero of the epic which bears his name. In the early sixth century B.C., Ezekiel addresses the prince of Tyre (28:3):

Art thou wiser than Daniel?
Hath he not equalled thee in all hidden lore?[118]

Note that the word used for 'hidden, esoteric lore' is the same in Psalm 51:8 and Ezek. 28:3. Elsewhere (14:13, 19) Ezekiel mentions Dan'el with Noah and Job as an

[116] Though not hitherto noticed, the word θεὰ has obviously been dropped by *homoioarkton*.

[117] Here again we have an obvious influence from Hellenistic-Roman theosophic speculation in the manner of Plutarch, *De Iside et Osiride*. These 'allegories' were merely myths.

[118] A rhetorical question with LXX.

archetype sage, and Jubilees 4:20 states that Enoch's wife, Edni, was the daughter of Danel, thus continuing the Dan'el tradition into the second century B.C. In the epic Dan'el is called 'man of Harnam', and since the latter town must have been identical with the Harnam of the Egyptian account of the battle of Kadesh, we can safely locate it at Hermel, near the source of the Orontes (not far from Ba'albek).[119]

Continuing down the line of Phoenician hierophants as reported by Philo Byblius, we come upon two basically historical figures, Thabion and Eisirios. About them Philo reports as follows: (1. 10, 39):

All these things Thabion as[120] the first hierophant of all Phoenicians born from of old, speaking in allegories and mixing natural with cosmic happenings, transmitted to the ecstatic votaries and prophets who initiated the mystery rites; but they, contriving in every way to increase the delusion, handed them down to their successors as well as to those brought in from outside.[121] One of them was Eisirios, the discoverer of the Three Books; he was the brother of Chna, whose name is equivalent to 'Phoenician'.

Immediately before this quotation, Tauthos is called 'god' and is followed by the 'first' human hierophant Thabion, who is himself followed by ecstatics and prophets, including especially Eisirios, author of three mysterious books (see below).

The name *Thabiōn* is actually found in its original form at Ugarit, where it appears as a personal name *Tabiyanu* in the fourteenth century B.C.[122] The transcription is per-

[119] BASOR 130 (1953), 26 f.

[120] The Greek text is corrupt; I suggest reading, instead of the impossible θαβιωνος or the syntactically awkward θαβιων ος (= ὃς) simply ὧς.

[121] That is, to men who did not belong to initiated families, but were initiated 'on their own'.

[122] PRU III, No. 16.249, line 13, written *Ta-bi-ya-nu*. The name was originally Hurrian (like Ethan below), as we know from the

fect, since *thēta* reflects Phoenician aspirated *t* (*taw*), not *ṭ* (*ṭēth*), and the *a* in the penultimate syllable is unquestionably short,[123] yielding Phoenician *Tabiōn* instead of *Tabiûn*, as it would if this *a* were originally long. Thabion thus belongs to the same ethnic group of hierophants as we find in biblical Ethan, transcribed *Eytān* (where the original *a* of the name had to be short) and Heman (*Heymān*), where the same is true.[124] 'Ethan' stands by a common shift, now well attested in North-west Semitic, and normal in Accadian, for the Ugaritic name *Attuyanu*,[125] alphabetic *'Atyn* (**Atyănu*⟩ **Aytănu*⟩ **Eytān*). In Hebrew these two figures appear among the greatest sages of antiquity, who were allegedly excelled only by Solomon (I Kings 5:11 = Eng. 4:31). They were considered in Israel as the founders of the two most important Davidic musical guilds, but their names may be used simply as a designation for schools of musicians. These names ending in *yănu* were mostly Hurrian in origin, as was true of this hypocoristic ending.[126] It is interesting to note the fact that Ethan and Heman were archetype musicians, just as Thabion was believed to have founded dramatic reli-

ending *yanu*, which was properly a Hurrian gentilic ending, also used for hypocoristica; cf. *Masriyanu*, 'Egyptian (land)' (so [!], spelled Mašriyan-), *Talmiyanu* from the fuller *Talmi-Tešub*. Cf. also the Hurrian hypocoristicon written *Tabeya, Tabiya, Tapaya* (NPN, 147), which have nothing to do with Accadian names beginning with *Ṭāb-*.

[123] Originally short *a* followed by one consonant, which became *ā* in Hebrew, changed to *ō* as in *dāgōn* for *dăgăn*; cf. PPG 30, § 78.

[124] Over twenty years ago I presented a paper on the Ugaritic names ending in *yn* but have never published it. See provisionally ARI², 127, 210 (n. 99).

[125] See PRU III (1955), 243b for several occurrences, spelled *A(d)duyanu* and *Attuyanu* = *'Atyn*; cf. the Hurrian Adduya, son of Itḫip-šarri (NPN, 40a). Note that cuneiform *d* and *t* reflect the same Hurrian phoneme.

[126] See above on this ending. There is, e.g., no doubt at all about *Šukriyanu* (PRU III, 255) = *Šukri-Tešub* (NPN, 137, borne by a score of different persons).

gious rites, in which music played a dominant rôle. The name *Eisirios* is unparalleled, and it may well be a corruption of *Sisirios* (CICIPIOC instead of EICIPIOC). This again may be *Sisera'*, name of a famous enemy of Israel in the twelfth century, as well as of the putative ancestor of a class of foreign temple servants in Jerusalem; it can easily be identified with the cuneiform personal name *Sisaruwa* (written *Zi-za-ru-wa*),[127] which sounds Luvian. Such origin is scarcely surprising, since the region north of Ugarit and the Plain of Antioch was occupied by Luvians. Eisirios or Sisirios is said to have been the 'discoverer of the Three Books (τῶν τριῶν γραμμάτων εὑρετής)'. These books have been a complete mystery, but they have perhaps turned up lately in the Aramaic 'Elect of God' text from Cave IV at Qumran. In this text, from about the first century B.C., we are told of the birth of Noah, 'who will not possess knowledge until the time when he comes to know the Three Books'.[128] Since this pseudepigraphical literature contains much material from ultimately pagan sources, they may be identical with the enigmatic Three Books found by the Phoenician sage.

The other ancient sages compared unfavourably to Solomon (I Kings 5:11), are called Chalcol and Darda, the sons of Mahol. As I pointed out in 1942, the designation *Bĕnê Māḥōl* refers to members of a guild of dancers or singers—probably combining both, as so often in an-

[127] PRU IV, 286 (19.68: 33 ff.), where *Sí-sà-ru-wa* appears three times as the name of a fourteenth-century prince in north-western Syria said to be hostile to Ugarit. The sign *zi* is regularly used to transcribe the Hittite affricative *z* (probably *ts*) and the similar Canaanite *samek* in LB tablets. *Samek* shifted from *ts* or *č* to *s* at some time in the early part of the Iron Age.

[128] On this text, published by J. Starcky, see most recently J. A. Fitzmyer, S.J., CBQ XXVII (1965), 348–72, especially pp. 357, 362 f. In my own opinion, this fragment comes from a second copy of the Genesis 'Apocryphon', and takes its place in a missing column of the latter.

tiquity.[129] 'Chalcol' appears also as the name of a female musician of the thirteenth century B.C. at the temple of the god Ptaḥ-prince-of-Ascalon.[130] The name is written in Egyptian syllabic orthography, and must be read either *Kurkur* or *Kulkul*, according to the now generally accepted transcription of syllabic orthography.[131] Needless to say *Kalkōl* is a normal Hebrew dissimilation of original *Kŭlkŭl*.

In evaluating this material, we must remember that music, dancing, and poetry were all considered to be the necessary concomitants of esoteric religious 'wisdom', as may be illustrated by a wealth of material from ancient Mediterranean lands. Note also that Greek *prophētēs* is used of ecstatics, whereas *hierophantēs* is employed for sages who were believed to have originated or organized the practice of religion. The Greek translation of *nabî'* as *prophētēs* is thus intimately connected with the ecstatic tradition in both Phoenicia and Israel. This fact was well known to the Israelites; cf. the references to ecstatic prophets of Baal as *nĕbî'ê Ba'al* in I and II Kings. The prophets of Israel, as we have seen above, composed nearly all their oracles in verse, which was always (as far as we know) either sung or chanted, often to the accompaniment of instruments. Habbakuk was primarily a temple musician and only secondarily a prophet. It should be obvious that one of the prerequisites for being considered as a true prophet was native poetic genius. In this connexion we may recall the Talmudic dictum (*Baba Bathra* 12a), 'The wise man is more excellent than the prophet',

129 ARI², 126 f.

130 ARI², 210, nn. 97, 100.

131 VESO (see especially p. 60); W. F. Albright and T. O. Lambdin (JSS II [1957], 113–27); numerous papers by Elmar Edel, and the more elaborate, but essentially identical, system of W. Helck, BAeV (1962), especially pp. 380, 480 (where he reads *Kurkur*, not having seen my discussion in ARI).

which reflects the attitude of a more mature age, which distrusted charismatic figures. In Israel we know that the canonical prophets were far from being mere charismatics, but we also know that they were regarded with distrust by the priests, who took a position characteristic of professionals when faced with amateurs in all ages. In Phoenicia the sages were often practical men, to whom inventions and discoveries as well as esoteric knowledge were attributed. This does not seem true of early Israel, but under Phoenician influence it was not long in developing. Note also that diviners and sages of Aramaic background, such as Balaam,[132] Lemuel and Agur of Massa,[133] come under quite different categories.

In estimating the influence of legendary Phoenician wise men on Israel, we must not forget that the biblical references to them come chiefly from Kings, Psalms, Job, and Ezekiel in contexts dating in general from the seventh or early sixth centuries B.C. in their extant form. This was the period in which Phoenician literary influence reached its climax. Earlier Canaanite influence came in mostly before the establishment of Israel as a commonwealth or in the time of David and Solomon.

E. SOME MAJOR ASPECTS OF PHOENICIAN LITERARY INFLUENCE ON ISRAEL

In Chapter I we dealt with Canaanite literary influence on the verse of early Israel. As pointed out there, the tenth century marked a great change in basic stylistic

[132] On Balaam see JBL LXIII (1944), 207–33 and BASOR 118 (1950), p. 20; another study is in preparation.

[133] On these figures see my study in *Studi Orientalistici in onore di Giorgio Levi della Vida* (Rome, 1956), 1–14, especially pp. 6 ff., where I analyse the structure of the poems attributed to them, noting the archaic Canaanite background, in spite of Aramaic influence on details.

features of Israelite poetry. Owing to lack of material, we must depend for a *terminus ante quem* upon tenth-century Psalms such as Psalms 78 and 18, in which such a date is highly probable. Characteristic of these Psalms is a stylistic reaction against repetitive parallelism of any kind; instead we have a strong tendency to eliminate repetitive elements and to vary wording for the apparent purpose of using as many different words as possible. It would, therefore, seem highly probable that Canaanite poetry was already giving up repetitive parallelism and replacing it by maximal variation of vocabulary, within the limits of what were then considered to be good taste and respect for the sacred. Since we now know that Hebrew music and, naturally, musical compositions were then under particularly strong Phoenician influence,[134] it is incredible that the new aversion to repetitive parallelism can have developed independently in Israel. If other evidence is needed, it may easily be drawn from a study of the prophetic writings of the eighth century B.C., where there is virtually no repetitive parallelism. As pointed out in Chapter I, occasional cases of repetitive parallelism in later Psalms and the Prophets, as well as in other parts of the Bible, are clearly archaic survivals—that is, either drawn from much older sources (as in Habakkuk),[135] or picked up from the mouth of the peo-

[134] I have long been intending to discuss this whole question in detail, following the concise survey in ARI, but have not had time. Meanwhile, I adhere firmly to my 1942 position on the Davidic date of the establishment of the musical guilds, as well as on their non-Israelite origin.

[135] See SOTP, 1–18. Here I may add my present interpretation of the puzzling verse Hab. 2:5a which I first discussed in BASOR 91 (1943), 40, n. 11. I then pointed out that the enigmatic *HYYN* of MT may reflect Ugar. *Hyn*, another name for the craftsman god Kôshar. The subsequent discovery of the Habakkuk commentary, reading *W'P KY' HYN* (or *HWN*) *YBGWD* (next colon like MT), yields a better text (see also W. H. Brownlee, *The Meaning of the*

ple, where they had been handed down without change for centuries (as in Canticles).[136] Where we do have attempts at original repetitive parallelism, as in the sixth-century *Šîrê ham-Maʻalôt*, it is so irregular and so different from archaic repetitive parallelism that its authors obviously did not understand the rules of the style they were attempting to imitate. In some Psalms such as 29, the text of which is very corrupt, it is quite impossible to tell what the date of the original composition may have been. I suspect that it passed through a number of different stages between Middle Bronze and its final redaction about the fifth(?) century B.C.

The recent publications of Mitchell Dahood have made it clear that Canaan exercised profound influence on Israelite lyric style in all periods after the end of the Patriarchal Age, and that it is absurd to try to isolate any aspect of Hebrew literature from Canaanite-Phoenician influence.[137] What is true of Psalms applies also to the

Qumrân Scrolls for the Bible, New York, 1964, 24 ff.). My present interpretation is:

> And even though he be as crafty as Hîyôn,
> A cowardly man will not succeed.

The Hebrew form *Hîyôn* corresponds to a probable Ugaritic *Hayyân*; Heb. *yahîr* is derived from the same verb as Arabic *wahrah*, 'fear', etc. Kôshar corresponds closely in some ways to Greek Hermes.

[136] See my essay in *Hebrew and Semitic Studies Presented to Godfrey Rolles Driver* (Oxford, 1963), pp. 1–7. Cf. also the review by J. C. Greenfield, JAOS LXXXV (1965), 257, with all of whose corrections I agree except that *elēlu* (CAD IV, 40a–b) and *šūlulu, mēlultu, melēlu* do refer to dancing to music, etc. (from *ḥll* = *ḥwl*). Incidentally, we should clearly emend the Greek text of Cant. 7:1 to read—ἡ ὀρχουμένη, '(she) who dances', instead of ἡ ἐρχομένη, '(she) who comes'. The Hebrew should then read ⟨*meḥôlélet*⟩ *bi-mḥôlát maḥanáyim*, 'dancing in the dance of two armies' with the corrected Greek text and variant Massoretic MSS (correct my remarks on p. 5 of my paper accordingly).

[137] See especially his major work, *Psalms* (Anchor Bible), to appear in three volumes, the first of which has already appeared

wisdom literature collected in Proverbs, as pointed out successively by Cullen Story[138] and Pierre Proulx,[139] and most recently by Mitchell Dahood,[140] with a wealth of new data. Father Proulx has shown that, while there is no repetitive parallelism in Proverbs except towards the end of the book,[141] the stylistic and syntactic phenomena which we do have are generally in accord with similar phenomena in Ugaritic verse. Mitchell Dahood is now demonstrating that a host of obscure passages in Proverbs may be clarified from the vocabulary, grammar and style of Ugaritic and later Phoenician sources. Since Proverbs contains the largest body of secular literature in the Bible, we should expect Phoenician influence on it to be disproportionately high. Criticisms levelled against the interpretation of biblical texts, particularly of wisdom literature, on the basis of Ugaritic material are groundless. In the first place, if we omit proper names, the vocabulary of the Hebrew Bible consists of about 3,000 words—varying according to the norms used to distinguish words from one another. Judging from the Egyptian and Accadian dictionaries, the total number of words—including all known Canaanite and Aramaic dialects between c. 2000 B.C. and A.D. 500—could not be appreciably less than 15,000. Accordingly, we may not know more than a fraction of the total Hebrew vocabulary in biblical times. It is, therefore, absurd for biblical scholars to insist that we must limit our vocabulary to Hebrew words found in standard Hebrew dictionaries. In principle, the

(New York, 1966) and the second of which is in press at the time of writing.

138 A Johns Hopkins master's essay, published in condensed form in JBL LXIV (1945), 319–37.

139 A Johns Hopkins doctoral thesis, *Ugaritic Verse Structure and the Poetic Syntax of Proverbs* (1956). Unhappily it has not yet been published in printed form.

140 *Proverbs and Northwest Semitic Philology* (Roma, *Scripta Pontificii Instituti Biblici*, 1963).

141 See my treatment referred to in n. 133.

late F. X. Wutz was quite correct in recognizing the fact that there must have been many hundreds of words in the original Hebrew Psalter which have been lost in transmission. He was wrong in trying to reconstruct a more elaborate Hebrew vocabulary through attempted retroversion of the Greek translation into a Hebrew text of his own creation with the aid of words in other Semitic languages. It is naturally impossible to know without specific examples in published literature just what words which appear in other Semitic languages may also have been employed in a Hebrew dialect or literary category. In spite of the lack of extra-biblical North-west Semitic sources, he correctly explained *rôkēb ʿarābôt* in Ps. 68:5 as a mistake for *rôkēb ʿarāfôt*, 'rider on the clouds' (Ugar. *rkb ʿrpt*, of Baal).

Even such an outstanding example of derivation from an external source as the material from the Proverbs of Amenemope (Prov. 22:17–23:11) was, in my opinion, almost certainly borrowed through Phoenicia. We now know that Amenemope was composed no later than the twelfth century B.C. and perhaps as early as the thirteenth.[142] Relations between Phoenicia and Egypt in these centuries were extremely close, as we have seen above. It is no accident that Israelite wisdom literature was particularly indebted to Phoenicia for literary inspiration. A highly sophisticated trading civilization is always likely to be interested in practical advice. Examples of the popularity of such aphorisms among cultures of this type are so numerous that we need scarcely dwell on them: mention of the Chinese, Scots, East European Jews, and Levantines is enough. Ugarit has yielded important remains of the oldest known wisdom book from South-west Asia, the Teachings of Shuruppak (which

[142] See my remarks in VT, *Supplements*, III (1955), 6; A. H. Gardiner in *The Legacy of Egypt* (Oxford, 1942), pp. 67–70; J. M. Plumley in DOTT, 172 ff. (1958); R. S. Williams, JEA XLVII (1961), 100–6.

have also been found lately in fairly extensive Sumerian fragments at Tell eṣ-Ṣalābîkh, dating from about the twenty-sixth century B.C.).[143]

When we turn from Proverbs to Job and Ecclesiastes, we find that Phoenician influence continues to grow. This is perhaps due to the fact that Proverbs, though containing some obviously Phoenician material also includes many orthodox Israelite sayings, as well as collections attributed to various special sources, both Israelite and non-Israelite. It is improbable that the book was edited before the sixth century B.C., and its final redaction may come down to the fifth.[144] Job and Ecclesiastes, on the other hand, are highly personal compositions; Job probably dates from the seventh century B.C., though an early sixth-century date is by no means impossible; only in the last chapter do we find passages added in later times.[145] Ecclesiastes dates almost certainly from the fifth century B.C. and is also the work of a single man.[146] Neither book contains specific quotations from earlier, now canonical, Hebrew literature and it is, accordingly, impossible to judge these writings on the same basis that we can judge a work containing chiefly traditional material. Both the authors were heretics in their own way, and it is most unlikely that their works would have survived if it had not been for their outstanding literary qualities, as well as for the fact that they deal with 'existential' themes

143 R. D. Biggs, JCS xx (1966), 78; W. G. Lambert, *Babylonian Wisdom Literature* (Oxford, 1960), 92 ff.

144 The best general survey now available of the place of Proverbs in wisdom literature is that of R. B. Y. Scott, *Proverbs* (Anchor Bible, 1965), pp. xv–liii and 3–30.

145 For the date of Job see especially Marvin Pope, *Job* (Anchor Bible), pp. xxx–xxxvii; my own arguments for the same date are largely different, but do not conflict. For a full discussion see my forthcoming *Experience on the Road to Reason: Phoenicia, Israel and Ionia.*

146 See the treatments, recent and forthcoming, cited below, p. 259, n. 147, and p. 261, n. 151.

which are scarcely touched on in earlier biblical literature.

In a forthcoming book to be entitled *Experience on the Road to Reason: Phoenicia, Israel and Ionia*[147] I shall deal with the origins of the new ways of thinking which seem suddenly to appear among the Greeks in the early sixth century B.C. I trace them back to a general intellectual movement which probably appeared first in Phoenicia, from which it spread more or less contemporaneously to Israel on the one hand and to the Aegean shores on the other, taking different forms in the two very different cultures. The roots of this movement can be traced in the earlier literature of Israel as well as in the active intellectual ferment which began with the foundation of Greek colonies all around the eastern Mediterranean in the eighth–seventh centuries B.C. This is not the place to go into detail about this movement, which can be best followed by analysis of the legal institutions of the Old Testament and the early Greek world. It was an age of increasing scepticism, with intensely cosmopolitan cultural transfusion in which the old polytheistic superstitions seemed more and more out of date and men struggled towards a more rational way of explaining the world in which they lived. While we have only fragments of native Phoenician literature before the sixth century B.C., we have in Sanchuniathon a rich source of information with regard to the growth of scepticism. In fact, Eusebius was so horrified by the impersonal character of the cosmogony of Taauth, where the ancient gods became natural phenomena, that he burst out: 'A cosmogony which leads directly to atheism! (κοσμογονία ἄντικρυς ἀθεότητα εἰσάγουσα)'.[148] Sanchuniathon was emphatically not influenced by Greek philosophy in any form known to

[147] See provisionally my forthcoming paper in PAPS, entitled 'Neglected Factors in the Greek Intellectual Revolution'.

[148] This reminds one of St. Augustine's reaction to the sceptical philosophy of Anaximander, but is stated more forcefully.

us, nor is there the slightest evidence for any Greek philosophical influence either on Job or on Ecclesiastes—though I formerly believed, with many other scholars, that the latter was composed in the third century B.C. under eclectic influence from popular Stoicism and Epicureanism.[149]

Actually, Job and Ecclesiastes are both so full of Phoenician language, economic practice, cosmology, astronomy, and imagery, that it is increasingly difficult to believe that either was written outside of the Phoenician sphere of higher culture. It is perfectly absurd to consider Job as an outgrowth of Edomite, still less of Arab, culture. The story of Job is, of course, much older, and probably goes back to an epic narrative which arose between the age during which the name *Ayyābum* was popular (first half of the second millennium B.C.) and Israelite times. The references to North Arabic districts are characteristic of the early first millennium B.C., and the names need not imply any personal acquaintance with the places in question. The name *Bûz*, for example, is typically Phoenician in form, since the native pronunciation, followed in Accadian, was *Bāzu* which would become, by normal rules of phonetic development, *Bûz* in Phoenician.[150] Allusions to the Chaldaeans and Sabaeans point to a relatively early date, before the two peoples had settled down completely, substituting caravaneering for raiding. A date after the middle of the seventh century B.C. would be difficult. It is most significant that there is not a single scriptural quotation in the whole of Job, devoutly monotheistic though its author is. Since it is written in Hebrew, in spite of its rich Phoenician colour, it contains many idiomatic Hebrew expressions which also occur in the

[149] FSAC[2] (1957), 351 f. The most extreme recent view of the lateness of the alleged Greek influence on Ecclesiastes is in the late Moses Hadas' *Hellenistic Culture: Fusion and Diffusion* (New York, 1959), pp. 140 ff.

[150] For its location see the Alt *Festschrift, Geschichte und Altes Testament* (Tübingen, 1953), pp. 8 f.

pre-exilic books of the Bible. One might expect scriptural quotations, but there is none. This suggests a period before the work of the Deuteronomist in the late seventh century B.C., or at least before the work of the Deuteronomist had become widely known. Even more surprising, if possible, is the lack of any quotation from the Hebrew prophets, since we should certainly expect to find such quotations if the author had been strongly influenced by them. His Phoenicianizing Hebrew may have come from North Israel or from the non-Israelite coast of Palestine, whose culture was Phoenician but whose population was certainly in part Israelite. The author was familiar with the Assyrian practice of compulsory exchange of populations, a fact which points to a date after c. 740 B.C. Had he written after the fall of Jerusalem there would surely have been some allusion to it, direct or indirect. Above, in dealing with the Phoenician hierophants, we have pointed out that some of our best material comes from Job. In our forthcoming volume, referred to above, we shall try to show in detail the extent of Phoenician influence on cosmogony, cosmology, and astronomy.

After many years in which I insisted on a third-century date for Ecclesiastes I accepted Mitchell Dahood's late fourth-century date.[151] More recently I have changed my mind again, going back successively to the early fourth century and then to the fifth century B.C.—preferably to the second half, though a date in the first half does not seem at all impossible. It is noteworthy that here also there are no scriptural quotations. In fact, we are in an atmosphere which is considerably more sceptical than the approach in the book of Job. We no longer have an author who can be called 'a devout Yahwist', yet he evi-

[151] See Dahood's study 'Canaanite-Phoenician Influence in Qoheleth' (*Biblica*, XXXIII [1952], 30–52; 191–221), and my remarks in VT, *Supplements*, III 14 f. [See now Dahood, *Biblica*, XLVII (1966), 264–82.]

dently considered himself as a good Jew. In fact, the difference is roughly on the order of a Leibnitz followed by a Schelling or, in more recent American terms, of a Borden P. Bowne[152] followed by a Paul Tillich. Furthermore, Qoheleth contains a very much higher proportion of Phoenician elements than Job. Yet it must be emphasized that not one of the supposed influences from Greek philosophy can be sustained. On the contrary, we have in Qoheleth some of the raw material on which the earliest Greek philosophers built their metaphysical structures. Note also that in Qoheleth we have three Persian loanwords,[153] with no Greek words at all. Note also that the content, including particularly the many occurrences of the expression 'under the sun', has its closest parallels in the Phoenician inscriptions of Eshmunazor and Tabnit in the early fifth century B.C. and the work of Sanchuniathon about the second quarter of the sixth century B.C., to say nothing of Euripides in the second half of the fifth century B.C. Examples—literary, quasi-philosophical, and historical—are now fairly numerous and all point in the direction of a date in the fifth century B.C.

But we must not suppose that literary influence was all from Phoenicia on Israel. Some of it was certainly in the opposite direction. We are told by Porphyry that Sanchuniathon wrote on Jewish history,[154] using information which he had obtained from a priest of the god called *Ieû*, that is, the North Israelite pronunciation of *Yáhû*

[152] Bowne (1847–1910) was the Methodist founder of the 'Personalist' philosophy.

[153] *Pardés*, *pitgám*, *zemán* (Syr. *zĕván*, *zavnâ*). Until recently I have oscillated between Acc. *simānu*⟩ *Síwān* and Old Iranian *zṛvan* as the source of *zemán*, but I have lately accepted the latter.

[154] Karl Mras pointed out long ago (Austrian Academy: *Anzeiger*, 1952, No. 12, p. 175), that it was Sanchuniathon, not Hierombal, priest of Ieu, who dedicated a history of the Jews to Abibal, king of Byblos. Contrast C. Clemen, MVAeG XLII:3 (1939), 4.

(*Iaō* in Greek).[155] Eusebius takes occasion to remark that this material was reported accurately by Sanchuniathon.

Our treatment has necessarily been uneven because of the fragmentary nature of our Canaanite and Phoenician sources. But the swelling tide of discovery has brought the evidence needed to prove the remarkable accuracy of Israelite tradition. The biblical sources make no attempt to disguise the extent to which Israel was influenced by the paganism from which it had emerged and to which it was always exposed. There is no evidence that any Israelite author or editor held 'historiosophic' views about the Hebrew past, to use Y. Kaufmann's phrase. Theirs was always a fundamentally empirical approach, and the errors which they sometimes made in interpreting tradition were natural and inevitable, not the result of a distorted world view.

The contrast between Canaanite and Phoenician paganism, on the one hand, and the faith and practice of Israel, on the other, was relatively just as great as that between Graeco-Roman paganism and Judaeo-Christian monotheism in the time of the rabbis and church fathers. Israel learned the arts of civilization, including music and belles lettres, from Canaanite-Phoenician neighbours, just as later Jews and Christians learned how to reason systematically from the Greeks. In the process of acculturation heresies arose. There were syncretistic cults and movements at every known stage of the development of

[155] *Praep. Evang.* I.9, 21. The critical apparatus of Mras lists Codex A as reading Ιευ, while Theodoret read Ιαω; the other codices read Ιευω. As well known, *Iaō* stands for *Yahū*; *Ieu* reflects the typical North-Israelite and Phoenician dissimilation, like *Yēšûʿ* for *Yôšûʿ*, *Yēhûʾ* for **Yōhū* (original **Yahuhûʾ*, Assyr. *Iauʾa*), *ʿēdût* for **ʿôdôt*<*ʿâdôt* (**ʿahdôt*, 'oaths, covenant'), etc. The Gnostic figures of Ιαω and Ιευ are doublets, the former reflecting the old southern, the latter the old North-Israelite pronunciation.

Yahwism. Gnosticism had its forerunners among Israelites and Samaritans, even though we can only see dimly at present. But significant pagan influences always came from the older and richer cultures, not from the nomads and semi-nomads of Sinai and North Arabia, as romantically imagined by many biblical scholars. It is high time that we turn from such imaginative fantasies to the real world of antiquity, which has so much to tell our own world of today.

Addenda

CHAPTER I

(a) Ch. I, § A, n. 3. On Wellhausen's Hegelianism see now Lothar Perlitt, *Vatke und Wellhausen* (BZATW 94, 1965). However, he forgets that a scholar may be strongly influenced by a school of thought (e.g. Platonism) even when he is quite unconscious of that fact. Wellhausen was certainly not interested in philosophical speculation. In this respect he resembled two eminent scholars whom I knew well: Paul Haupt and C. C. Torrey, both of whom considered themselves free of philosophical bias.

(b) Ch. I, § B, n. 20. Father Mitchell Dahood, S.J., whose work on archaic features of biblical poetry has been outstanding in both quantity and quality, informs me that he now has isolated over 200 such pairs of words common to both Hebrew and Ugaritic verse. Even if a number of them should prove to be coincidences, this impressive total compels us to recognize stylistic dependence of the former on the latter.

(c) Ch. I, § C, n. 51. Following E. A. Speiser, *Anchor Bible: Genesis* (1964), 361–72, I am now calling Gen. 49 'The Testament of Jacob' instead of 'The Blessing of Jacob'. In addition to his bibliography on p. 372, note Hans-Jürgen Zobel, *Stammesspruch und Geschichte* (BZATW 95, 1965). Though the latter did not come to my attention until I had nearly completed intensive research on Gen. 49 (which began in the autumn of 1966, several weeks after the manuscript of this volume had been completed), it has influenced me substantially. (The original impetus to return to this challenging poem came from my former student, Rev Dr Francis I. Andersen, in a letter of 14 October 1966.) Since I must be concise, I will say here that the content of the 'Testament of Jacob' is surprisingly heterogeneous. All the passages containing obvious plays on words are late, in accordance with our present knowledge of Hebrew stylistic development. Several individual tribal sayings are composite, containing both early and late passages. The consonantal text has been remarkably well preserved, though there is much archaism of language and not a little wrong division of a continuous text (as in the Sefîreh treaties of the mid-eighth century B.C.). The sayings about Naphtali and Benjamin are very archaic and point to a nomadic atmosphere. Late Patriarchal are sayings about Issachar, Judah, Reuben, Simeon and Levi, Dan, and especially Joseph (which is historically very important). The sayings about Asher and Zebulun are later and have obviously been interchanged. No early saying about Gad has been preserved. A single illustration must suffice; the beginning of the Issachar saying (Gen. 49:14) may be read, without changing a single consonant: *Yiśśakar ḥammôr gēr marbîṣ bên (ham)mišpetáyim*, 'Issachar is a (resident) alien donkey-driver/ Who camps between the (camp-fire) hearths'. Since a donkey does not bend his shoulder to accept a burden, the usual vocalization *ḥămôr*, 'donkey', will not do; the word is the North-Israelite pronunciation of later Hebrew and Aramaic *ḥammār*, Arabic *ḥammâr*, all meaning 'donkey-driver' (cf. early Hebrew *pārāš*, 'horseman', for **parrāš*. [See below, Addendum (r) for additional confirmation.] A. Alt's historical explanation of the passage in KSGVI I, 167 f. still holds; the settlement of Issachar probably began well before the fourteenth century B.C.

(d) Ch. I, § D, n. 67. In subsequent papers, Cross has further developed his views of the Old Palestinian and Proto-Lucianic recensions; see HTR LVII (1964), 292–9; IEJ XVI (1966), 81–95. At the same time our views appear to be diverging with respect to the relative importance of contractions and expansions of the text; I hold firmly to my long-standing position that in the Pentateuch and the Former Prophets (Joshua-Kings) 'losses' far outweigh 'glosses'.

(e) Ch. I, § E, n. 86. Father Dahood (*Anchor Bible: Psalms* I, 1966, p. 100) calls attention to the fact that the *tmn* of the dragon *Yam* in Ugaritic is parallel to his *pnt* (Baal Epic, IIIAB, A: 17 f. and 26), just as *tmnt* is parallel to *pānîm*, with reference to Yahweh, in Psalm 17:15. Both should be translated 'glory' or 'majesty' (note that when Baal fells the dragon, the latter's *pnt* is weakened [*nǵṣ*] and his *tmn* is exhausted [*dlp*]). These and other considerations make the rendering 'image' (vocalized *temûnāh*) still more unlikely.

(f) Ch. I, § E, n. 105. I have to thank Dr Menahem Haran for making me aware of a grammatical impossibility in my rendering (BASOR 163, 52) of *melek šĕlôm⟨ōh⟩* as 'a king allied to him'. In his remarks (*Annual of the Swedish Theological Institute*, IV, 1965, 48, n. 14), he gives the correct translation, '*the* king with whom he (Abraham) has peaceful relations'. Subsequent correspondence shows that the correction was inadvertent (i.e. it was dictated by his sense of Hebrew grammar), since he does not accept it himself. That it is idiomatic Hebrew is shown by the two pairs *malkê ḥesed* (I Kings 20:31) and *'îš ḥesed* (Prov. 20:6 with Greek and Syriac) versus several occurrences of *'îš šĕlômî*, *'anšê šĕlômkā*, etc., and our probable *melek šĕlôm⟨ōh⟩*. I now see that there is reason to consider Melchizedek as king of Jerusalem, as maintained by Haran; the original text (oral or written) may have been worded approximately, 'And Melchizedek, king ⟨of Jerusalem, the king⟩ who was ⟨his⟩ ally, brought out . . .'. This, or a similar, restoration of the original text would involve nothing but simple haplographies. It may be noted that the relation between Abraham's people and the king of Jerusalem would be analogous in some ways to that described in the Yaḫdun-Lim inscription of Mari, from the second quarter of the eighteenth century B.C. Here the two 'Apiru tribes of Ubrapû and Awnānum, as well as the similar tribe of the Rabbûm, are each allied to a different city king of the Upper Euphrates Valley (G. Dossin, *Syria*, XXXII, 1955, 14 f.); on these tribes and their biblical counterparts see Ch. II, § D.

(g) Ch. I, § E, last paragraph. For the use of historical analogies and models see AHAEBT, 3 ff., 60 ff.

CHAPTER II

(h) Ch. II, § A, n. 3. See now G. Posener's forthcoming paper in Syria, 1967, and my observations in BASOR 184, pp. 28, n. 10, and 35, addendum.

(i) Ch. II, § A, n. 9. Note that all efforts to push the royal tombs of Byblos back before the end of the nineteenth century B.C. are rendered impossible because none of the three now known lots of Execration Texts, dating roughly between 1925 and 1825 B.C., mention any native princes but only 'tribes' at Byblos, though they contain many other names of Palestinian and Phoenician chieftains of much less important places than Byblos. On this question see BASOR 184, 27 ff.

(j) Ch. II, end of § A. See below, Addendum (x) on Ch. IV, § A, n. 1.

(k) Ch. II, § B, n. 18. Two very recent efforts have been made to fit the kings of Byblos now known into the so-called 'middle' Babylonian chronology (that accepted in CAH[2]): J. Van Seters in a paper read at the New Haven meeting of the American Oriental Society in April 1967, and K. A. Kitchen, *Orientalia* XXXVI (1967), 39–54. The former operated with a very early date for Abishemu I of Byblos (c. 1840–1820), against which see above, Addendum (i), as well as with an impossibly short reign of Zimri-Lim, king of Mari, against which A. Goetze protested at the meeting; see also on Kitchen's similar view, below. Kitchen's treatment of the material from Byblos is excellent, but he has also become a victim of Dr H. Lewy's synchronisms (*Die Welt des Orients*, II, 5/6, 1959, 438–53). Since G. Dossin's exhaustive collection of the known year-names of Zimri-Lim (*Studia Mariana* [DMOA IV], 1950, 50–61), it has been quite certain that Zimri-Lim reigned at least 32 years, not 18 as assumed on the basis of dubious synchronisms by Dr Lewy. This would mean that he was on the throne from c. 1728 (or earlier), following the low chronology, to 1697. It is most unlikely that the letter ARM IV, 20, from Ishme-Dagan, son of Shamshi-Adad I of Assyria to his brother Ishme-Adad, was written after their father's death. The whole tone of the letter shows that the former (installed at Ekallatum on the Tigris, south of Assur, or at Assur itself) considered himself as still only a little superior to his brother; in other words, Shamshi-Adad was still alive, residing at Shubat-Ellil, and his elder son was only the heir apparent, not the reigning monarch. It is thoroughly improbable that the expression *ana kussî bīt abīya ērub*, 'I have entered the throne(room) of my father's house' has the same sense as the familiar *ina kussî abīya ūšib*, 'I sat on the throne of my father'. Similarly, the year-name of Eshnunna [H. Lewy, *op. cit.*, 440, n. 1 (a)], (MU) *Daduša ana bīt abīšu īrubu* probably means 'Year in which Dadusha was installed in his father's palace' (there is nothing to prove that this year was the year after his accession as sole ruler). When, for example, a year of Ishme-Adad at Mari is dated by the formula (*Studia Mariana*, 53) (MU) *Nergal ana bītišu īrubu*, this does not mean that the god Nergal became king but that he was installed in a new temple (= palace). It stands to reason that the young co-regent was immensely proud at occupying the redecorated (or rebuilt) palace of his father, wherever it was. I should date Shamshi-Adad I c. 1750–1718, and his younger son's co-regency at Mari during the middle years of his father's reign, before Zimri-Lim's accession in or before c. 1728. Reducing these results to the 'middle' Babylonian chronology Zimri-Lim would have reigned c. 1792–1760 and Shamshi-Adad I c. 1814–1782, dates which would make the almost total absence of references to Egypt or imports from Egypt totally inexplicable, besides creating insoluble problems for the historian.

(l) Ch. II, § B, n. 22. See also the extremely useful survey by Paul Garelli, *Les Assyriens en Cappadoce* (*Bib. Arch. et Hist. de l'Inst. Français d'Arch. d'Istanbul*, XIX, 1963), *passim* (see Index) on donkey caravans and drivers in the nineteenth century B.C.

(m) Ch. II, § C. Note also my concise presentation of the material from the standpoint of historical analogy in AHAEBT 22–41.

(n) Ch. II, § D, n. 50. E. Sollberger has, however, in *The Business and Administrative Correspondence under the Kings of Ur* (1966), No. 6 (pp. 73 f.), collated the tablet published by Kraus and refers it to the Third Dynasty of Ur instead of to Accad. But it remains highly improbable that the three SA. GAZ men in question, who resided in the town of [Bára-s]i$_{11}$-ga(KI), were actually robbers as he supposes.

(o) Ch. II, § D, n. 53. See now especially the critical edition and translation of the 'Curse of Accad' by the late Adam Falkenstein, ZA LVII (n.f. XXIII), 1965, 43–124. He has also shown that the text was already being copied in the Ur III period, c. 2000 B.C.

(p) Ch. II, § D, n. 69. I have long since pointed out that such words as Amorite *naḫraru*⟩ Accad. *niraru*, Amarna *ennirir*, Amorite *šunuḫra* are derived from the same stem *ʿrr* as Heb. *ʿatar* and *heʿtîr*, 'pray for help', *neʿtar*, 'come to (somebody's) help'; Arab. *iʿtarra*, 'beg for help'. See JPOS XIV (1934), 122, n. 105, and BASOR 78 (1940), 24, n. 5. Note that the clan-name *ʿEr* also appears in I Chron. 4:21 as the name of a son of Shelah, younger brother of Er and Onan—a typical case of the confusions in clan genealogies which are so common in early Hebrew and Arab tradition. The same clan name may also appear in the eleventh-century patronymic *Yaʿōr* (*ketiv* in I Chron. 20:5), which corresponds phonetically to the Mari variant *Yaḫurru* and early Assyrian *Ya'uri* (see above, n. 68). There is no way of telling whether the name in the Berlin Execration Texts which I tentatively identified with biblical *ʿEr* (JPOS VIII, 1928, 238) is really the same name or not, since it may be transcribed as Semitic *ʿlm* or *ʿrm*.

(q) Ch. II, § D, n. 92. There is a remarkable parallel, hitherto completely overlooked, between the situation among the early Asiatic (ʿApiru) donkey caravaneers, and the semantic development of New Egyptian *šwwty*, 'huckster, trader', whence Coptic *ěšôt*, 'trader'. The material is too extensive to be discussed here in detail; it is enough to say that the word *šw* (vocalized probably *šaw*-) appears in the funerary inscription of *Bby*, a late Middle Kingdom notable from El-Kab in Upper Egypt who was the provisioner of the ruler (*wʿrtw n ḫ3wt ḥq3*, published by H. Brugsch, *Thesaurus*, 1527 f.; Porter and Moss, *Topographical Bibliography*, V, 184). Among the offerings were grain, 20 bovides (large cattle), 32 bubalis antelopes (often included with the bovides in such gifts), 8 *šw* donkeys (with clear determinative), besides the usual spices, ointments, etc. The donkeys are unusual in such lists and presumably were connected with donkey caravans used in bringing supplies to the ruler's court; the name may be connected with Eg. *šw*, 'dry, desert'. Several different words are derived from this stem, including especially *šwwty* and the contracted *šwty*, who appear in the Nineteenth

Dynasty as hucksters trading especially with Syria (see also the Amenope list published by A. H. Gardiner, *Ancient Egyptian Onomastica*, I, 94* f., where *šwwty* appears as No. 210 followed immediately by Canaanite *m*(*u*)*ḫr*, 'buyer' (No. 211) and *mukiru*, 'seller' (No. 212). In the Papyrus Harris (early twelfth century) the class is so numerous as to be labelled 'unlisted' (*nn rdysn*). In the Nauri Stele of Sethos I (late thirteenth century) the expression *šwyw* (not *šwtyw*) *n ḫ3st*, 'foreign donkey-drivers', is found in a long list of labourers in the mines, followed immediately by 'refiners' (*qu-ra*, plural) and 'gold washers'. The extensive ramifications of this subject will be fully discussed elsewhere. (It is unlikely that there is any connexion between these words—despite the fact that all are written with the feather sign—and the Transjordan land of *Šwtw* in the Execration Texts [which I have identified with *Benê ŠT*, the archaic name of the Moabites] or the *'3mw n šwt*, 'Asiatics of Šwt', in the contemporary Beni Ḥasan tomb paintings, or even the much older *t3 šwt*, 'land of the feather', one of the 'Nine Bows'.)

(r) Ch. II, § D, n. 96. Note also that when Hamor appears as 'the father of Shechem' in Gen. 34, this term simply means 'founder' of the city in question, and that Shechem became a clan (district in the eighth-century Ostraca of Samaria) of Manasseh in the genealogical tradition of Israel. I strongly suspect that here again (see Addendum (c) above) we have a North-Israelite pronunciation *ḥammôr* for Hebrew *ḥammâr*, 'donkey-driver'. In this case, the Greek spelling *Emmōr* (which is the normal transcription of a Hebrew *Ḥammôr*) confirms my suggestion directly. I have long since accepted the Greek reading *Chorraios* instead of Hebrew *Ḥiwwî* in this passage. In the tradition preserved in the JE recensions of Gen. 34, Shechem was thus founded by Hurrian caravaneers, who were displaced (presumably in the fourteenth century B.C.) by Semitic 'Apiru.

(s) Ch. II, § E, n. 99. Contrast W. G. Lambert in *Iraq*, XXVII (1965), p. 11, appendix. The argument from half-a-dozen spellings ᵈ(ÍD)I-id in the Assyrian Law Code is alone decisive.

(t) Ch. II, end of § E. At the New Haven meeting of the

American Oriental Society (April 1967), S. N. Kramer described new fragments of a Sumerian mythological text which recounts a feud between Ellil and Enki (Ae, Ea), creator of mankind, in which the former brought about confusion of tongues among men. This proves the Sumerian origin of yet another early story of beginnings in Genesis.

(u) Ch. II, § F, paragraph following n. 129. His important paper has now been published in *Textus* V (1966), 34 ff. (see my remarks quoted by G. E. Wright in BASOR 169 [1963], note on pp. 28 f.) based on Dr Iwry's original observations, as stated.

CHAPTER III

(v) Ch. III, § C, first paragraph. The sacrificial tablet RS 24.643 (which actually contains what amounts to a third copy of the Ugaritic pantheon) has now been discussed in detail by M. Astour in JAOS LXXXVI (1966), 279 ff.

(w) Ch. III, § D. It may be considered quite certain that the references to the restoration of the temple of the Egyptian goddess Nut and the appellation 'beloved of Nut' in the seventeenth-century Byblian texts Nos. 1 and 2, refer to Anath, who was also called 'Mistress of Heaven'. For the material see P. Montet, *Kemi*, XVII (1963), 61–8; Albright, BASOR 179 (1965), 39–40; K. A. Kitchen, *Orientalia*, XXXVI (1967), 52 ff.

CHAPTER IV

(x) Ch. IV, § A, n. 1. For the latest competent treatments of the Hyksos problem see Jürgen von Beckerath, *Untersuchungen zur politischen Geschichte der Zweiten Zwischenzeit in Ägypten* (Glückstadt, 1964); John Van Seters, *The Hyksos: A New Investigation* (New Haven, 1966); Donald B. Redford, *History and Chronology of the Eighteenth Dynasty of Egypt: Seven Studies* (Toronto, 1967), pp. 39–49. My own treatment has been deferred repeatedly, chiefly because my work on the Hyksos alphabetic inscriptions on scarabs must remain hypothetical until more data are available.

(y) Ch. IV, § A, second paragraph. See also above, Addendum (c).

(z) Ch. IV, § A, fifth paragraph. See also above Addendum (q).

(aa) Ch. IV, § A, n. 26. My synchronism between the destruction of Ugarit (probably by the Sea Peoples before the Tablet Oven with its priceless contents could be opened) with the Assyrian invasion of Khatti in the first full year of Tukulti-Ninurta I, has been criticized by a number of scholars, but they have not been able to produce any solid argument against it. Two wars between the Assyrians and the Hittites are known to have taken place during the last generation of Hittite imperial history; the first under Tudhaliya IV of Khatti, Ini-Teshub of Carchemish and the contemporary rulers Amishtamru of Ugarit and Shaushgamuwa of Amurru (referred to in the clearest language by documents from Ugarit and Boğazköy); the second in the time of Ini-Teshub's son Talmi-Teshub and Amishtamru's son Ammurapi', the last king of Ugarit (a war known from Assyrian and Ugaritic texts). Suppiluliuma II was almost certainly king of Khatti at that time. An important study by H. G. Güterbock (JNES XXVI, 1967, 73–81) seems to have settled the problem of the relation between Khatti and Cyprus (Alashiya) in the reigns of Tudhaliya IV and his son Suppiluliuma II, in complete agreement with the evidence from the Tablet Oven and contemporary tablets of Ugarit; the father conquered Alashiya after defeating its king, whereas the son defeated 'the ships of Alashiya' and 'enemies from Alashiya' on sea and land. In other words, the Sea Peoples and their allies were already in control of the island. There is clear evidence, which I had overlooked, for the second war between Assyria and Khatti in the triumphal epic of Tukulti-Ninurta in which he celebrates his victory over Kashtiliash of Babylonia. Towards the end of the poem (as far as preserved; see E. Ebeling, *Mitteilungen der Altorientalischen Gesellschaft*, XII, 2, pp. 19–21), after reciting some of the deeds of his recent ancestors, including the final conquest of Mitanni by his father Shalmaneser I, the Assyrian king mentions the 'Hittite (king)' (*Ḫa-at-tu-ú*, col. v: 40). If we accept the sequence of events in the royal inscriptions of Tukulti-Ninurta, the attack on

Khatti in the first full year of the king was followed successively by repulse of the Hittite 'allies' in the northern mountains and by the defeat of the Babylonians, who had long been in alliance with Khatti. These events cannot well be separated by more than a year or two in time. If we take 1160 as the official beginning of the Second Dynasty of Isin, with J. A. Brinkman in 1962 (JCS XVI, 1962, 103) and add the seventy-one regnal years of the last eight kings of the Third Dynasty of Babylon as recorded in King List A, we arrive at a date, c. 1232 B.C. for the dethronement of Kashtiliash III. The insertion of an interregnum of seven years for the Assyrian occupation is *a priori* improbable, and there is no likelihood that any clear synchronism can be set up between Egypt, Khatti and Babylonia during the reign of Ramesses II (1304–1238). These considerations leave us with the year 1234/3 for the Assyrian attack on Khatti and the destruction of the Tablet Oven, followed by the war against the eastern 'allies' of Khatti and about 1232–30 by the punishment of Babylonia. Of course, this last date is not exact and may have to be lowered by a few years—and possibly even raised by one year.

(bb) Ch. IV, § D. With reference to the ephod as the visible heavenly glory of the invisible God of Israel (fifth paragraph from end of chapter), see above on the heavenly glory (*pnm/pnt*) and majesty (*tmnt*) of Yahweh in Addendum (e). Much more significant is the forthcoming treatment of the *'ānān* of Yahweh (which corresponds even more directly to the *melammû* of the Accadians) by G. E. Mendenhall, who has presented his views in lectures and papers (note especially the second series of Lovejoy Lectures given by him at Johns Hopkins University in March, 1967).

(cc) Ch. IV, § D, notes 113, 116. On the mortuary character of the whole area around the Temple aux Obélisques at Byblos see now BASOR 184 (1966), 26 ff.

CHAPTER V

(dd) Ch. V, § B, third paragraph and n. 30. For the latest surveys of Phoenician penetration into the western Mediterranean in the early first millennium B.C. see S. Moscati in the *Atti della Accademia . . . Lincei*, CCCLXIII (1966), *Memorie (Classe di Scienze morali . . . , Serie* VIII, Vol. XII), pp. 217–50; G. Garbini in *Studi Etruschi*, XXXIV (1966), 111–47. There is at present a strong reaction towards earlier dating. The Nora inscription is now dated by virtually all scholars in the ninth century; for the latest treatment see J. Ferron in *Rivista degli Studi Orientali* XLI (1966), 281–8, with a useful survey of recent interpretations. It must again be emphasized that the inscription cannot be complete: the alleged right edge is no original edge at all, since the letters along it are not aligned vertically; the resulting text cannot possibly be Phoenician, since it violates the normal rules of Phoenician grammar and orthography. B. Mazar's extension of my original suggestion that the right edge of the stone was cut off to include the left side as well, is the only reasonable view. The original stone block (which presumably included only part of the text) must have been cut into paving slabs or building material of similar shape.

(ee) Ch. V, § C, n. 86. See now the valuable survey by S. Moscati: 'Il sacrificio dei fanciulli' in *Rendiconti della Pontificia Accademia Romana di Archeologia*, XXXVIII (1965/66), 1–8. There can be little doubt that the term 'tophet' has been correctly used, though the word was probably not actually found in Phoenician. On the etymology of the word and its congeners see Koehler-Baumgartner, *Lexicon in Veteris Testamenti Libros*, s.v. *'ašpôt* (p. 95), *špt* (p. 1006), *tofet* (p. 1038). The stem *špt/tpt* is now generally identified with Ugar. *ṯpd*, 'set, place', as I first pointed out in JPOS XII, 18, n. 83; *tpt* (*tofet*) is not necessarily Aramaic but may be dialectal Hebrew like *tannôt*, 'recite', in the Song of Deborah. In HUCA XXIII (1950/51), Part I, p. 22, I pointed out that Heb. *miš-petayim* (Gen. 49:14, Judg. 5:16) and *šefattayim* (as vocalized in Psalm 68:14) is the dual of a word for 'hearth, fireplace' (see P. Haupt, AJSL XXIII, 1907, 236, n. 57) and must be identical with Ugar. *mṯpdm* in the Baal Epic, V AB, A: 79, where I should still render *ṯn mṯpdm tḥt 'nt 'arṣ* as 'the two fire-places under the fountains of the earth', i.e., hot springs.

(ff) Ch. V, § C, n. 105. This rendering of line 33 in the new funerary tablet of Ammiṣaduqa, *u rēdûm ša ina dannat bēlišu imqutu* has imposed itself ever since I received a copy from Prof. J. J. Finkelstein in the spring of 1965. The word *dannatu* is well attested in the sense of 'pit, dungeon, etc.' His translation 'and the soldier(s) who fell while on perilous campaigns(?) for their (lit: "his") lord' (JCS xx, 1966, 97, 113 f.) seems to me exceedingly forced and intrinsically improbable.

Index

1. Subjects and Authors

2. Biblical References

(Verse numbers cited according to the Hebrew text)